LABOUR AND EQU

A Fabian Study of Labour
1974–79

D1151537

THE EDITORS
Nick Bosanquet, *Lecturer in Economics, The City University, London*
Peter Townsend, *Professor of Sociology, Essex University*

THE CONTRIBUTORS
Paul Ormerod, *Research Officer, National Institute of Economic and Social Research*
Vincent Cable, *Research Officer, Overseas Development Institute*
Chris Pond, *Director, Low Pay Unit*
Robert Taylor, *Labour Correspondent of The Observer*
Michael Meacher, *MP for Oldham West*
Ian Martin, *Director, Joint Council for the Welfare of Immigrants*
Patricia Hewitt, *General Secretary, National Council of Civil Liberties*
David Piachaud, *Lecturer in Social Administration, London School of Economics*
Ruth Lister, *Director, Child Poverty Action Group*
Tessa Blackstone, *Professor of Education, University of London Institute of Education*
Malcolm Wicks, *Research Director, Study Commission on the Family*
Adrian Webb, *Professor of Social Administration, University of Loughborough*

LABOUR AND EQUALITY

A Fabian Study of Labour in Power, 1974–79

Edited by
NICK BOSANQUET
and PETER TOWNSEND

HEINEMANN

Heinemann Educational Books Ltd
22 Bedford Square, London WC1B 3HH
LONDON EDINBURGH MELBOURNE AUCKLAND
HONG KONG SINGAPORE KUALA LUMPUR NEW DELHI
IBADAN NAIROBI JOHANNESBURG
EXETER (NH) KINGSTON PORT OF SPAIN

Labour and equality.
1. Great Britain – Social policy 2. Great
Britain – Social conditions – 1945–
I. Bosanquet, Nick – II. Townsend, Peter, *b.1928*
300'.941   HN390

ISBN 0–435–83105–4
ISBN 0–435–83106–2 Pbk

Set in Monophoto Times and printed in Great Britain by
Richard Clay (The Chaucer Press) Ltd, Bungay, Suffolk

Preface

The main aim of this book is to review the record of the two Labour Governments which were in office between 1974 and 1979 (the first for some months in 1974, the second from 1974 to 1979). The stated intention of these governments was to redistribute income, wealth, rights and resources towards the poorer sections of the community. How successful were they in doing this?

The book begins by looking at the economy and international relations because they show the context within which, and the constraints under which, the Labour Governments worked. It then examines the policies for influencing inequality within the labour market and for dealing with discrimination.

Finally, the contributors turn to the government's own direct attempts to influence patterns in society through policies for income support and the social services. Compared with the earlier volume which we also edited (*Labour and Inequality*, Fabian Society, 1972), we have deliberately given greater attention to individual rights in society within Britain and beyond because this seems to reflect the increasingly broad conception of social policy being adopted in public and specialist discussion.

Contributors were asked to deal with some common questions: the meaning of equality; changes in philosophy; the record between 1964 and 1974; policies since 1974; the impact of these policies and plans for the future.

There is no one agreed line or conclusion held by the contributors – nor indeed by the editors. We hope, however, that the book will contribute to the debate on how a Labour Government can be really effective. Labour Governments have been in office for 11 out of the last 16 years, but the results must be considered intensely disappointing. Our earlier volume documented this sad fact for the period 1964 to 1970. Labour in government seems to become more conservative even as Tory Governments become more radical or at least daring.

We believe that the Labour Party can and should light a flame in a world of injustice and inequality. We hope that this book will contribute to the changes needed to bring this about.

Nick Bosanquet and Peter Townsend
July 1979

Contents

Acknowledgements

We are grateful to Dianne Hayter and to the other staff of the Fabian Society, particularly Betty Clarkson, Suzannah Davies and Anne Solomons, for their help and good humour, which was severely tested at times. We would like to thank members of a Fabian Seminar in February 1979 whose discussion contributed to the improvement of earlier drafts. Anonymous Fabian readers have also provided most useful comments. Finally, we would like to thank our families for putting up with a number of interrupted weekends.

Notes and References

In some of the chapters note indicators are not used in an unbroken sequence. When the order is broken by a number previously used, reference is being made to that source which has been cited earlier in the chapter. Notes and references for all chapters begin on page 297.

PART I

Introduction

1 Social Planning and the Treasury

by Peter Townsend

History shows that socialists are apt to speak too kindly about the latest acts of Labour Governments, especially at the conclusion of a term of office. I remember reading with dismay Tawney's new epilogue which he added in 1951 to his book *Equality*. The old master's principles and command of the English language remained intact, but he did not acknowledge the extraordinary loss of socialist momentum during those six years in office and took a rather sanguine view of Labour's achievements. I remember feeling much the same about the attitudes struck in 1970 by some (certainly not all) socialist colleagues and friends about Labour's rule from 1964. There were those who seemed prepared to go to extraordinary lengths to argue that sows' ears really were silk purses. They included people, especially former ministers, whose motives were in part self-exculpatory, and those who took the view that the test of a democratic socialist government was whether it could manage the 'system' as efficiently as any alternative administration. But they also included people in all parts of the Labour movement who did not want to believe that their expectations had not been fulfilled because that would have threatened life long political beliefs. Disillusion can be profoundly self-destructive, and unconscious as well as conscious defences tend to be erected against that experience. But of course there was another motive at work, which we can recognise equally well today. People dared not express too publicly, or too emphatically, their disillusion with Labour's performance for fear of destroying its chances of re-deeming itself in office. And loyalty tends to be approved more than candour.

For such reasons, the whole truth about the failures and successes of the Labour administration 1974–79 is not easy to tell, or even discern. Analysts vary in their expectations of a Labour Government and in their values. Those writing so recently after the 1979 election as the authors in this book are bound to remain sensitive to the feelings that have been expressed keenly by different groups and they are frustrated by lack of information about key events, especially for the last year of office. Nonetheless, it is important to begin the process of examining the record. Socialists need to understand whether more was possible and, if not, why not, so that the consequences for the Labour movement and national institutions and for Labour policies can be drawn and a future Labour administration can capitalise on the mistakes and shortcomings of its predecessors.

Like a previous collection of essays which covered the years 1964–70,[1] the present book attempts to limit a vast subject by concentrating on the themes of 'equality' and 'social policy'. Of course, both concepts are given different meanings and are properly controversial. 'Equality' for many is predominantly an economic concept but, as explained by Marx in his *Critique of the Gotha Programme* (1875), there can be a big difference between distribution on the basis of work performed and need, even when the means of production are publicly owned, and in his view a socialist society may have to accommodate itself for a long time to the former before it can advance to the latter. Similar conflicts of meaning also apply to other aspects of equality – like social, political and legal equality.

In the history of the Labour Party, equality has always been a dominant preoccupation. Part of clause IV of the party constitution reads: '(4) To secure for the workers by hand or by brain the full fruits of their industry and the most equitable distribution thereof that may be possible upon the basis of the common ownership of the means of production, distribution and exchange, and the best obtainable system of popular administration and control of each industry or service ... (5) generally to promote the Political, Social and Economic Emancipation of the People, and more particularly of those who depend directly upon their own exertions by hand or by brain for the means of life....'

Concern with 'equality' is also evident in party literature and especially its manifestos. In fact the allusions and direct references are so frequent as to amount in opponents' minds to an obsession. The party's aims, as distinct from particular items in its programmes, were expressed in the 1974 manifesto (which of course is most relevant to the present book, though also to the years 1946–51 and 1964–70) as to:

(a) Bring about a fundamental and irreversible shift in the balance of power and wealth in favour of working people and their families;
(b) Eliminate poverty wherever it exists in Britain, and commit ourselves to a substantial increase in our contribution to fight poverty abroad;
(c) Make power in industry genuinely accountable to the workers and the community at large;
(d) Achieve far greater economic equality – in income, wealth and living standards;
(e) Increase social equality by giving far greater importance to full employment, housing, education and social benefits;
(f) Improve the environment in which our people live and work and spend their leisure.[2]

All six of these aims draw on a complex idea of equality and provide a standard by which to judge performance in office, even if there remain differences of opinion about how the aims would be spelt out in practice.

The concept of 'social policy' is also problematic, but academic as well as Left wing opinion has been moving in favour of a wide and also more integrated concept. As with its predecessor, this book deliberately treats employment, income, wealth and fiscal policies as well as health, education, welfare, housing and social security as part of social policy. Its authors do not consider that the kind of aims set out above can be pursued or their implementation evaluated except in relation to the *combined* contribution of different policies.

One further preliminary comment deserves making. In the aftermath of the 1979 election, there was one major difference, compared with 1970, in the attitudes struck by socialists. In 1970 it was less easy for any of them than in 1979 to proclaim the different effects of periods of Tory and Labour office. For example, the expansion of public expenditure, especially on the social services, under a Tory administration in the early 1960s had been greater than under Labour during 1964–70. The influence of rather exceptional Tories, like Harold Macmillan, Iain Macleod and Edward Boyle (supported at the time by civil servants and others in key positions) had been considerable upon public housing policy, education and health and welfare services. The experience of the Heath government changed all that. In crucial respects – taxation, public housing, new means tests, even the management of the National Health Service – there was a reversion to form. The early months of the Thatcher government, in terms of the prospects for social services and social equality, are even worse. There can be no doubt at all that, even with a weak administration, a Labour victory in 1979 would have mattered more to the poor and dispossessed and for the preservation of those social services helping the working class than the Tory victory which occurred. Even if our criterion were to be the prevention of inequalities becoming greater rather than the more positive criterion of eliminating or reducing poverty and inequality, this would still be true.

Planning for equality

Any review of social policy in 1974–79 must begin with planning. The most critical problem was the failure to define social objectives in any detail and set up the administrative apparatus to control and monitor social planning so that the management of the economy could be properly informed. This is the single most important act for a government which seeks to lay claims to socialism and represents the greatest single domestic failure of the governments of 1974–79. In studying the record, it goes without saying that Britain is deeply involved in an international system of trade, finance, investment, diplomacy and military alliances, and any government would be forced to come to terms with certain trading, balance of payments, military and political realities which have been determined predominantly by others. No doubt there always will be an argument about the extent to which we remain masters of internal conditions within our own society. The point is that if the definition of what those internal conditions should be and how they can be brought into effect goes by default, then the argument that external constraints prevent internal changes rings decidedly hollow.

Perhaps the need for planning for equality requires summary re-statement. From any comparative perspective, Britain could not be said to be, in 1974, despite two post-war spells already of Labour Government, one of the most equal of the world's relatively rich countries. Different economists writing in the 1960s and 1970s believed the concentration of wealth to be greater than in the United States.[3] On a rough standardised measure, there was more of the population in poverty in the early 1970s than in Sweden, Norway and Germany.[4] In 1972, the UK was ranked twelfth of 17 OECD countries in public 'income maintenance' expenditure, expressed as a percentage share of GDP.[5] Britain's ranking on the distribution of income among relatively rich countries has been neither low nor high.

Harold Lydall found that the countries distributing employment income most equally were Czechoslovakia, Hungary, New Zealand, Australia and Denmark.[6] On different distributional and social indicators (such as infant mortality), Britain's ranking has fallen.

It is instructive also to compare the performance of state socialist countries. A recent review concluded that on the whole the distribution of income in these countries was significantly more equal than in capitalist countries at comparable levels of development. They did not have the small minority of individuals with huge holdings of means of production normal under captialism and their élites, including members of most professions, were significantly worse off than the élites of capitalist countries, though this had to be tempered with the fact that senior party officials, together with leading members of the military, police and state and trade union agencies, were several times richer than the average citizen.[7] Nonetheless inequality remained marked in these countries and there was substantial poverty by national standards.[8] In terms of the living standards guaranteed to the dependent minorities in the population, some capitalist countries, especially those with a long history of social democratic government such as Sweden, stand favourable comparison. The comparison becomes a lot sharper if characteristics like the desperately poor living standards as well as loss of freedom of the much higher proportion of detainees per 1,000 of the population in countries like the USSR are also weighed. 'The main reasons for the persistence of inequality under state socialism appears to be the division of labour, the family, the sexual division of roles and the role of the state in state socialism.'[9]

The instruments of planning in 1974

In 1974 there was an unprecedented opportunity to develop the 'social contract' into a reasoned socialist manifesto. It really did seem that previous policies of wage restraint, masquerading as 'incomes' policies, were going to be replaced by a plan to reconstruct wealth and incomes, or at least impose fair principles of desert on all sections of the community so that the nation could be steered from the chaos into which the previous administration had plunged the economy. The collapse of the social contract, or 'compact' as Harold Wilson originally called it, remains one of the mysteries of recent Labour history. The contract grew out of anger at the previous administration's divisive policies and for some months promised to be developed as a method of restricting profits, dividends and top incomes as well as wages. The social contract was concerned with improving the social wage, controlling prices, reducing unemployment and improving industrial investment, and not just pay restraint. This was also the period when the government had a clear mandate for decisive and progressive action on behalf of the nation as a whole. This was the occasion, if ever there was one, for moral leadership by ministers and for political education of the nation. But the outline remained an outline and the opportunity passed.[10]

The social contract was potentially an effective instrument of planning. But it was not the only one. There were other possibilities. The production in 1975 by the Central Policy Review Staff of *A Joint Framework for Social Policies* was a different and much more limited initiative, which called attention to the questions involved in deciding between different social priorities. But William Plowden, one of its principal authors, does not suggest that developments since its publication have been particularly brisk. For example, the 'strategic forum' for ministers seems to have met increasingly infrequently. One fascinating by-product of the debate in 1976 about child benefit was the use of a TUC–Labour Party Liaison Committee to defuse a potentially explosive wrangle between the Cabinet and the party. The committee played a vital part in changing government policy on child benefit. Some ministers are said to have argued that the document prepared by the Liaison Committee and approved by the TUC General Council and the NEC of the party in July 1978 should have been used as a basis of the 1979 election manifesto. For planning purposes, there is something to be said for machinery independent of government which would properly represent both the TUC and the Labour Party.

Public expenditure control

But the most important instrument for planning social policy was public expenditure planning. This was where the crucial battle for socialist control had, and has, to be waged. Hitherto it would be fair to argue that the machinery of public expenditure planning was developed by the Treasury to maintain its rule not only in economic but also social affairs. Despite protestations from some government departments, like the DHSS, that their planning is 'needs' conscious, the fact is that the exigencies of the economy, as decided by the Treasury, have led to the adoption of public expenditure control as the dominant form of planning approved by the Cabinet and imposed by Whitehall.

In recent years, it has come to be realised that most of the key decisions in social policy are taken during the sequence of discussions leading up to the budget in April of each year (though also some of the mini-budgets which became more common in the 1970s). It is preceded by the review of public expenditure. This takes place in the summer, is approved in the autumn, and published the following January. The Public Expenditure Survey Committee is chaired by a Treasury Deputy Secretary and consists of the Finance Officers from different departments and Treasury officials. The Committee's report goes to Cabinet and may differ considerably from the subsequent White Paper. The Committee makes estimates of the likely growth of the economy, revenue and departmental spending over the next five years. The system dates back to the 1950s and flows from the recommendations of the Plowden Report of 1961.[11] Neither the Committee nor the Cabinet engages in exhaustive discussion of all the major departmental proposals which may be put up. Instead, Treasury intimations of what can be afforded are communicated to the departments which, in turn, attempt to get departmental estimates agreed with the Treasury representatives on the Committee before the estimates are put to Cabinet for broad approval. The system is therefore cost- and not needs-oriented and has the effect of maintaining the *status quo*, including the divorce of public expenditure planning from any consideration of the organisation and development of the private sector.[12]

Successive governments have tried to reduce the power wielded by the Treasury over central social planning through its tight grip on public expenditure. The Department of Economic Affairs was set up in 1964 to formulate a national economic plan. However, the plan misfired and, one by one, the department's functions were taken away. In October 1969 it was finally abolished. Again, under Edward Heath in 1970, the Central Policy Review Staff was set up as part of the reorganisation of central government to bring planning under better ministerial and Cabinet control. This small body has no executive power and is regarded by Whitehall as carrying little weight. Many of its reports have been suppressed or, if published, have been firmly shelved.

During the mid-1970s, with balance of payments problems, high inflation and low or negative rates of growth, public expenditure control dominated other forms of planning even more comprehensively. There was a kind of departmental rearguard action. For example, the Department of Health published its priorities for the health and social services.[13] Taking the Treasury's allowance for future expenditure, the percentage increase was varied for different categories of service to show how progress towards desirable objectives might be made. Again, a report of the Resource Allocation Working Party on Health used a broad criterion of need (in this case the need for health services as indicated by differential mortality) to work out and so justify a redistribution of resources between regions.[14] While both these documents were restricted in scope and did not explain enough, they demonstrate that new efforts were being made *within* departments to deal more rationally with expenditure priorities and to consult representatives of outside opinion.[15]

But reasoned, if modest, adventures in planning were overshadowed by new central restrictions. Cuts were made in public expenditure plans and cash limits were devised as a means of financial control (and extended in scope by the new Tory administration in June 1979). Critics have even argued that the figures used by the government to justify the huge cuts were 'wildly wrong' and that an estimate of the Public Sector Borrowing Requirement for 1976/7 of £11.2 billion given in December 1976 to the IMF turned out to be £8.8 billion. 'It is extraordinary that the forecast which was fundamental to seeking a loan whose conditions were so savage should be so wrong.'[10] Table 1.1 summarises the trends. Throughout the 1960s, expenditure on the public social services increased by an average of 5 per cent per annum. This rate was maintained in 1970–74 but after rising temporarily in Labour's first year fell drastically in the next three years. The brunt of the cuts was borne by social services other than social security. Although expedients were adopted, like varying the method of uprating pensions, benefits could not be withheld from growing numbers of pensioners and of unemployed people. In the early part of the life of the 1974 parliament, increased pensions and new disablement benefits were accorded high priority.

The contraction of expenditure produced distortions in the services as well as variations locally in the interpretation of policy. Avowed priorities were not always fulfilled. Ancillary services for consumers or clients were much more vulnerable to economies than staff establishments. The collapse of growth in personal social services expenditure is particularly significant. After the Seebohm reorganisation of 1970, expenditure increased by 15 per cent per annum in the early 1970s but fell to a negative rate, as Table 1.1 shows, in 1976–77 and 1977–78. Priority services for disabled people and the elderly were actually cut in a large number of areas.[16] Paradoxically, the publication of plans to give priority to the development of community services coincided with negative rates of growth of those services!

Table 1.1   Rate of increase in expenditure (capital and current) at constant prices on the public social services (percentages)

	All social services	Social security	Educa-tion	Health	Personal social services	Housing
1959–64	5.5	4.9	5.9	3.2	7.4	10.3
1964–70	4.5	5.4	4.8	3.2	6.2	3.3
1970–74	5.0	3.0	6.3	4.3	13.6	7.4
1974–75	9.0	6.9	0.4	1.0	8.3	44.1
1975–76	2.1	8.3	1.8	3.2	6.5	−11.7
1976–77	1.0	2.9	−0.3	0.8	−1.3	−1.0
1977–78	−0.9	3.6	−3.6	0.8	−1.6	−9.4
1978–79	(7.0)	7.6	(2.0)	(3.7)	(4.5)	(2.8)

Source: *Public Expenditure White Papers*. Figures in brackets indicate expectations in January 1979 which seem likely not to be quite fulfilled.

The Treasury's social policy

Part of my theme, then, is the negative impact of public expenditure control on planning. But positive action to concert incomes, tax, pricing, subsidy, employment and benefit policies was also not taken in the five years. It scarcely needs arguing that these policies interact in determining living standards and changing the class system. That interaction is not very well understood – as the 1975 budget illustrates. During 1974–75 pensions and other benefits had been greatly improved, food subsidies introduced, furnished tenants protected from eviction, a new earnings related pension scheme and non-contributory benefit schemes for the disabled announced, a Green Paper on a wealth tax published and the social contract between government and trade unions widely discussed.

In the November 1974 budget, the Chancellor promised further help for 'those who are least able to withstand the impact of inflation – all in all, pensioners and families with young children, the groups among whom poverty is to be found on the widest and most tragic scale.'[17] The following April, the Chancellor (a) increased unemployment and accepted the responsibility for part of this increase; (b) did not announce any increase in family allowances or child tax allowances, nor bring forward a new scheme for child benefits; (c) did not raise the tax threshold for single and married

Table 1.2   *Real weekly net income at December 1978 prices* (£)

	Single person	Married man	Married 1 child under 11	Married 2 children under 11	Married, 4 children 2 under 11, 2 aged 11–16
1973–74	68.10	70.40	72.80	75.80	83.10
1977–78	72.20	65.80	68.30	71.20	77.40
1978–79	65.70	69.20	72.40	75.70	82.70
Real weekly net income as % of income in 1973–74					
1973–74	100	100	100	100	100
1977–78	91.3	93.5	93.8	93.9	93.1
1978–79	96.5	98.3	99.5	99.9	99.5

Source: *Hansard*, 26 January 1979, Cols *287–288*.

persons to match the increase in prices or introduce a reduced rate of tax for a first band of taxable earnings; and (d) announced the phasing out of food and fuel subsidies, with disproportionately large effects on those with low incomes. The combined effect of such measures cannot be reconciled with the priorities expressed in the Labour Party's manifesto nor with its long term aims.

The same point can be illustrated for the period as a whole. After 1973–74, real incomes fell and between 1974 and 1977 there was a reduction in real disposable incomes of approximately 7 per cent. By 1978–79 the living standards of most types of household had been restored almost to the 1973–74 levels (Table 1.2). By the summer of 1979, due to an improvement in the economy in the preceding 12 months, real net incomes were expected to have advanced beyond the 1973–74 levels. That in itself is scarcely cause for congratulation for five years of Labour Government. The figures derive from the New Earnings Survey (in which the low paid are under-represented), and tax rates and family allowance or child benefit rates are applied to earnings. The inequality experienced by different types of family as shown in the Family Expenditure Survey (FES) is greater. Thus while the *average* reduction in standard of living between 1974 and 1977 was, according to the FES, still 7 per cent, the cut in the disposable income of families was greater, and for families with four children was a chilling 20 per cent. The *expenditure* figures from the FES show the same trend, though not so sharply. In the mid-1970s, living standards of families with children fell by more than did those of other types of household.[18] All this can be said before taking account of the relatively greater increase in prices experienced by low income families.[19] The lack of planned protection of the living standards of families and poor people was due not only to the delays in resolving the problem of phasing out child tax allowances and family allowances in favour of child benefit but to a number of other elements in policy: the inadequate uprating of tax thresholds, the radical reduction of food and fuel subsidies (though not the subsidy to maintain the price of European butter), the failure to increase low pay and the incomes of the unemployed and the sick by as much as long term benefits and the fall in incomes of social security recipients because of high rates of inflation during the months preceding upratings in November.

Another illustration is to be found in the history of child benefit – rightly believed to be a Labour measure of great importance but not yet implemented at a level high enough to buttress against the basic costs of bringing up children. The emergence of the scheme cannot be interpreted as a consolation prize produced by the government for Labour and Child Poverty Action Group activists. The danger is in forgetting the previous value of child tax allowances and the erosion in the 1970s of the combined value of child tax allowances and family allowances. Since the level of child benefit is central to the structural problem for a socialist administration of equalising living standards between households with and without dependants, its treatment in 1974–79 has to be assessed carefully (see Chapter 11 by Ruth Lister, especially Table 11.1). Child benefit had a chequered history and there was a major struggle before the government introduced it in a number of stages in 1977–79. The introduction of a £4 rate of child benefit in April 1979 does not, for

1979–80, restore the value of family support available up to the late 1960s, except for families with one child only. (In April 1979, the Chancellor announced a projected increase to £4.50 from November 1979, but this proposal was not pursued by the incoming Tory Government.) Table 1.3 puts the same point in a rather different way. It shows how great the gap became between what was paid in child benefit and what was needed to maintain the relativities to net income achieved in 1965.

Table 1.3   Combined weekly value of child tax allowances and family allowances (children under 11) to standard rate taxpayers, actual and maintained relative to net incomes, 1965–1979 (£)

	1 child	2 children actual value	3 children	4 children
1965 (Oct)	0.91	2.10	3.35	4.60
1978 (Nov)	3.63	7.27	10.90	14.54
1979 (Nov)	4.00	8.00	12.00	16.00
1965 values, updated relative to net income in 1978–79				
1978 (Nov)	3.57	8.21	13.30	18.65
1979 (Nov)	4.11	9.44	15.30	21.45

Source: DHSS for 1965 and 1978. Author's estimates for 1979.

Planning and the distribution of wealth

The disavowal of proposals to tax wealth during the five years provides more disconcerting evidence of unwillingness to develop a framework of planning to bring about a significant reduction in inequality. In February 1974, Denis Healey announced the government's intention, following the promise in the manifesto, to introduce a wealth tax. Subsequently a Green Paper was published.[20] As Professor C. T. Sandford writes, in a succinct account of Labour policies, this was

> ... a remarkable document. ... The green paper was unique amonst green papers on taxation. Other green papers, like that on *Local Government Finance* and on *A Possible Inheritance Tax in Place of Estate Duty* had left as many options open. Other green papers, like that on VAT or the Tax Credit Scheme, had

committed governments to a particular tax. But none had, at the same time, committed a government firmly to the principle of a tax whilst leaving virtually everything else open. If we assume that the government was sincere in its desire for a wealth tax, the position it took up in the green paper was essentially illogical. If the government was so vague about the desired objectives and methods of achieving them, it should hardly have been prepared to commit itself to the principle. The structure of a wealth tax depends essentially on the purposes it is intended to fulfil. There is not really one wealth tax, but a number of possible wealth taxes with very different implications and structures.

Later he added,

The lack of research and lack of preparation by the party are likewise revealed by the vagueness of the green paper; although the Labour Party had been publicly advocating a wealth tax for something like ten years, when it came to implementing it they apparently had very little idea of what they wanted or what the implications might be.[21]

In December 1975, the Chancellor announced the postponement of the introduction of a wealth tax in that session and in 1976 further announced that it would not be introduced in the present parliament. Michael Meacher discusses this chapter of Labour's policies in detail later in Chapter 7.

Taxation allowances and the Treasury
Since Richard Titmuss first called attention to the importance of the fiscal welfare state (in 1955), increasing efforts have been made to argue for the co-ordination in planning of tax and cash expenditures. But only after the House of Commons Public Expenditure Committee reviewed evidence from overseas of administrative and political consideration of the aggregate cost of different tax allowances was a list of tax expenditures published in January 1979 in the Public Expenditure White Paper. Leaving aside a long list of items which could not be costed, or which were small in value, a total cost for these allowances of £26 billion for 1978–79 was reached, compared with total public expenditure of £65 billion. It is more than surprising that the Labour Government did not review the possibilities implied by any consideration of this list (including £6.6 billion for the married man's tax allowance, £1.8 billion for the wife's earned income allowance and £1.1 billion for mortgage interest tax relief). Stricter control of tax allowances as well as tax avoidance and

evasion could greatly enhance a Labour Government's opportunity to devise fresh policies for income tax or public expenditure. Among the detailed possibilities are the phasing out of a substantial part of the married man's tax allowance in favour of direct cash allowances for families bringing up infant children or households caring for dependent disabled people.

Another possibility is action to relate employer welfare benefits to wages and salaries. In its third report, the Diamond Commission reproduced revealing examples of the substantial value of these benefits to the higher paid and showed that they had increased proportionately to earnings.[22] However, the full value of employer welfare benefits was not aggregated and related to trends in net disposable personal income.

The absence of an employment policy

Above all, the consequences of economic policy for high rates of unemployment in 1974–79 were not fully appreciated and a positive full employment policy did not form part of national planning. The decline of the manufacturing labour force and the failure to establish new industry on a sufficient scale, together with the restrictions now placed on the growth of the public sector, caused unemployment to grow remorselessly. From 615,000 in 1974 the numbers of unemployed grew to over 1.5 million in 1978 and then fell slightly in the months leading up to the election. In the spring of 1979, another 200,000 would have been out of work but for the special employment and training measures and, according to various official and independent surveys, there were probably another 500,000 unregistered unemployed. There were 335,000 people who had been out of work for a year or more, 54,000 of whom were under 25 years old.

Much of the discussion of the problems of unemployment has concentrated on the living standards of unemployed people. Less than 50 per cent now draw unemployment insurance benefit and only a fraction of them an earnings-related supplement. The increasing number of people who have been unemployed for one year or two years or more are not entitled to the long-term rate of supplementary benefit. Neither do many of them receive additional discretionary payments. Information from the DHSS about the net incomes of unemployed couples with one child, two children, three children and four children (for December 1977) shows that for most types of family net incomes were half or less than half the *average* net disposable income of families of their type. Even in the case of married couples with four or more children, the net income was only a little over two-thirds of the average income for families of that size. Contrary to the impressions created by press campaigns, the real incomes of unemployed people are desperately low. And although there is evidence that, just before the election, government ministers were coming round to the view that the unemployed should be allowed to draw a higher rate of supplementary benefit after one or two years; the fact is that more and more families were having to live for long periods on benefit rates designed only for the short term. Although some ministers resisted antipathy voiced against 'scroungers', stringent measures were newly introduced by the government against fraud in the supplementary benefits scheme but not to the same extent, for example, in the taxation system.

Comparatively little attention has been concentrated on the employment implications of different components of economic policies and possible alternatives to the special employment and training measures introduced gradually during the mid- and late-1970s. In 1975, the government gave the impression of feeling its way cautiously; the job creation and other programmes at that time were little more than diversionary window dressing. But there are now a whole battery of programmes which assist about 250,000 people a month and will cost £612 million in 1979/80, including the temporary short time working compensation scheme started in April 1979 to avoid 55,000 redundancies during 1979–81. Real expenditure amounts to probably not much more than half this total, since social security benefits would otherwise have to be paid to those assisted by the schemes. The Youth Opportunities Programme (covering 65,000 aged 16 to 18), the Special Temporary Employment Programme (providing temporary jobs to 10,000 people aged 19 to 24 on schemes of benefit to the community) and the Temporary Employment Subsidy (helping to maintain employment for 95,000 short time workers in textiles, clothing and footwear) account for the great bulk of present programmes.

The crucial feature of most of the schemes is that they are temporary. They make no long term contribution to full employment and, although the evidence is patchy, do not seem to be very satisfactory either to employers or to employed. Some peripheral temporary roles have been invented and many of those assisted have felt stigmatised and insecure. But few would deny that they are at least better, if only for a short time, than the vacuum of unemployment.

In 1978/9, the cost of unemployment benefits will be in the region of £1,500 million. To this should be added lost revenue from taxation – probably of the order of at least £1,500 million again. An alternative cost of lost production might be made. Even at a modest estimate of £4,000 per unemployed person at 1978 values, the 'excess' unemployment of about 1,000,000, compared with the mid and late 1960s, would represent a loss of about £4,000 million per annum.

Calculating the costs helps to demonstrate the need for alternative policies. Deprivation due to loss of income takes many different forms. Those who become unemployed tend to be people with insecure and poorly paid jobs. Because of that, they are already predisposed towards deprivation in housing, environmental amenities, dietary conditions, clothing and material possessions, and partly because of bad working conditions, a greater risk of poor health. Unemployment reinforces tendencies already there. There is evidence of the psychological impact of unemployment and of the association between insecurity and poor working conditions, low occupational status and poor health.

Detailed interview studies (for example, by Dennis Marsden) bring out more sharply the plight of people, especially men, who become unemployed. Relief from bad working conditions and exposure to the risks of industrial illness and accidents may be counterbalanced by the greater economic deprivation of the household and the risks of stress-related illness.

Few studies have been made in Britain of the socio-economic factors related to illness and mortality. Social inequality, and especially class inequality, is the major factor for study. But we need to relate the distribution of wealth and income better to analyses of mortality and morbidity by occupational class of individual and combined class (of origin and occupation) of income units or households. The experience of unemployment is only one aspect, not the most important, aspect of that inequality.

Employment has to be studied in relation to the entire population. In the nineteenth century, children were gradually removed from the labour force. In the twentieth century that process has been applied to people regarded as chronologically old. And the position of married women has been ambiguous. There is not a simple division into the employed and unemployed. At one extreme there are those in whole time secure employment. At the other there are those who are continuously unemployed. In between there are different ranks of intermittently, seasonally and occasionally unemployed, the mobile between jobs and those in insecure employment. In a society in which incomes favour the employed, the factors which control the *size* of different groups of the employed and the non-employed, are as important as those which determine the *levels* of incomes which are distributed.

It is not just people's general relationship to the labour market, as conditioned by the development of a market economy, which has to be analysed if we are to explain the facts of unemployment, subemployment and associated poverty. Social and not merely industrial forces have created a more finely differentiated *hierarchy* of roles – both in employment and unemployment – together with a set of discriminating rules by which the characteristics of those who will normally be recruited to these roles are defined. In studying poverty, too much attention is paid to the characteristics of the unemployed instead of to the characteristics of job or role structure. We have to distinguish between the number and characteristics of jobs, and the characteristics of the people occupying them.

If no change is made in 'orthodox policies', the Cambridge Economic Policy Review Group predicts some 2,900,000 unemployed in 1980–85, and 4,600,000 in 1985–90. This takes no account of those among the elderly, young and among women who are consigned to 'dependency'. There is no doubt that the reconstruction of employment and, as part of that, the reduction of dependency (on the part of women, the disabled and the elderly) is the predominant task for a future Labour Government. The reconstruction must take at least two forms. One is the creation of new industry, including enterprises supported by the National Enterprise Board. The other part is community service. Had the social services continued to benefit from a controlled growth in public expenditure during the mid-1970s, the living standards and quality of life of many people in the minority groups in Britain would have been a lot better by 1975 than in fact they are. The cost of a large public sector programme would have been small. The wages and salaries of additional home helps, day care assistants, other ancillary workers and social workers would have been offset by savings in unemployment benefits.

Treasury domination
Although other departments and institutions played a part in the general policies reviewed here, the mid-1970s represented years of particular Treasury dominance in the evolution of social policies.

Different histories have traced its 'restrictionism' in previous decades over social policy.[23] The values which underpin the management of the economy and surfaced in key decisions about the postponement of the wealth tax, the relaxation of corporation tax, the determination to create incentives for private investment, the quixotic treatment of tax thresholds and tax allowances generally, quite apart from the more stringent governance of public expenditure, and the failure to develop a true incomes policy, are the dominant factors determining social conditions during this period. What was new, and especially important, was the attack on public expenditure (long before the IMF laid down its conditions for the terms of its loan in late 1976, as Paul Ormerod points out in Chapter 3) and the justification for unemployment.

I will leave to others the task of tracing the full sorry story about public expenditure. Before 1975 it could be noted that although Labour's years in office could hardly have been said to have marked a dramatic advance towards socialism, they continued to mark commitments to the public sector of the economy and to the social services in particular, which obstinately survived successive economic crises. Cabinet ministers as far apart as Tony Crosland and Barbara Castle reflected and upheld that commitment. But in 1975, to the chagrin of socialists everywhere, the Labour Government committed a savage act of self-injury.[24]

Behind, and in substantial measure penetrating, the Labour administration has been the senior civil service and especially the Treasury. The single source which can be said to have been most influential in shaping social policy throughout this period has been the Treasury, its principal spokesman being the Chancellor of the Exchequer. Its influence throughout the period 1974–79 has been disastrous. This can be expressed or measured in many different ways. It has adopted economic policies which have created more unemployment than was necessary. In particular its crabbed and irrational attitude to public expenditure has prevented re-employment of hundreds of thousands of people and stunted services for the most vulnerable people in society. In reducing real standards of living, it failed even to confine the cuts to those who could bear them easily, and it would have done even more damage but for intense efforts by ministers such as Barbara Castle and Stanley Orme to protect the incomes of pensioners and those with families. In particular the Treasury fought a long battle to frustrate the child benefit scheme, which I hope will in time be made public so that socialists can fully digest the lessons. It is dominated by values – monetarist, material, market and means test – which are thoroughly antithetical to socialist values. It would be wrong to attribute too much of the failure of the last five years to one institution – but it would be equally wrong to neglect the enormous responsibility of that institution.

Lessons for social planning

Two lessons can be drawn from such a general review. The first is that socialists have wholly underestimated the power to control and initiate policies of senior civil servants and especially senior Treasury officials. More important than the mobilization of opinion within the Labour movement on behalf of new policies is the analysis of establishment organisation and methods linked with proposals to control and reduce that power.

The process of policy making by a range of departments deserves open public scrutiny. A start was made, for example, by a former junior minister Michael Meacher when he wrote:

There are three main ways in which the civil service subverts the effect of the democratic vote. One is the manipulation of individual ministers, an exercise in man management which is skilfully orchestrated and on which a great deal of time and care is spent. Second is the isolation of ministers and the resulting dependence on the Whitehall machine, for which a heavy price in policy terms is paid. Third is the exploitation of the inter-departmental framework, in order to circumvent ministers who may be opposing the Whitehall consensus.

In addition there is the close inter-lock with establishment interests outside, which often means officials are acting in concert with the extra-parliamentary power structure against ministers rather than in support of the political manifesto of the governing party.

A further factor is the selective restriction on the dissemination of information, which keeps the power of decision-making limited in fewer hands and rebuts undesired ministerial or public intrusion, especially into the most sensitive areas of policy.[25]

A complex argument about the control of policies is difficult to summarise in an article and Michael Meacher did not spell out the institutional or structural basis of this power. The stranglehold of the Treasury is more a question of administrative organisation, traditions of procedure and cultural associations as well as selective recruitment than a question of conscious conspiratorial communication. For their part senior civil servants, at least in my experience, are often surprisingly unaware that they are taking an interested view of crucial issues as they arise in the 'guidance' which they give ministers. An immense educative task has to be undertaken by British socialists, and this involves more than taking the Fulton Commission's proposals off the shelves where they have been gathering dust. It involves taking action after an election to change the administrative structure, including departmental and inter-departmental committees and semi-autonomous bodies at the apex of the pyramid and the appointment of a large number of Labour supporters to occupy administrative as well as political advisory positions. All this will be necessary before a long term form of central administration can be created.

A second lesson follows form the first. The clumsy contradictions of social policy making have become uncomfortably clear during 1974–79. No longer can they be left largely to private machinations within the Treasury. A Social Development Council needs to be created with direct responsibility to the Prime Minister but with a duty to consult the public. It would consist of outside specialists as well as representatives of consumers and providers of services. It would have to be staffed by an office or department of social planning, and a sub-committee of the Cabinet would meet regularly to consider its reports and commission particular ventures. The Council would have the particular responsibilities of examining (a) expenditure priorities *between* spending departments and (b) the wider balance of priorities among public and private social services, employment pro-grammes and fiscal and incomes policies.

I would not wish to imply that a piece of machinery can solve deep-seated problems but machinery must reflect the approach that governments take to problems and make policies possible to implement. The central problem of the next years will be the precise definition of institutions to enforce that relationship. Public expen-diture control without regard for social needs has penetrated and stultified thinking about policy inside and outside the public social services and at every level of administration. The change in policy making symbolised by the creation of a Social Development Council would also influence approaches to planning in individual depart-ments and the publication of statistical and other data. The interrela-tionships of policy would be better recognised and administration become more flexible and collaborative.

Policies are, of course, crucial to the motivation to reorganise party and government. The obstacles to the effective administration of democratic socialism deserve to be better understood, so that they can be overcome. Better accountability to the party and closer liaison between the trade unions, the party and the administration are part of the solution. Much also depends on the trends in the collaborative instincts and relationships of the people. But above all there need to be changes in planning and central administration, as I have tried to argue.

It must be remembered that in 1974–79 a long term public expenditure cut was substituted for socialist planning, traditional pay restraint was preferred to an effective social contract or a statutory incomes policy, the numbers in the population living below the state's unemployment doubled and a wealth tax was deferred. That is not a record of success in establishing socialism.

2 Labour and Public Expenditure: an Overall View

by Nick Bosanquet

Socialism may be a faith – but it is one daily fortified by evidence. The evidence is of bias towards inequality inherent in the world economy and in British society. Left to themselves, market forces and the class system would produce an even more unequal society. The aim of public spending and policy is to redress this inherent bias towards a restoration of income and opportunity for the less well off. In this book we are looking at issues which go to the heart of a Labour Government's work.

The search for equality has to begin from consent. Before 1945 – and even before 1914 – it was possible to think of redistribution as being principally from the 10 per cent of wealth holders and rentiers to everybody else. The divisions now are more complex. Henry George saw economic progress as an 'immense wedge ... forced not underneath society but through society'.[1] It has much the same effect today. The 'haves' are, or feel themselves to be, well placed in the labour and housing markets and have all the opportunities in education and health care which they want. For other people, life is a struggle with inadequate income, with the actuality or fear of exclusion from the labour market and often with poor health. The search for consent is about persuading a majority – in a time when a sense of financial pressure is common to everybody.

The 1974–79 Labour Governments faced the most severe economic crisis since 1945. The recession with its pressures on public spending and on the employment of those at the end of the labour queue was bound to mean a severe increase in the inherent bias towards inequality. In this case there was another crisis which had to be faced on top of the imbalance in the economy – this was the crisis of belief in public spending. The period thus saw both a recession and the break up of a consensus.

Most of this book charts the reaction to these crises in particular areas of policy. But we also need to look more generally at the record in public spending. Did the 1974–79 Labour Governments succeed in shifting the balance of income and opportunities in society? Did it succeed in creating a fairer society? We begin by looking at questions which are mainly ones of fact: about the context within which the government worked, its policies and their effects on the distribution of income. We then turn to a judgement on the record and to some suggestions for the future.

The context
From the first, policy had to be made in an atmosphere of economic crisis, as such events are conventionally measured. It will be a matter for judgement as to whether this could have been avoided or its consequences mitigated – but its severity and prolonged nature are clear. It was not until 1977 that the atmosphere began to lighten a little.

The short term crisis in the economy was obvious enough – but the government also inherited problems of longer standing within the tax and benefit systems. The level of direct taxation was not yet the central issue in politics – as it became in the late 1970s – but there was already anxiety about the tax system. There had been the episode of the 1969–71 wage explosion. Research seemed to suggest that rising levels of direct taxation as a consequence of the 1967 devaluation had contributed to this. There was also strong criticism of the 'poverty trap' from 1971 on.

The new government also inherited anxieties about the social security system. There was pressure towards improving pensions which had fallen in relation to average earnings. There was anxiety about family support for people at work. The 1966–70 Labour Government had made a half attempt at reform through raising family allowances and clawing back tax allowances. This had pleased few people and the Conservative Government's FIS (Family Income Supplement) scheme had pleased even fewer. There was other unfinished business too in the Finer Report for single parent families and the obvious needs of disabled people below retirement age. The benefit system was in disrepair and many changes had been far too long postponed. This was not just a question of the value of benefits but of the complexity of the system and its reliance on means testing; this was not simply inefficient, but an affront to dignity.

The pressures on the benefit system had been increased by changes in the labour market. Inequality in 'original' income had increased while the methods used in redistributing it had become more ineffective. The sources of change in original income were to be found in worsening unemployment among groups that were most likely to be in poverty: falling participation rates among the elderly and the disabled; and employment difficulties among single parents. The evidence of the Diamond Commission suggests that employment income was becoming even less important for the poorest 20 per cent of households.[2] Even without these changes there would have been a shift towards greater inequality as the means of redistribution became less effective. The fall in the tax threshold and the reduced level of family support affected families in work. The fall in the relative standing of pensions affected pensioners. Income support to single parents remained at the short term supplementary benefit rate and was affected by the relatively slow increase of the short term rate compared to the long term one. Finally the disabled were affected by the growing inadequacy and complexity of the benefits for which they could apply. While the labour market was reducing the gross income of various groups, political and administrative decisions were affecting their net incomes. To all this was soon to be added the effects of higher unemployment.

The government faced major demands for improvements in income support. There was also the need (although not nearly the same political demand) for particular expansions in services. The numbers of very elderly people were growing and were particularly dependent on services. It was recognised that single parents would be helped by an expansion in day care. Community care for the mentally ill and the mentally handicapped was still far away.

The change in relative unemployment was only one part of a wider shift within the labour market. There were signs that the labour market was becoming increasingly divided. On one side there was a primary sector characterised by job security, good levels of pay and of fringe benefits and often by strong trade union organisation. On the other side there was the secondary sector of insecure work, low pay, lack of union organisation and weaker labour intensive firms. The Labour Government tried to deal with some of the effects of these changes within the social security system but without really having any plan of campaign against increasing original inequalities in pay, fringe benefits and job security.

The new government in 1974 also had to work in a changed context of views about the sources of inequality in society. In the older view, social policy was primarily concerned with the inequalities created between people by natural events such as old age, the coming of family responsibilities or ill health. The role of government was to provide a basic minimum of income, to correct for differences in 'equivalent' income and to give insurance against certain risks through services. The other main type of inequality was between children of different class backgrounds which was to be remedied through education. Thus equality of opportunity was set as an aim alongside equality in terms of a basic minimum.

These notions underlay the Beveridge approach to social policy. We now see poverty more in relative than in absolute terms, but our view of the sources of inequality has also changed. We have come to fear the effects of the tax and social security system on inequality. The attempt of various bureaucracies to correct for deficiencies in original income has had various highly undesirable side effects. We have also become much less optimistic about whether the educational system can ever contribute very much to equality. The government was thus faced with the challenge of inequality arising from all the old natural sources and also with a greater challenge of finding a more equitable way of financing public spending. The redistributive effects of public spending might well be undermined by the increasingly regressive way in which it was financed. In the old view, a redistribution in terms of services which was mainly horizontal (between different stages of the life cycle) could be financed by a progressive tax system which brought about some 'vertical' redistribution. The changing nature of the tax system and the continued bias in the enjoyment of the more attractive forms of public spending towards the middle classes had weakened both sides of this old equation.

How can we sum up the pattern of original income distribution facing the new government in 1974? We can best describe it in terms of three main groups of households. The poorest 30 per cent of households had then and still have little income from the labour market – about 5 per cent of the total. There was then a middle band in which 50 per cent of the households had about the same proportion of total income; finally the top 20 per cent of households had about 45 per cent of total income. Within the top band, the top 1 per cent had about 6 per cent. However the most important inequality was probably between the 20 per cent of the managerial and professional élite and everybody else.

Change in the labour market had strengthened the position of this top 20 per cent through a remarkable expansion in the number of well paid non-manual jobs. These jobs have greater stability of income, as compared to the pay of manual workers. Change in the labour market has been lowering the share of the bottom 30 per cent. Within the middle band there have been two main pressures. Rising unemployment has made for greater insecurity of income for some; higher participation rates for married women has affected many households. If a family has a second income, it is likely to feel well off. Change in the labour market has increased the dispersion of income within this middle band. Finally, a surprising number of the very poorest in terms of original income are excluded altogether from the figures. These figures are based on households living independently. They exclude single people living in institutions or without a home. These may amount to about one million people.[3]

The state intervenes to redistribute original income through the tax system and through income support. The tax system as inherited in 1974 took about 20 per cent of the income from poor households and then was roughly neutral across the whole range of income, taking direct and indirect taxes together. Cash benefits raise the income of the poorest 20 per cent. The main redistribution such as it is comes about through services. The main groups to benefit overall are the elderly through cash and families through services.

This picture drawn from *Economic Trends* deals in averages but it conceals the increasingly tortuous way in which transfers are made. The tangle does not affect the top 20 per cent of households very much. They ride clear on their high levels of original income, helped by the shadow welfare state of tax allowances. The effect of change in the labour market and in the benefit system taken together has been to increase the variety of fortune within the middle band. From some points of view, the changes may seem random but they work towards favouring certain types of household against others. As between families with only one wage earner in it, there have been important changes in the relative net incomes of families below average earnings compared with those in average earnings or just above. This can be seen if we compare gross and net earnings for men with two children under 10. In terms of gross earnings, there was a difference of 100 per cent between average earnings and half the average in 1977 (from £81 to £40.50). In net terms on the assumption that all benefits were claimed, the differential was reduced to 26 per cent (£63 to £50). Rising participation rates also raised significantly the incomes of households in middle age. The main 'losers' were households around average earnings where the wife did not go out to work.

These changes created new points of affluence and difficulty across the life cycle – and also new feelings of inequality, even of rage and bafflement. To the old problems of distribution between top and bottom were added new issues of distribution within the middle band. The government had to work not only in a context of uncertainty about the economic management of the tax and social security systems, but in one of growing feelings of discontent about them.

At the same time the whole basis of the welfare state was coming under much greater questioning. For many years, the 'welfare state' has been under attack from groups which are variously called the 'Right' and 'liberals'. The IEA since the early 1960s has perhaps been the most notable spokesman for these views. There were a number of grounds for attack. One was that the extension of state activity restricted choice; it was also argued that it led to dependence. Finally it was argued that state activity was generally inefficient and that the private market could do the job more effectively. The argument was psychologically about the effect on individual character and economically on the microeconomic operation of individual markets. These strands of criticism remained, but a new and important addition was made to them in the years after 1976. This was the thesis about the macroeconomic effects of the public sector which was put forward most notably by Bacon and Eltis.[4] The earlier criticisms of the public sector had never found much favour within the Labour Party. This new theory however not only appealed to a wide spectrum of opinion in the country but even found converts among Labour Cabinet ministers.

The argument was that the increasing share of public spending had crowded out the growth of 'tradeable' output. The main evidence presented was the fact that public spending had grown significantly in the last few years relative to other types of output. The case was also made by David Smith in a more tightly argued way.[5] He carried out a study of the relationship between the growth of the public sector and economic performance for 19 industrial countries. This showed that there seemed to be some relationship between the two when public spending was defined in terms of spending on goods and services; there appeared to be little relationship, however, when transfer payments were also taken into account. His conclusion was that the growth of the public sector might have contributed to Britain's low growth rate but that it was certainly not the major or the only explanation. The mechanism by which the public sector affects other parts of the economy is not made clear in this or other studies. There could be effects through financial markets if public borrowing raised the cost of funds to the private sector. On the other hand, there could be effects through competition for scarce production resources at times of high demand.

The Labour Government fell heavily for the Bacon and Eltis thesis when first announced. Later analysis suggests that a greater degree of scepticism might have been appropriate. The international evidence suggested that Britain's public sector was no larger than that of most other developed countries and, in fact, smaller than some of them. Most important of all, it was possible that the low rate of growth had come about through quite other reasons (to do with the poor performance of British firms in export and domestic markets) and that without expansion of the public sector there would have been even more unemployment. The Bacon–Eltis thesis lacked a view of causality. It left unanswered the possibility that growth in the public sector may have been a sympathetic response to a pattern of low growth that had already established itself rather than the cause of the low growth originally.

The final school of criticism was again new and came mostly from within the Labour Party itself. This was the view that the particular method by which the public sector was financed may have led to increased inflationary pressure. The increased burden of income tax on the wage earner may have led to greater frustration and increased wage demands. Another criticism associated with the name of Anthony Crosland looked askance more at how the results of public spending were distributed rather than at the way it was financed. The middle classes were held to take a disproportionate share of the fruits of public spending. There was certainly some weight in this criticism, although there might well be incompatibility between the aims of universality in a service and the aim of concentrating help away from the middle classes.

The record in public spending

We now turn to the government's policies. How did it react to the crisis of belief in public spending and to the crisis of balance in the economy? Public expenditure showed very rapid growth in 1974–75 but was slowed after this. The growth was much greater for transfer payments and for public sector pay than for other kinds of spending. It was greater for transfer payments than for services; and within the services there was additional spending on public sector pay but reductions in capital spending.

From 1976 on, the government was attempting to hold back the growth of public spending. This restraint continued for the rest of its period in office. The government's short term reaction to the economic situation was gradually transformed into a social philosophy and a social policy for the longer term. The government went out of office committed to reducing the share of public spending in GDP. In his 'Letter of Intent' to the IMF, the Chancellor wrote that 'an essential element of the government's strategy will be a continued and substantial reduction over the next few years in the share of resources required for the public sector'.[6] He may not have been entirely successful in this. But overall the share of government spending on goods and services in GDP fell from 24.5 per cent in 1973/4 to 23.5 per cent in 1978/9. Total spending (excluding debt interest) fell in real terms between 1975/6 and 1978/9.

The effect of such restrictions can be seen on a service such as the NHS. The net share of GDP, after an early rise, fell from 5.5 per cent to 5.3 per cent from 1976/7 to 1977/8 and then remained unchanged at 5.3 per cent.

The distribution of income

What was the record in terms of income distribution? We look first at the effects of the tax system (cols. 1 and 2 of Table 2.1). We are limited to comparisons between 1972 and 1977 as the only years with comparable data. These show that the tax 'take' from very low incomes fell slightly with the decreased emphasis on indirect taxes. For the other brackets, proportions of income paid in tax rose but remained roughly constant across the range. The ratio of the proportion of income paid in tax by the bottom decile as compared to the top decile fell from 63 to 53 per cent. Thus the tax system at the extremes got a little fairer but above the third decile the basic feature remained the constancy of the proportion paid in tax.

Table 2.1 Changes in taxation and income, 1972–77

Deciles of original income	(1) (2) Total tax paid as % original income plus cash benefits		(3) (4) Income after all taxes and transfers as % original income		(5) (6) Final income after all taxes and benefits as % original income		(7) (8) Income after taxes and transfers as % original income top decile		(9) (10) Income after taxes and transfers as % average original income	
	1972	1977	1972	1977	1972	1977	1972	1977	1972	1977
1 (lowest)	22.0	20.2	230.0	664.0	310.0	857.0	9.4	12.0	24.2	31.4
2	24.2	21.7	220.4	351.8	277.5	457.1	12.1	12.4	31.3	32.6
3	29.0	27.9	102.6	131.5	127.7	165.0	17.3	17.1	44.8	44.8
4	32.8	34.8	78.9	83.3	95.6	104.4	20.7	20.3	53.5	53.2
5	33.4	35.6	73.5	73.8	89.1	90.7	24.5	24.0	63.3	62.9
6	33.5	37.3	71.3	69.1	84.6	84.2	28.0	27.5	72.4	72.0
7	33.8	37.2	69.9	67.7	81.7	80.7	32.2	31.8	83.2	83.1
8	34.1	37.3	68.9	66.6	79.5	77.5	37.2	36.6	96.1	95.8
9	34.4	37.7	68.1	65.2	77.2	75.4	44.5	43.5	115.0	113.9
10	34.8	38.1	66.7	63.9	73.2	71.2	66.7	63.9	172.3	167.3
All	33.2	35.8	75.6	75.7	88.3	89.9	29.3	28.9	75.6	75.7

Source: *Economic Trends*, 1979.

Turning to changes in final income, we must look both at final cash income and at income including the social wage of services. By both these measures, there were significant relative gains in the incomes of the poorest households (see Table 2.1, cols. 3 to 6). The comparison year is 1972 but a check of intervening years in *Economic Trends* suggests that the change came about after 1974. There was also a slight reduction in the relative incomes of households in the top 40 per cent but little basic change in the pattern above the lowest decile. The same results hold looking at cash incomes as proportions of the original incomes arising from employment. There was some improvement in the relative incomes particularly of the poorest households (cols. 7 to 10, Table 2.1). The main change was for income at the lowest decile which rose from 24.2 per cent to 31.4 per cent of average original income.

The evidence does suggest some movement towards additional help for the elderly during the Labour period. This book charts some of the policies which brought this about, notably the big relative increase in pensions in 1974/5. The child benefit scheme at least held out the promise of fairer support to families. But there were still deficiencies in income support affecting single parents and the long term unemployed. Within services, the government did make some attempt to redistribute spending towards the worst off both within the NHS and within the education service.

Against these successes, have to be set the effects of the recession in adding to pressure on the less well off, particularly among families. There was a large increase in the number of households below the usual poverty line in the most recent period for which figures are available. Although a part of this can be explained by the improvement in the real value of the supplementary benefit scale the recession certainly contributed. The numbers at or below the supplementary benefit level are set out in Table 2.2.

Thus the numbers counted as poor among the elderly and the long term sick showed little change or they fell, while the numbers of working age rose. The government was able to temper the effects of the recession to some people who were out of the labour force completely. It was not able to prevent a great intensification of difficulty for many families of working age.

The judgement
Turning from questions of fact to those of judgement, is the record a creditable one? There is certainly much more to debate here than

Table 2.2   Numbers in households dependent on supplementary benefit or with estimated incomes below SB level, 1974 and 1976 (thousands)

	1974	1976
Pensioners (as % total)	2,680 (52)	2,800 (44)
Under pensionable age family head or single parent		
Unemployed	450	1,080
Normally in full time work	360	890
Sick or disabled	480	280
Others	1,170	1,300
Sub-total (as % total)	2,460 (48)	3,550 (56)
Total	5,140	6,350
of which:		
In large families	760	1120
Single parents	840	1120

Source: DHSS, quoted in *The Rising Tide of Poverty*, Low Pay Unit, 1978.

there was about the record of the 1964–70 Labour Governments. We can ask whether the government could have avoided or mitigated the recession by a different policy for public spending. We can also ask whether, within the policy which it did adopt, the composition of public spending was sensible. Did the government get as much value as possible for the most vulnerable in society?

Some would argue that the government's overall policy was forced on it by the requirements of a capitalist economy.[7] By this view, public services have only a very limited role as a kind of casualty clearing station in the struggle for growth. Certainly an open mixed economy sets up strong pressures towards inequality of income. Growth requires capital accumulation. This implies higher profit shares and higher relative rewards for managers. A growing mixed economy also requires stimulus from the demand side. This will often conveniently take the form of increased private consumption of consumer goods which in turn implies an increase in purchasing power for those with the most free income over and above that required for food, housing and heating. Growth also requires favourable conditions on the financial side which are often thought to imply a reduced financial claim from the public sector in order to avoid crowding out the private sector. All these requirements may limit the scope for increases in public spending.

Certainly these constraints exist but they are neither total nor inexorable. A Labour Government still has some room for manoeuvre and some scope for changing the distribution of income and opportunities set by the market and by the class system. For all their defects, the establishment of the National Health Service and the more recent improvements in living standards of pensioners both show what can be done. Over the long term the share of resources going to public spending *has* risen very significantly. At present, apathy and our own lack of a clear philosophy seem as serious obstacles to change as do the requirements of the economy.

We turn now to a more specific proposition: could the government have used public spending to avoid the worst of the recession in 1975–76? There had been a big rise in public spending in 1974. This was accompanied by a rapid increase in the rate of inflation, a rising balance of payments deficit, a rising Public Sector Borrowing Requirement (PSBR) and rising unemployment. By 1975, the British inflation rate was running at over twice the average for the major OECD countries. A different policy would have required, as a first stage, a higher PSBR. This would have meant a further rise in interest rates which would have increased the severe pressures on corporate liquidity and thus led to higher unemployment. Over the medium term there would also have been further falls in the exchange rate which would have fed back into domestic inflation. Thus the case for more public spending in 1975–76 has to show how such spending could have been financed and how it could have been compatible at just that point in time with a reduction in the rate of inflation and in unemployment.

The government had little choice but to rein back the growth in public spending in 1975–76. It proceeded however to turn this change, which had begun as a short term economic adjustment under duress, into a longer term social philosophy. There are certain compelling reasons in the longer term why certain forms of public spending should grow at least as fast as national output. There are growing numbers of people who are outside the labour force. Some of the most important public services are labour intensive and cannot show the same rate of productivity growth as capital intensive forms of output in the private sector. The 'normal' expectation would be that some items in public spending would rise slightly faster than national income, simply to maintain existing standards, even before allowing for the effects of recession in raising certain kinds of spending. Much was made of supposed inefficiencies in the public sector. Certainly these exist although we rarely get a careful comparison of managerial slack in the private sector. However it is dangerous to base a general judgement about the future of public services on anecdotes about surplus administrators in the NHS or even in local government. There may have been waste, poor levels of 'output' and inflexibility in some public services, but such problems called for more active management rather than for general reductions in the share of the public spending which in any case would affect most those services which were trying to adjust to change. In the event the government ended up with the worst of all worlds. It was attacked by its own supporters for trying to reduce the share of public spending in national income, while it was accused by the Conservatives of extravagance.

The public sector includes many different elements. The total level of public spending is now a sum with only ambiguous meaning in social terms although it may have greater relevance for demand management. We can get a clearer view of the record by looking at the four core programmes which do have an immediate impact on equality (Table 2.3). Between them, these four kinds of spending accounted for about half of total public spending. Over the period, only health and social security registered a major increase in share. Much of the increase for the NHS reflects the effect of pay and cost changes in 1974 and in relation to the evidence of need contained in demographic change the service was severely stretched. The effects of the fall in education's share may have been partly offset by falling school rolls but there was certainly little room for

Table 2.3   *Shares in GDP at market prices (percentages)*

	1973/4	1974/5	1978/9
Education	5.9	6.2	5.6
Health and social services	5.0	5.4	5.3
Housing	2.9	4.4	3.2
Social security	7.9	8.8	9.8
Total	21.7	24.8	23.9

Source: *The Government's Expenditure Plans, 1979/80–1982/83*, Cmnd 7439, HMSO, 1979.

any improvement in standards. These figures suggest that the resources available to the services were very much affected by the government's newly acquired philosophy. Peter Townsend showed in Chapter One just how drastic were the reductions in rates of growth compared with the past.

It may be that recession in 1975 was unavoidable. It is difficult to see how the government could have gone for a radically higher level of public spending at that time particularly when much of local government, which spends most money on goods and services, was soon to be under Conservative control. The real question is about the longer term philosphy. Labour left office committed to rather low rates of growth in the core public services. For example, the White Paper on public spending published in 1979 projected a rate of growth on spending on the NHS below the most likely rate of growth of GDP and even below the growth of spending on defence.[8] As a practical point, such a plan hardly seemed feasible and certainly it seemed undesirable. We have argued that, in the normal course of events, these services would be expected to take a rising share of national income just to maintain standards and before allowing for the many new initiatives required both in income support and in the services. The government seemed to lack any belief in the positive role of the core public sector. In this sense it has to be judged as being far too pessimistic and defeatist.

The lack of aspiration for better services was linked to the total failure to reform the tax system and the benefit system. The well known defects of the tax system were just as serious when Labour left office in 1979 as they had been in 1974. The only real gain was in the indexation of tax allowances and the re-introduction of the reduced rate band which between then stopped the tax threshold from falling even further and made income tax a little more progressive. The poverty trap remained, as did the shadow welfare state of tax allowances. The corporate sector remained very lightly taxed. The political consequences of this conservatism were to be all too drastic.

Looking at the record within the given total of public spending, how sensible was the balance? The most important change was in the increased importance of transfer payments. This came about partly because of the real increase in support to pensioners but it also reflected changes in the numbers qualifying for pensions and the effects of unemployment which increased the numbers of people who were eligible for supplementary benefit. Finally, transfer payments rose because of the shift from child tax allowances to direct payments.

There are two main successes. One was in the increase in the real level of pensions. The other was in the child benefit scheme which held out hope of improved support to families with a head in full time work. The child benefit scheme should mean that families are less dependent on means tested benefits and on FIS. The record was however much more disappointing for single parent families and also for disabled people under retirement age. Aspirations towards improving benefits for these groups came under increasing pressure because of the rising level of unemployment. This created a new and major priority for improving support to the long term unemployed. In the field of pensions and of family benefits there were fundamental reforms of the systems of benefit. In the case of pensions, these would have effects which were admittedly long term but which would be major. No similar reform of the system of benefits for the unemployed was forthcoming. The system was still dominated by the idea of unemployment benefit as relief for a temporary interruption of earnings. The income support for those who were below retirement age but out of the labour force for long periods remained both inadequate and tended to decline the longer people had left the labour force. Nor was there any higher level of support or any more consistent scheme of benefits for single parents. Apart from automatic factors, the improvement in transfer payments such as they were tended to reflect pressure on behalf of groups with strong political support.

Local government spending fell from 28.6 per cent of total government spending in 1973/4 to 25.4 per cent in 1978/9. The declining role of local government spending mainly reflected declining expenditure on roads and housing. There were also signs however of increased pressure on other services and particularly on social services. The growth rates of spending on community services for the elderly were low and rather below the increase in the numbers of the very elderly. Local government was coming under increased financial pressure first because of the rates crisis of 1974–75 which left scars; later the proportion of spending financed out of the rate support grant was static. Thus local government was not in a strong position to finance new services even if the political will to do so had been there. This was an important change given the relevance of many local government services particularly social services and housing to many deprived groups. Finally the NHS in particular suffered a drastic decline in its capital programme. Joint funding only stopped an even greater fall. It did not give any new impetus.

The net effect of all these changes was to create a greater problem of balance between income support and support to services. Some forms of income support were now indexed and also, in the case of pensions, had assurances of long term improvements. The services were suffering from heavy pressure which inhibited new development and which in some cases even made it difficult to carry on the existing level of care. At the same time, there was a growing tendency even within the service category to give attention to problems which could be defined territorially while neglecting the interests of groups such as single parents or the elderly mentally confused who were scattered around in small groups. Thus overall there was some success in improving income support to pensioners and to families but much else in the pattern of need went by default.

Conclusions

The Labour record had some promising early beginnings but became more discreditable with time. On balance, there were more constructive changes for the future than might have been expected. The child benefit scheme and the new pension plan were useful beginnings. The central failure was not in handling the recession of 1975 but in turning the short term imperative of restraint into a permanent philosophy for public expenditure. The government seemed to have no belief in public services. It put much weight on the element of waste in the public sector. For years we had anecdotes about the surplus bureaucrats of the NHS and falling reading standards in the schools. These tales often turned out on close examination to have little substance or to be fairly minor issues but they had a major impact on opinion. The Labour Government itself contributed greatly to the crisis of opinion about public spending. If we did not appear to believe in the public services ourselves, how could we expect others to?

The government did little to reform the ways in which public expenditure was financed. It was unable to deal with the problems of the 'poverty trap', the shadow welfare state of the allowances and the lack of progression in the tax system. Thus it added to the genuine and understandable worries which many people had about these problems. Its approach to the tax system was one of diffident conservatism; it did not believe in the present system but it was unable to find the courage to change it.

Little attempt was made to influence inequalities in the labour market at source after a promising start with the Employment Protection Act. The great difference in working conditions and fringe benefits between manual and non-manual workers remained. The government continued to operate a peculiar kind of minimum wage called the wages council system but again without believing in it. Its approaches on women's rights and the rights of the immigrant minority were rather more active, however, and more creditable in their results, as was its approach to equality in the international sphere.

Lessons for the future

The activities financed from public spending have become much more varied and some of them have little to do with social equality. But we can mark out a core which is important. This must surely include expenditure on social security, education, the NHS, social services and housing. On a normal expectation, the proportion of GDP going to these forms of spending must rise simply to maintain existing standards, in the face of pressures from demography and from relative costs. In addition, there are many urgent claims from the deprived such as single parents and the mentally ill who have little chance of improved opportunities except through public initiative. It is hard to see how we can move towards a fairer society – a more even distribution of income and life changes – unless this core of the public sector has an expanding share of GDP. Even with such expansion there would be no guarantee of success. It would all depend on how the extra money was used; but higher public spending remains a necessary condition for a fairer society. Arguments about waste in the public sector (many of which in any case relate to activities outside the 'core') should not be allowed to obscure the strength of the case for more public spending.

Such a case must go on to show how the extra spending can be financed. Some would see public spending as desirable in itself but would argue that it involves excessive costs either in terms of lost growth or in terms of a net worsening of income distribution. The Labour Government was trapped here partly by myths and partly by reality. The reality is unpleasant enough. A long time ago a certain amount of horizontal redistribution was financed through a progressive tax system but the tax system is no longer progressive except for very low incomes. On paper, marginal rates of income tax would seem to be high but in practice they are abated by tax allowances. The current pattern of indirect taxation with its reliance on the alcohol and tobacco duties is extremely regressive. The tax system took 35 per cent of an original income of £2,703 in 1977 and 38 per cent of an income of £11,079. In net terms, the corporate sector hardly pays any tax at all and Britain has the reputation of being a corporate tax haven. Against this reality has to be set deeply rooted and widely believed myths which the Labour Government failed to dispel. There is the myth that the top 20 per cent of household incomes (which have in any case derived so much benefit from changes in the labour market) are highly taxed and that the burden of taxation is crippling the better off. There is the myth that the burden of corporate taxation is crippling investment.

The case for higher public spending will certainly never have a fair chance within the present system of taxation. Labour must abandon its approach of hesitant conservatism. We need a series of fundamental reforms which will include a reduced emphasis on tax allowances within the income tax system, a broader base of expenditure taxation and a gradual increase in taxation of the corporate sector until Britain loses its offshore status in relation to Europe and even to the Cayman Islands. The most important aims are to increase the buoyancy of revenue and the progressiveness of the system as a whole rather than to have a sudden increase in the taxation of higher incomes. Unless the Labour Party has such a plan, it will be vulnerable to the same assault as felled it in 1979. At present the case for public spending is drastically weakened by the narrowness of the tax base and the many inequities and anomalies which riddle our taxation system from the bottom to the top.

The case for public spending is also weakened by examples of waste, inefficiency and poor service to the public. All too often there has been an incredible slowness in taking decisions and in trying to change patterns of service. We do need more courageous, active management of the public services. No doubt we lack full and careful comparisons with the private sector, yet public services will always be more visible and more open to judgement on a day-to-day basis.

Without active management, there will be little hope of making sure that extra spending really does help the least well off. In social security, we need a new will to redistribute towards groups such as single parents. Within education this means spending relatively more on the compulsory years of schooling. In the social services it means facing up to the poor record in community care. It means, too, greater activity in making sure that all local authorities provide minimum standards in some vital services.

The public services should not, however, bear the whole weight of the struggle for equality. The evidence suggests a widening gulf within the labour market between the organised, primary sector and the rest. There is also still a great division between the conditions of work and fringe benefits of non-manual workers and those of manual workers. For a period after the second war change in the labour market was, if anything, favourable towards equality. This has certainly not been so in the last fifteen years. Unless we can alter the trend at source, it is bound to have effects on the core public services which, especially in the case of education and of social security, tend to be very much affected by changes in the labour market. The first essential here is to reduce unemployment, which has been the most powerful force making for inequality in the recent past. For socialists there will also be a strong case for a major campaign to improve the conditions, fringe benefits and job security of manual and of secondary workers. The Employment Protection Act and the Health and Safety at Work Act have been small beginnings. They have at least established the principle of intervention. Many of these inequalities in status and conditions seem to reflect apathy, social convention and low expectations rather than some deep-laid plan on which the whole economy depends.

The increasing division in the labour market also creates a new case for a minimum wage. At present we have the façade of a minimum wage system. It was often argued that a minimum wage would be inflationary as people moved to restore their differentials but in the current conditions of the British economy, a sensibly managed minimum wage might help to settle inflationary expectations through providing a point of reference. It could set a standard in a labour market. It may also be argued that such a measure will have employment effects. These will certainly exist but they will mainly affect a fringe of poorly paid jobs which are characterised by high turnover in any case. A minimum wage would make sense as one part of a more socially responsible approach to determining pay in Britain.

Some – perhaps many people in the Labour Party – would argue that we can never make progress towards equality within the setting of a mixed economy. This book, by implication, rejects this nihilistic view. Socialism is much more likely to develop from example than from exhortation. The example of public spending and public services at work in reversing the inherent bias towards unfairness in society would be a powerful one. For some, socialism will only emerge from an apocalypse but in practice socialism in the next few years is much more likely to stand or fall on whether we can make the case for equality through better and more fairly financed public services. Labour Governments have been in office for 11 out of the last 16 years and the results must be considered intensely disappointing. Labour Governments seem to have become increasingly conservative even while the Conservatives have become bolder and more radical. We want to see a Labour Government that will make a real difference to the many people in our society who are still desperately deprived in life chances. We hope that in this book we have pointed some directions for such a government.

PART II

The Economy and International Relationships

3 The Economic Record

by Paul Ormerod

The socialist response to the problems of capitalism has always been to expand the role of public ownership and control in the economy. The social democratic section of the Labour Party has questioned the relevance of these arguments in the post-war years, preferring to rely on the indirect influences of taxation, subsidies and public expenditure. The period of office of the Labour Government 1974–79 was characterised by an even more marked shift in the philosophy of the majority of the Cabinet reflected in the government's intention of reducing the share of public spending in national income.

A strong and efficient economy is essential for movement towards socialism in a democracy. Without such an economy, the ideals of socialists are frustrated and, far from advances being made, painful retreats will often have to be endured. A rapid rate of growth is needed for reasons which are fundamental for socialists – for example, to eliminate the 'backlog of social investment' of which Crosland[1] wrote 25 years ago and which remains today. It will be argued that an expansion of public expenditure can be a causal as well as a consequential factor in rapid economic growth; but for sustained expansion of public services such as health and education, a fast rate of economic growth is needed.

Growth is also required in order to generate employment and preserve the right to work. Unemployment is still a cause of suffering in our society, particularly since benefits are in general much lower than the working wage even after tax. It is the disadvantaged in society who suffer the most from increases in the overall unemployment rate: for example, older workers who became unemployed experienced much longer spells and other groups suffered disproportionately – the unskilled, the disabled and young coloured people.

Between 1974 and 1977, when total unemployment increased by 120 per cent, unemployment amongst coloured workers increased by 350 per cent. The problems of the disadvantaged are illustrated in a Manpower Services Commission Report on youth unemployment.[2] A disproportionate number of the young unemployed had fathers who were employed in manual occupations and there was a strong relationship between lack of qualifications and the length of time spent unemployed. The concentration of unemployment in areas and amongst social groups was shown by the fact that 14 per cent of the survey had fathers who were unemployed, 22 per cent had at least one unemployed brother or sister, and 19 per cent lived in households where no-one had a job. Further, nearly four out of five in the sample had some friends unemployed. In general, however, the average spell of unemployment is lower for younger than for older workers, but the incidence of unemployment amongst youth is disproportionately high in a recession: a 1 per cent increase in male unemployment has been associated in the past with a 1.7 per cent increase in unemployment amongst young males, whilst for young females the figure is 3 per cent.

A stagnant economy is also obviously the worst climate for acceptance of socialist ideals amongst the voters. Since 1973, the annual average rate of growth of real national output has been less than 1 per cent a year, with no growth at all in the key manufacturing sector. During these years, we have seen the development of increasingly bitter attacks upon the redistributive function of the state. There has been vilification of the trade unions, whose existence is fundamental to the extension of the rights of the working class as a whole. In trying to defend their members against the inadequacies of the system, they are made the scapegoat for these inadequacies.

The received wisdom is that once again a Labour Government was 'blown off course', resulting in measures of austerity being imposed upon the government by the external pressure of the International Monetary Fund at the end of 1976. But, in fact, the strategy of a reduction in the share of the public sector in total output was already in existence by then. The first steps had been taken within months of Labour being returned to power in October 1974. A more positive approach had been adopted initially by the government after the February 1974 election and this was not formally abandoned until the April 1975 budget. This was in response to the formidable external problems which faced the country after the oil price rise in the winter of 1973/4. The huge increase in oil prices (some 250 per cent) not only added about £2,500 million to our import bill in 1974 but also increased the domestic price level directly by some 2.5 per cent. Apart from the domestic inflationary consequences, the oil price rise and the dislocation of supply associated with it eventually led to a severe recession in the world economy in 1975.

The potential consequences of the oil price rise for the industrialised countries were accurately predicted by the National Institute in their February 1974 *Review* when they wrote: 'The impact of the oil price rise on individual industrial countries will be severely deflationary. There is a danger that they may react by intensifying the deflation which the oil price rise causes ... if they can act in common and at the same time they can avert this deflationary impact. Some kind of international agreement is needed on a compatible set of 'target' (balance of payments) deficits, and on the reflationary policies needed to achieve them'. The oil price rise was effectively equivalent to an indirect tax increase, reducing purchasing power in the rest of the world. The correct response for the West was therefore to take reflationary action to counteract the oil price rise and to ignore the adverse movements in the balance of payments which it caused. A reduction in indirect taxes such as VAT would have been ideal to offset the increase in the domestic price level due to oil. The oil price rise represented a real shift of resources away from the industrialised world but the existence of spare capacity meant that the actual level of real output could have remained unchanged if the appropriate reflationary action had been taken. Although the Labour Government did not go far enough, nevertheless its overall fiscal policy was expansionary during the financial year 1974/5[3] with the result that unemployment rose relatively slowly. However, the industrialised countries as a whole, with the minor exceptions of Canada and Sweden, intensified the deflationary impact of the oil price rise by deflationary domestic policies; these were introduced partly to remove the induced balance of payments deficit and partly in the mistaken belief that restrictive policies would moderate the rate of inflation. The result was that in the industrialised countries in 1975 the level of demand and trade collapsed in a manner unprecedented since the war.

There were undoubtedly limits to how far the level of domestic output and employment could have been preserved during 1974 and 1975 by the use of traditional techniques of economic management alone. Surrey and Ormerod argue that a sharply reflationary policy could have kept the level of unemployment down to about 750,000 by the end of 1975 compared to the actual level of 1,170,000 without unduly adverse financial consequences, either internal or external.[3] But in the hypothetical case, just as in reality, the level of unemployment would have been rising, and the scope for further reflation through orthodox measures more or less exhausted. The adoption of protectionism and an interventionist industrial strategy would have been essential to insulate the British economy from the consequences of the world recession.

During the winter of 1974/5, the Cabinet was faced with a critical choice on economic policy. The strategy of moving to a planned, protected, expansionist economy was a genuine political option for a government which had just been returned to power with a small but effective majority. Instead, the government conformed with the other major industrial countries and chose a strategy of deflation which reduced the share of the public sector in the economy as a whole. The April 1975 budget was the first public announcement of this strategy. In it Denis Healey stressed the need for resources to be diverted into the balance of payments. To secure this aim, the public sector borrowing requirement (PSBR) was to be reduced by £1 billion in the financial year 1975/6, and by a further £3 billion in 1976/77. In addition, indirect taxes were increased, adding some $2\frac{3}{4}$ per cent to the Retail Price Index over the next three months. This budget explicitly forecast that unemployment would continue to rise to about 1 million by the end of 1975, whereas even the 1964–70 government baulked at the thought of unemployment rising above 600,000. Healey predicted that unemployment would fall during 1976, not as a result of the traditionally effective responses to rising unemployment such as tax cuts or public expenditure increases, but as world trade recovered. In the July *Attack on Inflation*,[4] the government pointed out that work was in hand to bring about extensive use of cash limits in 1976/7 as a means of curbing public expenditure. In August 1975, Anthony Crosland announced a 'standstill' in local authority revenue expenditure for grant purposes in the following year. This was to be limited to the equivalent in real terms of the 1975/6 level of spending. In November, at a meeting of the NEDC attended by senior ministers and representatives of the TUC and CBI, a major shift in economic priorities was announced, away from public expenditure and towards the regeneration of Britain's industrial structure.

The culmination of these measures was the White Paper on the government's public expenditure plans to 1979/80.[5] In this, the government declared its intention of bringing about a sharp fall in the public sector share of total national output: in other words, to bring about substantial cuts in the levels of public expenditure below what they would otherwise have been. Explicit reliance was placed upon the private sector to expand to fill the gaps left by public expenditure cuts and to promote growth and employment. As Glennerster and Ormerod commented 'the present government thus intend to achieve something which even recent Conservative administrations have not – namely to reduce the share of economic activity devoted to public expenditure'.[6] They further argued that 'if the government sticks to its strategy ... 1976 may still see another round of cuts'. The strategy of cuts in public expenditure was therefore established well before the visit of the IMF at the end of 1976. The cuts announced in December of that year were simply part of the overall logic of the government's strategy, which was subsequently maintained throughout the life of the government, its most recent expression being the January 1979 Public Expenditure White Paper[7] in which public expenditure was planned to grow in real terms by an average of 2 per cent a year through to 1982/3. However this was in the context of an assumed annual growth in real national output of $2\frac{3}{4}$ per cent. So the share of the public sector in total output was projected to continue to fall into the early 1980s. The implication was that if the target growth rate for national output was not met, then the growth in public expenditure would have to be cut back accordingly, despite an explicit projection of a level of unemployment of 1.3 million in 1982/3, excluding school leavers.

The White Paper of February 1976 exaggerated the share of public expenditure in national output, quoting for the first time the misleading figure of 60 per cent, which is still used by the far Right as part of their sustained attack upon the public sector.[8] Indeed, such men as Milton Friedman and Roy Jenkins saw in this figure threats to the very existence of democracy in the UK. Yet the figure of 60 per cent was a gross exaggeration. Firstly, the government chose the smallest available figure with which to measure national output, GDP at factor cost, rather than GDP at market prices (the difference being that the latter includes indirect taxes such as VAT whilst the former does not). The latter is more appropriate in this context, and subsequent White Papers have in fact used it rather than GDP at factor cost. Yet the difference between the two was not insignificant in 1975, the figures being some £92,000 million and £103,000 million respectively. Dividing public expenditure by the smaller figure obviously produces a bigger number for the share of public expenditure in the total. Secondly, and more importantly, the White Paper itself pointed out the fraudulent nature of the 60 per cent figure by noting that 'this ratio compares two disparate magnitudes – transfer payments are included in the total of public expenditure but do not constitute part of GDP'.[5] Transfer payments comprise pensions, unemployment benefits and similar benefits and although the ratio of public expenditure including transfers to GDP may have some relevance to the financing of spending, it gives a quite misleading impression of the use of resources in the economy. The latter concept is better illustrated by the ratio of general government expenditure on goods and services to GDP. Table 3.1 sets out the two measures.

Table 3.1   Ratios of public expenditure to GDP at market prices

	Total public expenditure	General government expenditure on goods and services
1973/4	40.5	24.5
1974/5	46	26
1975/6	46.5	27
1976/7	44	26
1977/8	40.5	24
1978/9 (est)	42	23.5

Source: Cmnd 7439, *1979 Public Expenditure White Paper.*

These figures put the notorious figure of 60 per cent in perspective, and the figures for spending on goods and services show that the government was successful in its declared objective of making reductions in the share of public expenditure.

It is instructive to quantify the scale of these cuts. A conventional defence of government policy has been that although there has been restraint, nevertheless public expenditure has continued to grow in real terms. In fact, even this is not completely true since public expenditure excluding the technical concept of debt interest actually fell by 1.2 per cent in real terms between the financial years 1975/6 and 1978/9. If interest payments on outstanding debt are included, there was a rise of just 0.2 per cent between these years. However, to measure the scale of the cuts, the relevant figure is not simply what actually happened to public expenditure, but the difference between what happened and what would have happened if public expenditure had been maintained at its 1975/6 share of total output. In other words, how much higher would public expenditure have been if the government had not determined during the course of 1975/6 that they would reduce its share in total output. The relevant measure of public expenditure in this context is general government expenditure on goods and services (col. 2 of Table 3.1) rather than total public expenditure (in col. 1). For, in a recession, national output is lower than it would otherwise have been, but total public expenditure is higher as more is paid out on unemployment and supplementary benefits. So the share of total public expenditure in national output automatically rises in a recession, exaggerating its share in an artificial way. This is not the case, however, with general government expenditure on goods and services which represents real claims on resources, and which is the definition of public expenditure used in the calculation of Table 3.2. It might be argued that it is more appropriate to calculate how much higher (or lower) public expenditure would have been if the 1973/4 share of total output had been maintained, rather than the 1975/6 level. But this argument implies that the 1975/6 level is in some way 'excessive', and is in any case not appropriate to the discussion of the record of a government which was in principle committed to an extension of the public sector. Table 3.2 sets out the amount of public expenditure which has been lost by this policy.

Table 3.2   *Additional public expenditure on assumption of 1975–76 'share' in GDP (£ million)*

	1976/7	1977/8	1978/9	Totals 1976/7 1978/9
Goods and Services	1,300	1,000	800	3,100
Fixed Investment	1,600	2,100	1,000	4,700

Source: *Economic Trends*, October 1978 and estimates from Cmnd 7439.

In other words, had the 1975/6 share of public spending been maintained, there would have been £4,700 million more investment and

£3,100 million more current spending over the period to 1978/9.

These cuts had a substantial effect on unemployment. The Treasury's own computerised model of the economy can be used to estimate the increase. Properties of the model are described elsewhere[9] but the model can be used to show that public expenditure cuts led to unemployment in 1978/9 being 600,000 higher than it would otherwise have been.

It is possible that the latest version of the Treasury model (not yet available to the public) would produce a slightly lower estimate than 600,000, but even so the increase in unemployment due to the cuts would still be of the order of half a million.

It should be emphasised that these figures represent not just the direct impact of changes in public expenditure upon unemployment but also the indirect effects after allowing for the effects of changes in public expenditure on the exchange rate, the money supply and other economic variables. A common argument against public expenditure increases is that these entail an increase in the public sector borrowing requirement, which means that the government needs to sell more gilts if this increased borrowing is to be financed without excessive increases in the money supply. In order to sell more gilts, interest rates have to be higher than they would otherwise have been. The higher interest rates are alleged to deter private sector expenditure, particularly investment, so that the net addition to total national output (and hence employment) following increases in public expenditure will be the sum of two factors. Firstly, the positive effect of increased public spending and, secondly, the negative effect of higher interest rates on private expenditure, which is termed 'crowding out'. This is a perfectly respectable theoretical argument. The key question, however, is one of empirical fact rather than theoretical argument, namely *how much* private expenditure is 'crowded out' by increases in public spending. The empirical evidence for the UK economy suggests that relatively little does in fact take place,[10] so that increases or cuts in public expenditure make substantial net additions or reductions to the level of total national output. The Treasury model contains these theoretical linkages, the empirical effects of which are not very strong. The principal channel of 'crowding out' is slightly obscure but perfectly valid: higher interest rates lead to a (limited) capital inflow of foreign exchange, which drives up the exchange rate, leading to a (temporary) loss of trade competitiveness and consequent reductions in the volume of exports and increases in the volume of imports. Taking all of these factors into account, the Treasury model indicates that with £8,000 million more public spending, unemployment would now be about half a million lower.

The effects of public expenditure cuts can be seen not just from economic models but from the actual experience of the last few years. According to the government's strategy, the reduction in the share of the public sector in total output, combined with the increase in private sector profits, should have led to an increase in private sector investment sufficient to fill the gap created by public spending cuts. In reality, comparing the financial years 1975/6 and 1978/9, private sector investment has only increased from 8.8 to 9.4 per cent of total final expenditure, a rise of £1,300 million compared with a fall in public investment of £4,700 million. An investment intentions survey from the Department of Industry[11] suggests a slowing down in the growth of manufacturing investment during 1979, and the possibility of an actual fall in 1980.

The government hoped that restraint on public spending would permit more rapid expansion of exports and thus create employment. Superficially, this appears to have happened, with the share of exports rising as a proportion of total final expenditure by 2.5 percentage points between 1975/6 and 1978/9, or some £5,300 million. However, this is due to three factors quite removed from the public expenditure cuts. Firstly, 1975 saw the beginning of by far the deepest recession in world trade since the war, with the volume of trade in manufactures falling by 5 per cent, compared with an annual average increase of 10.5 per cent 1968–74. British exports depend upon the level of demand given by world trade, so that their share of total UK output was artificially low in 1975/6 due to the world recession; thus any rise from the 1975/6 share is an exaggeration of the real movement. Secondly, there is a historical tendency for the share of exports in UK output to rise if world trade expands more rapidly than UK output, which it has done at more than twice the rate since 1975. Thirdly, British exports have been exceptionally price competitive in world markets in recent years. A recent study by the Bank of England showed that UK exports were substantially more competitive in 1977 than in 1975 – in fact of the order of 10 per cent more.[12] Both the Bank of England's and the Treasury's economic models indicate that for every 10 per cent improvement in price competitiveness, UK manufactured exports eventually rise by 8 or 9 per cent in real terms. So the rising share of exports, while of course very welcome, is almost entirely due to factors which have nothing to do with the expenditure cuts. Public expenditure could have been kept up, and unemployment kept down, and the rise in exports would still have taken place.

It is useful to add that although world trade has expanded again since 1975, this is at a rate well below that experienced in the decade before the oil price rise. The government has placed great reliance on a recovery in world trade to lift the UK out of the recession[13] and has frequently been the initiator of the numerous 'summits' and high level international ministerial meetings held to discuss ways of co-ordinating reflationary policies by individual countries. Apart from relatively minor concessions, however, little of consequence has followed from these meetings, principally because of resistance to reflation from the Japanese and West German governments. Indeed, the West German initiative on the European Monetary System seemed designed to tie the rest of Europe into the German ranking of economic priorities, in which restraining inflation is given overwhelming preference to the reduction in unemployment.

Additional evidence about the restrictive effect of policy on expenditure and taxation since 1975/6 can be derived from the concept of the full employment public sector borrowing requirement (PSBR FE). One of the targets of government policy has been to keep the actual borrowing requirement within certain specified limits. Yet the adoption of the actual PSBR as a target suffers from the fundamental weakness that it fails to distinguish the influence of the budget on the economy from the influence of the economy on the budget. In other words, the lower is the level of economic activity, the higher will be government expenditure on such things as unemployment benefit, the lower will be government receipts from taxation and the higher will be the actual level of the PSBR. The idea of the PSBR FE is to attempt to correct for the effects of economic activity on the actual PSBR by calculating what government receipts and expenditure would be if there were full (or at least high and constant) employment and the associated level of income, rather than being based on the actual levels of employment and income. This concept has long been familiar in economics; its advantages over the actual PSBR have been accepted in the United States for many years. For example, the Committee for Economic Development in the 1940s recognised that low levels of output were bound to cause budget deficits, although it was not until 1962 that the concept of the PSBR FE became embodied in official American thinking in the *Economic Report of the President* of that year. The widespread acceptance in the US of the fact that there can be a substantial difference between the actual PSBR and the PSBR FE has, until recently, prevented the emergence of the near hysteria which has affected some British commentators over the recent size of the UK deficit.

There are a number of technical criticisms which can be made about the concept of the PSBR FE, all of which, however, are related to the need for more sophisticated adjustments to be made to the actual PSBR than are required to produce the PSBR FE; the latter variable is unequivocally superior to the actual PSBR as a measure of the effects of government policy on the economy. Of course, there is an inherent problem in trying to express the effects of the whole range of fiscal and expenditure policy into a single number. But the *changes* in the level of the PSBR FE from year to year are a useful indicator of the effect of the government's taxation and expenditure plans on the economy. Table 3.3 presents estimates of the PSBR FE calculated by the National Institute, along with the actual borrowing requirement for comparison.

Table 3.3   *Estimated PSBR at full employment* (£ *billion*)

	Actual PSBR	PSBR at full employment measure
1973/4	− 4.6	− 3.4
1974/5	− 7.6	− 4.6
1975/6	− 10.8	− 3.4
1976/7	− 9.0	− 2.0
1977/8	− 5.5	+ 2.4
1978/9 (est)	− 8.3	+ 2.4

Source: *National Institute Economic Review*, various issues.

A minus sign indicates that the overall budget is in deficit, and a positive sign that it is in surplus. In other words, a minus sign indicates that the government is putting more into the economy than it is taking out, and a positive sign the opposite. Thus the changes in the PSBR FE indicate that taxation and expenditure policy became increasingly contractionary from 1975/6, with the exception of 1978/1979 when the income tax cuts offset the expenditure cuts to produce no change.

This illustrates an important point regarding the financing of increases in public expenditure during recessions; a part of any increase in public expenditure will be self-financing through the reduction in expenditure on unemployment benefits and the increase in receipts arising from the increased levels of employment. The exact proportion will vary depending upon the particular type of expenditure which is increased and its employment-creating potential. But a reasonable calculation is that half of any increases in government expenditure on goods and services will be self-financing, assuming an average resource content although it is interesting that the Treasury model indicates that about two thirds of any increase on goods and services will be self-financing after two years.

Apart from unemployment, the other major economic problem with which the government had to deal was inflation. By the spring of 1974, the government was facing serious external inflationary pressures. The prices of basic commodities other than oil had been rising very rapidly during 1973. Between the fourth quarters of 1972 and 1973, for example, the price of food exports of the primary producing countries rose by 49 per cent, non-food agricultural products by 73 per cent, and minerals and metals by 66 per cent. The inflationary consequences of the rise in the price of basic materials and fuel were exacerbated by the system of threshold agreements which the Labour Government inherited from the Heath administration. Introduced in November 1973, before the bulk of the oil price rise took place, the threshold system involved an automatic increase of 1 per cent of the average wage (40p a week) for every 1 per cent increase in the Retail Price Index once it had risen 9 per cent above its November 1973 level. In other words, the usual lag between price increases and wage increases was eliminated by the threshold agreement. The additional increase in wages was transmitted into further price increases. Eleven threshold payments were made before the agreements expired in November 1974 and they played a major part in accelerating the annual rate of increase of earnings from $12\frac{1}{2}$ per cent in the fourth quarter of 1973 to $25\frac{1}{2}$ per cent in the fourth quarter of 1974. The 1974/5 Social Contract between the TUC and the government thus had little chance against a background of huge rises in the price of raw materials and of the effects of threshold agreements. If the government had made substantial cuts in indirect taxes in March 1974 to offset the effects on domestic prices of the commodity and oil price increases, perhaps much of the acceleration in earnings and inflationary expectations during 1974 could have been avoided.

What has been the 'great success' of the government's economic strategy is the reduction of the annual rate of inflation from 26 per cent in the summer of 1975 to 8 per cent in the winter of 1978/9. This success was mainly due to the two very tight incomes policies which were successfully imposed from August 1975 to July 1977. Stage one of the policy allowed a maximum increase of £6 per week, with a cut off point at £8,500 per year; it brought the annual increase of earnings down from $27\frac{1}{2}$ per cent in July 1975 to 14 per cent in July 1976. Stage two was unique in British experience in that it was tighter than the first stage; in previous attempts at constructing a second stage of incomes policy, a tight first phase had to be relaxed. Stage two allowed increases of 5 per cent, with a maximum of £4 per week: it reduced the annual increase in earnings still further to 9 per cent in July 1977.

But the success in reducing inflation through these incomes policies was entirely due to the sacrifices made by the ordinary worker. Substantial cuts in real living standards were accepted by the majority of the population during stages one and two, the real take home pay of most people being at least 8 per cent lower in June 1977 than in March 1975, prior to the April 1975 Budget (which raised prices almost 3 per cent) and prior to the introduction of stage one. In contrast, real gross trading profits of industrial and commercial companies rose between the first quarter of 1975 and the second quarter of 1977 by almost 40 per cent. The reasons for the sharp reduction in living standards were twofold. Firstly, the restrictive overall stance of government policy constrained real growth within the economy as a whole. Secondly, to the average worker, a reduction in the rate of increase of his money earnings at any point in time means a cut in his real standard of living in the immediate future as price increases already in the pipeline are passed through the system. It is only after some time (at least two years according to the economic models of the London Business School, the National Institute and the Treasury) that workers can realise real wage increases through reductions in the rate of increase of prices following their wage restraint.

The government clearly recognised the existence of the latter problem by introducing expansionary budgets in March and October 1977 and again in April 1978; these were partly designed to improve real take home pay through tax reductions. The expansion, however, was only sufficient to halt the trend to an increasingly restrictive fiscal stance and did not reverse this trend (see Table 3.3). Moreover, as Table 3.4 shows, even by September 1978 most people were no better off in real terms than they had been in March 1975.

Not surprisingly, resistance to further periods of wage restraint

Table 3.4   Real weekly net income at October 1978 prices (£)

	Single person	Married couple no children	Married couple, two children under 11 or between 11 and 16
March 1975	65.50	68.00	80.10
June 1976	62.30	64.40	78.80
June 1977	59.10	62.80	74.30
September 1978	64.40	67.90	80.10

Source: *Hansard*, Written Answers, 19 January 1979.

grew during 1977 and 1978. Stage three of the incomes policy through to July 1978 was not supported by the TUC. This policy, however, was loosely designed to permit increases of 10 per cent; in the private sector many groups of workers were able to evade the formal guidelines so that in the year to July 1978 earnings rose by some 15 per cent. Despite the opposition of the TUC and the Labour Party Conference, senior ministers attempted to introduce a very tight stage four of incomes policy, based on a maximum increase of 5 per cent. Further cuts in living standards would clearly have followed if this had been accepted, for the rate of inflation was around 8 per cent towards the end of 1978. The government resolutely refused to increase real earnings by expanding the economy sufficiently, and even threatened to increase taxation if money earnings were 'excessive'. After a period of phoney war during the autumn of 1978, determined attempts to destroy the 5 per cent policy were made by large groups of workers in the public sector; in this they were mainly successful. The government threw away a marvellous opportunity in the autumn of 1978 of reducing the inflation rate even further. Inflationary expectations were lower than they had been for some time, with the annual rate of increase of the Retail Price Index steady at just under 8 per cent since April 1978. Workers, principally in the public sector, simply wished to restore some of the increases in real take home pay which they had foregone during the previous three years of incomes policies[14] and as a result of the government's restrictive overall economic policies. A substantial expansion of the economy with tax cuts and public expenditure increases, perhaps coupled with a temporary price freeze on manufactured goods, could well have persuaded workers to accept single figure percentage increases in the pay round to July 1979 which would have further consolidated the reduction in the rate of inflation.

The overall economic record of the Labour Government 1974–79 in terms of its impact on equality can only be described as dismal. Far from creating the conditions in which a genuine move to a more equal and a more just society could be made, far from furthering the extension of socialism to which it was committed in its manifesto, the government deliberately reduced the share of the public sector in the economy and followed a highly restrictive strategy which led to large rises in the level of unemployment. After securing the co-operation of workers in bringing down the rate of inflation, at the cost of unprecedented reductions in real living standards, the government tried and failed in an attempt to impose yet further cuts on real incomes. In so doing, the gains made in reducing the rate of inflation were jeopardised.

Within months of the October 1974 election, the overall shape of the government's economic strategy was being constructed with reference to the politically motivated and misguided economics of the City and the financial markets and with very little reference to social and employment objectives. Harmful and misleading targets for the nominal level of the public sector borrowing requirement were accepted. In fact, the actual financial variable for which the government was supposed to have a target varied from time to time, seemingly according to which target financial opinion thought would lead to the most restrictive policies. Sometimes it was the PSBR, sometimes it was the increases in the money supply, and sometimes the increases in domestic credit expansion. In contrast, one of the important conditions attached to the 1976 IMF loan was the need to keep a competitive exchange rate. The City rapidly forced the government to abandon this condition, believing as it always has done in the (elusive) benefits of a 'strong pound'. Month to month and even day to day movements in financial markets were accorded the greatest degree of importance by the government, whilst the rising level of unemployment was effectively ignored.

Skidelsky produced a fitting epitaph on the 1929–31 Labour Government: 'It struggled to defend the working class as long as it knew how, and when it could defend them no longer it resigned.'[15] As other sections of this book indicate, the 1974–79 government did attempt to protect some groups, particularly pensioners, from the consequences of its strategy. But little good could come overall of such a strategy. Far from resigning, the government deliberately chose this strategy in preference to others and it implemented an ever increasing series of restraints on public expenditure during the last four years of its office.

It is not the purpose of this chapter or of this book to present detailed plans for the future, but the implications are clear. The social democratic approach of gradualism and indirect controls on the economy failed once again. The 1929–31, 1964–70 and 1974–79 Labour Governments all eventually felt that they had no alternative in the end but to adopt the restrictive monetarist policies of financial interests. Even the 1945–51 Attlee Government was not completely immune from these pressures, particularly towards the end of its period of office when the bulk of the 1945 manifesto had been carried out and further theoretical guidelines on the transition to socialism were lacking. The leading industrialised countries are proving unwilling to co-operate effectively, and in some cases are actually hostile to a massive co-ordinated reflation to lift the world out of recession. A move to a more planned economy is essential if British industry is to be restructured to enable it to compete effectively in world markets, if the level of unemployment is to be brought down to an acceptable level and if a strong economy is to be developed to facilitate the democratic transition to socialism.

4 Labour and International Inequality

by Vincent Cable

Reviewing the Labour Government's development policies during 1964–70, Seers and Streeten concluded: 'on the whole Labour's record was discreditable, especially in contrast to the promises before the election ... when it comes to the pinch, Labour is really very parochial.'[1] As in other areas of government, the socialist spirit had been generally willing, but the flesh, and the backbone, weak. Chroniclers of the 1974–79 period are most unlikely to find Labour less parochial, but their judgement of the government's record will probably be more equivocal, less indignant, and more world weary. Not a great deal has been delivered, but much less was expected. Levels of aid in relation to GNP are way below what was considered respectable 10 to 15 years ago, but the decline has been halted and British performance is slightly above the average for an industrialised country in quantity and rather better in quality. The aid programme has also been given a clearer poverty focus.

But 'North–South' relations are no longer about rich nations donating, or not donating, aid to poor ones. This is partly because the distinction between rich and poor is no longer as clear as it was with OPEC and 'newly industrialising countries' (NICs) distancing themselves from the rest of the Third World. But also, whereas development policy was portrayed as contributing through resource transfers to a crusade against poverty, the emphasis has now shifted from aid to trade issues. UNCTAD V has been dominated by discussion of protectionism and commodities. This reflects cynicism in developing countries about the motives behind aid, and its practical usefulness, and a conviction that more can be achieved by strengthening export earning capacity. The donor-recipient aspect of relations between rich and poor countries has been further blurred by events which have undermined some of the confidence of the rich and given some of the poor ones a taste of power, and even wealth—recession in Western countries, OPEC and the oil crisis, the growth of sophisticated manufactured exports from newly industrialising countries, the apparent geopolitical shift away from Western political dominance. The British response to the new turn of events, especially as it affects trade policy, has not so far been at all positive. This threatens to undermine improvements on the aid front.

The concept of international inequality

Only modest sensitivity is required to be aware that domestic inequalities pale to insignificance before those which exist internationally. Nonetheless the concept of international inequality is elusive, and it eludes not only those who find its implications uncomfortable.

At its simplest, international inequality is measured by the absolute gap between rich and poor countries. The gap between the low income group of developing countries (inhabited by 1.2 billion people, mainly in the Indian subcontinent, with an average per capita GDP in 1975 of $150) and the 685 million people in industrialised countries enjoying an average income of $6,200, would take 750 years to bridge even if the poor countries grew at 1970–76 average rates and industrialised countries stopped growing altogether. These average income aggregates are however misleading. A better measure of income levels is the 'purchasing power parity' which corrects for distortions introduced by the use of nominal exchange rates and differences in the prices of non-traded goods and services. Table 4.1 shows that correction for these factors narrows the differential by about half but it is still very large.

A more fundamental difference of approach questions the usefulness of talking about absolute inequality however measured. Many would reject the idea of 'catching up' with Western living standards which reflect aspirations alien to traditional (and some modern) cultures. Although it is often difficult to separate out genuine aspirations from the concerns of paternalistic leaders, some weight has to be given, for example, to the phenomenon of militant Moslem sentiment (even if not yet expressed very widely in material asceticism). In addition, attempts to suppress 'luxury' consumption in some developing countries reflect the belief that Western life styles are not

Table 4.1   GDP per head measured in purchasing power parity

	(world = 100)	
	nominal	purchasing power parity
Developed market economies[a]	279	242
North America	461	340
Europe	206	201
EEC	241	230
Other	130	138
Other[b]	179	191
Developing market economies[a]	21	38
Africa	17	30
Asia	14	28
America	57	86

Source: *Economic Journal*, June 1978.

Notes   [a] Main exclusions: centrally planned economies.
       [b] Japan, South Africa, Israel, Australia and New Zealand.

merely socially divisive in poor countries but also inherently wasteful.
But for Western socialists to shuffle off international obligations on
the grounds that people in poorer countries are less materialistic
would be not only based on a factually dubious proposition but also
morally cheap.

Another line of criticism of absolute inequality measures is that
relative differences are more important: 'most people (and governments) tend to think of the income of a nearby reference group ...
most people in poor countries do not regard rich foreigners as part
of their reference group and hence are not overconcerned with the
gap'.[2] The policy implication is that domestic rather than international inequality is intrinsically of much greater importance. This
is certainly true in some cases, mainly Latin American, where there is
a strong sense of grievance produced by apparently worsening
inequalities *within* countries which are on average still poor (or
middle income, but still a good deal poorer on average than us). The
argument is less compelling for poor countries (such as India) where
a good deal of redistribution, at least from the urban middle class,
has taken place. It also fails to deal with the uncomfortable fact that
some degree of domestic inequality may be inevitable if poor countries are to make advances in key areas such as food production, a
point now apparently accepted even in erstwhile models of equality
such as China and Tanzania. Moreover a framework of analysis

which places responsibility for inequality on the shoulders of Third World élites (while immensely comforting for armchair radicals in the West) ignores the way in which these local élites themselves acquire their expectations from their contact with the West, contacts which are unavoidable unless poor countries retreat into complete economic and political isolation. It could be argued that in a world of improved communications and mobility (at least for the educated), local reference groups are decreasingly important.

One way of avoiding the difficulties in defining inequality is to concentrate on absolute poverty, defined in terms of minimum standards of nutrition, shelter, education and health care. The World Bank, on its own (necessarily arbitary and not very generous) standards of absolute poverty, identified 800 million people in the category of 'absolute poor': 630 million comprising 52 per cent of the population of 'low income' countries and 140 million comprising 16 per cent of the population of 'middle income' countries.[3] Although this represents a potentially more manageable problem than the elimination or substantial reduction of international inequality, the Bank gloomily observes that 'elimination of absolute poverty in the low income countries by the end of this century seems impossible. A more realistic target would be to reduce the proportion to 15 to 20 per cent by the year 2000 leaving nearly 400 million in absolute poverty'. From a practical, as well as a humanitarian, standpoint, it makes sense to concentrate on alleviating this massive accumulation of distress. However, while the concept of minimum or 'basic needs' has attracted a good deal of support in Western countries (possibly because it makes rather limited material and moral demands on them), it is some way removed from international egalitarianism.

Conceptual problems also exist in tackling domestic inequality but there is one fundamental difference. Policies to deal with international inequality operate through independent governments. International negotiations between rich and poor take place through their governments and reflect not only grievances deriving from income or wealth inequality or from absolute poverty but also from the frustration of governments of more or less poor countries that they do not have a greater say in running the world economy (and, in some cases, their own economies). They are also concerned to shift the argument away from internal equity issues to the real or imagined inequalities of the international trading system, past and present. There is in this context a vigorous debate on the merits and demerits of the New International Economic Order (NIEO) proposals. Suffice it to say, it is possible to hold an egalitarian view of the world while questioning both the premises of the NIEO and the policy prescriptions which flow from them. The effect of some proposals, such as commodity price indexation, might well have a regressive impact, and to the extent that the NIEO represents a rationalisation of OPEC pricing policy, it is contrary to the interests of the populous poor oil-importing countries, such as those of the Indian subcontinent. Thus for various reasons the basic issue of gross international inequality has been allowed to slip out of focus.

Motives and objectives
The motives behind British development policy are complex and are not solely concerned with addressing the problem of international inequality. Before examining policy performance in detail, this mixture of motives and objectives needs to be clarified. Motives fall into two broad categories: the self-interested and the humanitarian. Trade and investment policy tends to reflect national economic interests while the aid programme incorporates what there is of a humanitarian motivation. But British aid policy has always had a strong dash of self-interest, especially aimed at trade promotion. The first real British effort in the aid field was the Colonial Development Bill of 1929, advocated by the McDonald government as a means of 'promoting commerce with and industry in the United Kingdom'. No political party opposed it.[4] Today, roughly two-thirds of the British aid programme is actually tied to the purchase of British goods though only one-third is acknowledged to be. Five per cent of the budget is unofficially set aside for the use of the Department of Trade as part of a 'credit mixte' policy (though on developmentally sound projects). Politically, one of the most persuasive arguments for more aid has been that many British jobs (40,000 directly and more indirectly) depend upon it. One of the most thorough investigations by this parliament of aid policy focused upon the lack of consistency between trade and aid policy,[5] and made practical recommendations for increasing Britain's share of orders from untied and multilateral aid. But the export promoting function is not the sole explanation for aid policy. There are, after all, more cost effective ways of promoting exports than giving them away (though the amount of arm twisting required to make India 'buy' free ships might suggest otherwise). If the British government wished to create employment by pump priming methods, it could as well stimulate domestic as foreign demand for British goods. If we were to take as our models the

export-led economies of Germany, Japan and Switzerland, the aid budget would be smaller in relation to GNP not larger. Thus, although economic self-interest is one motive, and a useful one for domestic political consumption, it is far from being the only one.

There is little doubt that some of our aid has a political function. Although we no longer often hear (as in the 1960s) arguments about aid being necessary to stave off communist or other revolutions, there is often an unspoken assumption that by helping economic development we help to promote political stability. There may be a few cases where aid has been sufficiently important for that to be a legitimate claim (Malawi or Kenya), but there are counter-examples and the experience of economic development in Iran has undermined conventional wisdom. By comparison with the French and American, British governments have given less weight to political considerations.[6] The 1965 White Paper reflected this disinterest, which was reinforced by the 1974–79 governments: 'aid is not a means of winning the friendship of individual nations'. That is almost certainly realistic as well as virtuous.

This leaves the humanitarian or egalitarian case. The moral justification for aid is variously presented in terms of combating absolute poverty, reducing inequality and/or making reparations for past or present exploitation. The least controversial of these is the generalised concern for the plight of very poor people in poor countries, a concern shared by most Tories as well as socialists. Conservative aid and development policy differs little from Labour's, and the moral (as well as the self-interest) rationale is expressed in almost identical language.[7] There has of course, on the Right, long been a dissenting view (expressed by Peter Bauer, Enoch Powell and *Daily Telegraph* contributors) that rich nations owe no moral obligations to poor ones, except possibly in disasters and through personal contribution to charity. However, by coincidence (rather than by a process of intellectual osmosis), their slogan of 'trade not aid' has now been taken up by the developing countries. Labour would claim that it has an internationalist tradition which makes it more sensitive to the plight of the poor overseas. Clause 4 of the party constitution invokes us to 'cooperate ... for the improvement of the social and economic standards and conditions of work of the people of the world'. From the 1930s, on development aid 'Labour has been the more vociferous critic, the more venturesome initiator, itself spurred on by a core of yet more vociferous critics'.[8] While this internationalism has been largely inspired by a wish to tackle absolute poverty and hunger, a powerful supporting factor has been uncomfortable awareness of the contradiction between domestic social policies designed to reduce social and economic inequality and much bigger and widening gaps internationally.

Inequality between nations has, however, failed to achieve for Labour the same ideological status as concern over domestic inequalities. There are several reasons for the lack of interest. One is that Labour is, if only because of the need to survive politically, a populist movement. Not only do foreigners not have the vote but helping developing countries is not popular. A recent survey of British opinion produced the somewhat unhelpful, if predictable, response from a substantial majority that Britain was already doing too much (but that other rich countries should undoubtedly do more).[9] A second, more commendable, reason is that international inequality is genuinely difficult to translate into national politics. There are rich people in poor countries, and poor people in rich ones. Official aid involves transfers between governments, not between social classes. In some cases transfers can be regressive rather than progressive. There is a contradiction between cosmopolitan standards of social justice and the fact that different and sovereign states are allowed to administer their own systems of justice.[10] Third, the problem of international equality is so immense that any politician with a practical turn of mind can be expected to ignore it for more tractable issues. Like world peace, international inequality suffers from the paradox of being too important to be taken seriously as a political issue. Finally, there are points at which international and domestic equality are in conflict. This is less obvious in the case of aid than trade, particularly where developing country exports compete with products made in Britain. Honesty, at least, demands that this conflict of (at least, short term) interests should be recognised.

Performance

Aid is not the only aspect of development policy, and the share of net aid transfers in GNP is not an ideal measure of its worth, but it is a useful place to start. Moreover, the fact that aid targetry is no longer in fashion is more of a reflection of embarrassment at a consistent inability to reach the targets than of any defect in the measures. In 1953, Harold Wilson wrote a book which suggested an aid target for rich countries of 3 per cent of national income.[11] In 1964, Barbara Castle argued in parliament for 2 per cent. The

1964 election was based on a 1 per cent pledge. This was reinterpreted in 1969, in the light of the Pearson Report, to mean 0.7 per cent, with the other 0.3 per cent in the form of private investment. By 1977, the annual figure achieved was 0.38 per cent, for net aid, the highest level since 1971 but an eighth of the level thought feasible by Harold Wilson a generation earlier, and just over half the 0.7 per cent target reaffirmed in 1974.

By international standards, British performance in volume terms is not impressive.[12] It ranks tenth of seventeen developed market economies in net overseas development aid (ODA)[13] as a percentage of GNP. Although below the median, it is slightly above the average level due to the poor performance of three major donors: the USA, Japan and Germany. UK performance on this measure is way behind the Netherlands, Sweden, Canada and Norway. Along with other developed countries, Britain has seen a steady decline in the share of aid in GNP in the last 15 years. Only Sweden, Netherlands and Canada of the main donors have managed to swim against the tide. Britain's aid performance decline has been more marked than any other Western country's except for the USA, France and Belgium. This decline does now appear to have been stopped. The 1974–79 Labour Government held the ratio at 0.38 per cent, fractionally up on the Heath government's 0.37 per cent (annual average), and it had promised to raise real aid volumes by 6 per cent annually in the next four years. It was one of the few sectors of public expenditure to be treated generously in the last round of cuts by Labour.

British performance is better in terms of the concessionality of its aid (Table 4.2). The grant element at almost 97 per cent is now one of the highest of the industrial world (it was 85.4 per cent in 1974). However, there has been a strong movement by most donors in the same direction, to a point where the grant element of all DAC aid is 90 per cent. Only Japan continues to give ODA with a limited grant component.

A further development in British policy has been Retrospective Terms Adjustment (RTA), relieving 17 of the poorest countries of interest and repayments on past loans. (For India, the biggest debtor with two-thirds of the total ODA debt, the repayments will be off set by money from the current aid budget which, instead of being tied to British exports, will be available for local costs.) The total debt repayment subject to RTA is £900 million, by far the largest write-off by any donor. Lest this provoke undue excitement, it must be stressed that the principal repayments (£60 million each

Table 4.2 Comparative aid performance, 1977

Country	(1) Net ODA (m. $)	(2) (1) as % of GNP	(3) % change in 1960–77 annual average of (2)	(4) Aid per capita $	(5) Grant equivalent of aid (%)	(6) Share of low income countries in net ODA (%)	(7) Share untied %	(8) Share of aid to (%)	(9) Share to multinational agencies (%)
Canada	991	.51	+.32	42	97.5	60	51.5	19.4	32.1
France	2,267	.60	–.75	42	93.4	26	40.8	8.3	13.0
Germany	1,386	.27	–.04	22	86.0	58	76.3	15.7	32.9
Italy	186	.10	–.12	3	99.2	20	81.2	11.5	74.4
Japan	1,424	.21	–.03	12	70.2	90	43.8	9.6	26.9
Netherlands	900	.85	+.54	65	91.1	38	48.0	27.3	25.3
Sweden	779	.99	+.94	95	99.8	77	80.8	15.1	31.7
UK	914	.37	–.18	17	96.8	56	46.7	21.2	34.5
US	4,159	.22	–.31	19	88.9	45	27.3	28.1	31.9
Total	14,696	.31	–.20		89.3	47	47.2	14.2	29.0

Source: Derived from OECD, *Review of Development Cooperation*, 1978.
Notes: (1) Net ODA consists of net (less repayment) disbursements of concessional official development aid.
  (5) Based on interest rate, maturity and grace value. The market rate of interest is taken as 10%.
  (6) Low income countries are those with per capita income under $400.
  (7) Share of gross disbursements.
  (8) Multilateral aid includes aid channelled through EEC. This constitutes 60% of French multilateral aid, 62% of German 65% of Italian, 27% of Dutch and 18% of British aid.

year) are taken from the aid programme so there is no additional flow of resources (the position on interest charges – £8 million a year – is less clear). The advantage to the recipient country is that what would have been in the form of tied aid is now untied.

As regards procurement tying, Britain is not one of the most generous donors. 47 per cent is untied (close to the average) but this contrasts unfavourably with Sweden's 81 per cent and Germany's 76 per cent. All these figures are overstatements of the degree of freedom since there are many informal and unreported methods of achieving the same objective.

Another measure of the quality of aid, since it reduces the degree and cost of procurement tying, is the share given via multilateral agencies. For the UK, the figure is 39 per cent of net aid (as against 27 per cent in 1976). The biggest slice (one half in our case) is directed to the World Bank (£86 million in 1977) though the EEC is now beoming a substantial vehicle for aid (£55 million in 1977).

Changing priorities in aid policy
In parallel with changes in the volume and financial structure of aid, there have been qualitative changes in the programme. The most important has been the attempt to develop a programme aimed at the poorest groups in the poorest countries. In addition there have been attempts to give human rights a place in aid allocation criteria. The main innovations, which owed a great deal to Judith Hart, were summarised in the 1975 White Paper, *Aid for the Poorest*.

The poorest countries
A key element in government thinking was that British aid should be concentrated on the poorest countries subject to assessment of the foreign exchange earnings capacity of the country, its ability to attract aid from other sources and the country's general prospects in the absence of aid. In 1977, the share of low income countries (under $400 per capita) in bilateral ODA was 56 per cent (the figure is higher if multilateral aid is included). This is better than average for developed countries and significantly better than for France (which gives substantial amounts to middle income countries like Ivory Coast and Gabon) and the Netherlands (which has committed itself to a big programme for relatively high income Surinam). India receives the lion's share, nearly 30 per cent of bilateral aid, followed by Bangladesh and Pakistan, Malawi, Zambia and Kenya. One departure from the poverty-orientated country allocation (though it

is not a major one) is the need to give generous quantities of aid (£41 million in 1977) to the remaining, small island, British dependencies and Associated States, most of which are negligible population and would not otherwise qualify on grounds of need. The credibility of the policy has been more seriously undermined by difficulties which have dogged the aid programme to India. Britain is the largest aid donor to India but the aid budget is consistently underspent. The main reason for this is a set of restrictions on use of the aid, notably the condition that most of the aid money be spent on British goods or services. The restrictions are primarily occasioned by India's abundant foreign exchange reserves (£3.5 billion) and India's trade surplus with the UK (circa £100 million). There are some small exceptions (local costs for family planning and untied funds for debt relief) but for the most part aid money is spent on British goods, either in the form of maintenance aid (spare parts, components, industrial materials) or capital goods for capital investment in new projects, mainly industrial (coal, power, fertilisers). Given the extra real economic cost of tied aid, India has become discriminating in its choice of donors, and at present (though not for long) it can afford to be. Even when British exports are competitive, aid is overwhelmingly confined to the foreign exchange element of projects. Where local (rupee) costs are dominant, as is the case in many rural and infrastructure activities, the aid is difficult to utilise in a way that meets the priorities of donor and recipient.

While the principle of concentrating genuinely concessional aid on the poorest countries is eminently sensible, it is important that this does not lead to an international 'poverty trap' in which poor countries are penalised once they are sufficiently successful in development, or fortunate, to escape into the category defined as 'middle income' countries. These are expected to benefit from trade, through preferential market access to developed countries and commodity agreements, but progress in neither of these areas is altogether secure. Many 'middle income' countries have a considerable appetite for borrowed capital and so far little attention has been given to helping them to secure finance on terms which, while not as generous as that available to the poorest, are better than purely commercial finance.

The poorest people

The Labour Government aid policy also tried to ensure that aid directly benefits the poorest sections of the community in developing countries. This originated in two convergent streams of thought. The first was that more attention should be paid to distributive policies within the developing countries. Cross-section and time series analysis shows that in general the share of the poorest groups in national income falls as countries pass through the early stage of development.[14] But this is avoidable, and has been avoided to various degrees, by countries which consciously applied themselves to equity questions (China) or managed to combine successful capitalist development with land reform (Taiwan, Korea). The second was that many developing countries struck the wrong balance between industrial and agricultural activity. Excessive attention to industrial development, especially the protected, import substituting kind, preempted investable surpluses which could have gone to agriculture, while the domestic terms of trade moved against the countryside where most of the people, and the poor, live. The main policy instrument allocating aid to the poorest people was a commitment to raise the share of project aid going to rural development.

Given the relatively small amount which aid contributes to development in the more populous countries, there would be little to show from aid policies which tried to impose improved policies, even if they were not actively resisted by recipient governments. There are also more fundamental problems which make poverty focusing 'easier said than done'.[15] The most serious of these is that rural development and equity objectives are not necessarily consistent. In India there are signs that an agricultural revolution is taking place. The spread of irrigation and with it multiple cropping, better fertiliser use and improved seeds have already transformed agriculture in the Punjab and Delhi areas and is now extending East down Ganges valley. The main agents of these changes are small-holder, *kulak* farmers, originally the beneficiaries of land transfer from absentee landlords and now small-scale landowners in their own right. They are not only economically successful but politically powerful. Their demands for a rural bias in development have struck a responsive chord amongst Indian planners and international agencies and they stand to gain most from general improved provision for farming and especially from the tractors and fertilisers being donated to India under rural aid programmes. But their interests conflict with those of the rural proletariat: over 100 million landless people, mainly of low 'untouchable' caste. They want land reform to be taken further. The smallholders do not. The seeds of a political as well as an agricultural revolution have been sown, and violence is already sprouting all over rural India. What line 'poverty focused' aid donors should take on this is far from clear, especially as exhaustive simulations of alternative policies show that all income distributive and welfare measures other than asset confiscation and transfers from the rural 'rich' (which is politically difficult when the 'rich' are very numerous and not very rich) are likely to achieve little or nothing.[16]

One way of resolving the possible contradiction between an 'aid for the poorest' strategy and aid to farmers is to concentrate on the provision of 'basic needs'. Although there is some confusion about the definition and measurement of 'basic needs',[17] the common sense of it is quite clear: the provision of goods and services (food, health care, shelter, literacy) necessary for a minimum level of existence. The choice of 'minimum' is necessarily arbitrary but since large numbers of people in poor countries fall below even the most conservative minima this is a somewhat academic problem. A more immediate and practical question is whether aid programmes can be usefully integrated into national efforts to meet 'basic needs'. As far as nutrition is concerned, the evidence suggests that, except on an emergency basis, food aid does more harm than good by discouraging domestic production.[18] And in India, where the largest number of absolute poor live, the problem is one of distribution (both physical and economic) rather than availability. There have been excess stocks of grain for the last two years. The other components of 'basic needs' provision require, above all, competent administration and good political motivation at a village level – as apparently obtains in China. If these are absent it is not clear how aid donors can provide them. Much of the current enthusiasm for 'basic needs' in Western thinking stems from a naive belief that it is possible to have the fruits of Chinese communism without the Chinese and without communism. A final difficulty is that (except for food aid) most 'basic needs' provision does not require a large input of internationally traded goods and services to which most aid is tied. It is not surprising therefore that British efforts in this field have been token rather than substantial. But they are being paid the compliment of imitation; several aid donors now have 'poverty-focusing' as a central objective, in the British manner.

Human rights

'Human rights' policy is a more recent and more politically charged innovation in the aid field. The British government deferred to it by not including in the RTA (that is, debt relief) five 'serious violators of human rights': Uganda, South Yemen, Cambodia, Vietnam and Ethiopia. Britain also pressed for a clause in the renegotiated Lomé Convention to make aid subject to some kind of measure of human rights performance. It is difficult to quarrel with the general proposition that political and social liberties are an ingredient in 'development' defined in the broadest sense.[19] Indian experience is standing reproof to those who question the political sophistication, and respect for political freedoms, of even the poorest people. Nor is it difficult to find examples where economic development is rendered largely meaningless by extreme political repression (Uganda, Equatorial Guinea, Haiti).

Unfortunately the manner in which the human rights qualification to aid provision is being applied suggests that it may do little to help human rights and quite a lot to harm aid programmes. One problem is that it cuts across attempts to introduce objective criteria (such as directing aid to a precisely defined group of 'poorest' countries), replacing them with more subjective ones. Political conservatives predictably find Left wing authoritarian regimes particularly offensive; the converse being true with socialists. It was precisely to forestall this kind of arbitrary political interference that developing countries have sought to have the principle of 'automaticity' incorporated in resource transfer mechanisms. The basic integrity of one of the innovations under the Lomé Convention, the Stabex commodity earnings stabilisation scheme, has been threatened because of the insistence of the British and Dutch governments that relatively small compensatory sums should not be allowed to find their way into the pockets of Amin, Bokassa and other undesirables.

A second problem is that economic and social progress in developing countries does not always go hand in hand with sensitivity to human rights. It is difficult to think of more than a handful where it does. Conversely, there are many examples, mainly in the Far East, of impressive economic and social progress, under both capitalism and communism where the rulers would not recognise a human right if they saw one. Finally, by showing a strong but selective concern for human rights, the British government has unnecessarily exposed itself to charges of inconsistency and hypocrisy. For example, in giving evidence to a Select Committee, the Foreign Secretary sought to make a virtue of inconsistency when justifying the wish of the British government to impose sanctions on erring Black African signatories of the Lomé Convention but not on South Africa. The answers failed to convince the Committee, including its Conservative members, which described them as 'legalistic' and they must have been incomprehensible in Lagos or Dar.[20] Perhaps the best case for incorporating human rights' criteria in aid policy is a more mundane one; it protects ministers, and the aid programme, from the charge that British taxpayers' money is going to help support dictatorships. Whether this is worth the cost is arguable. Ministers responsible for British aid have so far sensibly confined their human rights activities to the grossest cases.

The European dimension

One important by-product of British accession to the EEC is that we have adopted the Community's special trade and aid relationships with groups of developing countries, notably the Lomé Convention which now incorporates Commonwealth African, Caribbean and Pacific countries (ACPs). The implication for the British development effort is that a growing amount of the aid budget ($100 million out of $359 million multilateral aid in 1977) is now channelled through the European Community. The beneficiaries of the Convention also enjoy trade preferences, above those available to all developing countries. Evaluation of the overall impact of the Convention is difficult. There is a delicate balance to be struck between appreciating the positive if small impact which the Convention has on most ACPs (19 of whose 53 members are also in the group of least developed countries LDCs), while being apprehensive of the divisive effect of giving preferential treatment to some developing countries, chosen on a geographically arbitrary basis, but not to others, especially poor and populous countries in Asia.[21]

Hitherto, developing country non-members have taken a charitable view of the motives behind the Convention and its likely effects, regarding the Convention as a 'pilot fish' to show the way to more broadly based concessions by the EEC. It is too early to pass judgement on the results of renegotiating the all important second phase of the Convention. Of the many issues which emerged in renegotiation, two are worthy of comment. The first is that serious deficiencies have become apparent in the way in which the Community operates its Development Fund. A combination of insensitivity to recipient interests and incompetence (in the Community) have helped to ensure that the Fund is seriously underspent.[22] With four out of five years gone under Lomé, only 20 per cent of pledged funds have been spent. A second point is that, despite the efforts of British ministers, the imbalance in the treatment of the ACPs and poor non-associates is still stark. The Community has conceded the principle of non-associate aid but the sums are derisory (20 million ua in 1976 rising to 70 million in 1978). British ministers have been much less energetic in pressing the claims of the same group of countries for parity of treatment with ACPs in trade, an altogether more substantial issue, but one which creates protectionist apprehension in Britain about Indian and Pakistani competition. This leads directly to the trade aspects of development policy.

Non-aid aspects of development policy

Although the institutional role of the Ministry of Overseas Development inevitably focuses attention more on the aid aspects of development than on trade policy, this reverses the priorities which most developing countries have. Aid transfers account for a modest share of the foreign exchange earnings of developing countries ($20 billion as against $115 billion export earnings in 1977 for non-oil LDCs).

As expressed through UNCTAD, the Paris 'North–South' dialogue or the Commonwealth, developing country negotiating demands have given pride of place to trade issues, in particular to stabilising and/or raising commodity prices, and to the question of market access. On commodities, the British government has taken a fair amount of criticism for not, like the Dutch or Swedes, having embraced more enthusiastically the UNCTAD concept of a Common Fund co-ordinating a series of buffer stocks. One of the last actions of the Labour Government was however to support the setting up of a Common Fund albeit somewhat reduced in scale and scope from that envisaged by UNCTAD. But the British line of encouraging individual buffer stocking arrangements on their particular merits is more helpful than trying to strike superficially impressive political postures. The problem simply expressed is that, for many commodities, buffer stocking arrangements are largely irrelevant. In some cases (tea, jute), the problem is one of secular price decline though these may benefit from the proposed 'second window' of the Common Fund. For others, where price fluctuations stem from supply instability, price stabilisation may aggravate rather than reduce earnings instability. This said, there is little sign that

Britain, and other developed countries, are willing to come up with the kind of working capital which would be required to establish viable buffer stocks for those products where price instability is a problem and where instability does come from demand and not supply (such as copper). Of the remaining commodity schemes, the problem is as much one of lack of agreement between developing country exporters over quotas (for example, tea) than between producers and consumers. Interesting though these issues are it is easy to lose track of the egalitarian wood amongst the UNCTAD trees. The connection between setting up a buffer stock for copper and making a tangible contribution to reducing world inequality is, at best, tenuous. The main gains to poor countries would come from export organisation of beverages, but this is a remote prospect.

One important commodity where the EEC could be helpful to poor countries is sugar. Here the problem is one of excess production of European sugar beet which is undermining a recently signed International Sugar Agreement and, through the dumping of surpluses, depressing world prices. Britain has always been regarded as one of the voices of sanity on sugar and an ally of cane exporters seeking to combat the wilder idiocies of the CAP, as well as of domestic consumers. Unfortunately the rapid expansion with government encouragement of beet farming in recent years has created a conflict of interest, and British support for price and production quota cuts in the EEC is now more muted.

Sugar exemplifies in agriculture the more general reluctance of industrial countries to adjust to competing imports from developing countries. Protectionism is becoming a serious bone of contention in North–South relations,[23] and was near the top of the agenda at UNCTAD V. The issue is now important for only a small, but growing, number of newly industrialising countries but potentially for most others. These see the principle of liberal access for manufactures or processed raw materials as a guarantee that they can evolve from a dependent colonial trading arrangement to a more equal one. Unfortunately this has proved an extremely difficult issue for the UK. Britain has been singled out for criticism by the President of the World Bank among others for leading the protectionist pack, mainly as a result of the role which Britain played in the textile (MFA) renegotiations. There has undoubtedly been an adverse shift in policy and opinion in Britain. The TUC has drawn up a long shopping list of industries for which it wishes to reduce 'import penetration'. These industries include those in which the

UK has least long-term comparative advantage and developing countries most (clothing, shoes and leather goods, cutlery, radios, some electronic components). The Labour Party has also proclaimed the need to 'limit the degree of import penetration in British industry'.[24] Not surprisingly, given the pressures from producer lobbies and the Labour movement, ministers have periodically caved in to demands for protection and newly industrialising countries have borne the brunt of it.

This is not the place to rehearse the arguments about protectionism and import controls. But if Labour is to have a credible position on North–South issues (quite apart from a coherent economic and industrial policy), some rethinking will have to be done in the party. First, there is great confusion about the relationship between 'alternative strategy' solutions for the British economy, designed to raise employment, and how this relates to imports of particular items in weak sectors of the UK economy. Cambridge economists have pressed the case for non-discriminatory import controls. But either as a result of misunderstanding of, or disagreement with, their analysis, the pressure from the party and the unions is not for general but selective restrictions.

Second, the consequences of protectionism for developing countries are underestimated. One reason is that most LDC imports currently come from a few of the more industrialised Asian countries. Korea and Hong Kong do not attract sympathy as poor countries (though there is no justification for discriminating against them and in favour of other developed countries). But India, Sri Lanka, Pakistan and other poorer developing countries are now being affected by import restrictions too. In India in particular, millions are employed in highly labour intensive export industries (garments, carpets, leather, jewellery) some of which, notably clothing, face severe access barriers in Europe. Another reason is a feeling that manufactured exports from developing countries benefit multinational companies rather than the exporter countries. This no doubt happens in some cases but a large part of developing exports is traded on an 'arms length' basis, and many countries trying to promote exports of manufactures do not utilise multinational companies to any substantial degree (China, Yugoslavia, India and even countries like Korea which rely heavily on domestic capitalists for their export effort).

A final reason is the old fear of workers in rich countries that their wages and conditions will be undercut by 'cheap labour' overseas. The latest manifestation of this feeling is the demand from trade unions for a 'social clause' under GATT and EEC trade agreements to permit limitations on imports where adequate workers' standards are not complied with. There is an element here of purely idealistic concern with human rights in poor countries. Regrettably, the mechanism proposed is unenforceable (the EEC proposes for example to make access for imports conditional upon observance of a maximum 72 hour week) and is also open to use, and therefore abuse, by protectionist interest groups. There are much better ways of helping workers' organisations in poor countries. All this suggests that there remains a major educational and political effort to be made if British labour is to accept the adjustment implications of changing trade patterns. The issues are much harsher than in the aid field; thousands of jobs in import-competing industries are on the line and the pressures are coming most intensely at a time when there is serious unemployment in the UK. We may well be dragged into increasingly acrimonious conflict with developing countries over this issue.

These are, however, only two of the non-aid issues and not always the most important. Britain's relations with the Indian sub-continent, for example, are perhaps most critically affected by immigration policy and with other countries by British private foreign investments.

Conclusions

It is to the credit of the Labour Government that despite domestic financial crises and either indifference or hostility from the general public and even the Labour movement, some advances were made. Aid targets stopped receding. A clearly defined poverty-focused aid programme was developed. The modest achievements are now threatened by a Conservative Government. Before the election, Conservative statements on overseas development were bland and they found little in Labour's approach to quarrel with. Subsequently they have taken an axe to the aid programme, cutting £50 million, as part of the general 'pruning' of public expenditure. There are strong pressures to increase the degree of aid tying and to cut valuable institutions like the Tropical Products Institute, tropical medicine and overseas surveys. The Ministry of Overseas Development is also now subject to close supervision from the Foreign Office. The official line is now that developing countries should help themselves. At the same time, action is being taken on the trade front to make sure that they cannot. The Tories are showing themselves every bit as assiduous as Labour in responding to pressures for action against 'unfair' (that is, Third World) imports and for strict controls on Third World textile and clothing imports. Cynically, the CBI has just produced a bosses' 'guide' to the use of import controls. Those in the Labour Party who imagined that these controls were building blocks in the construction of British socialism will hopefully have been given some cause for thought.

If future Labour administrations are to give international equality higher priority, the need is less for better policies at a detailed level, at least for aid, than for firmer general commitment by the movement as a whole. Indeed there is already a tendency to seek refuge from the difficult wider issues by immersion in detail; aid to Bolivian tin mines or indirectly to Equatorial Guinea becomes more important than the size of the aid programme or the overall stance on development issues. This improved commitment will not be easy to obtain. There is an increasing tendency on the Left to see British problems in isolation, to become obsessed by the apparent uniqueness of Britain's declining industrial economy, to seek national solutions to international problems and to ignore Britain's interdependence with the rest of the world, including developing countries.

PART III

The Labour Market and Wealth

5 Low Pay
by Chris Pond

Introduction

The five year period with which we are concerned began with a period of optimism that the social contract might achieve a real improvement for the low paid. It ended in confrontation between the Labour Government and its own low paid employees in local authorities and the health service. This chapter traces some of the developments that led the Labour movement along this road from optimism to confrontation and examines what happened to the low wage problem in the years 1974 to 1978. It considers the policies adopted to alleviate the problem – and those which actually made it worse. The first part of the chapter considers what is meant by 'low pay' and whether its eradication was an appropriate objective for a Labour Government. It also suggests reasons for the failure to deal with low wages. It goes on to examine the extent of the problem and assess the policy response. Finally, it offers proposals for a strategy which might be adopted by a future Labour Government.

What is low pay?

A major constraint on the ability of the 1974–79 Labour Government to act decisively on low wages was the lack of agreement within the Labour movement as to what constituted low pay or, indeed, whether it was a problem at all. As in earlier years 'the laudable desire to offer preferential treatment to low earners has been outweighed by the fear that a precise definition would raise expectations and cause a flood of wage claims'.[1] Nevertheless, to make a realistic assessment of policies towards the low paid, we need to be clear just who it is we are talking about.

We might begin by relating minimum earnings to the Supplementary Benefit (SB) level – a 'convenient communally decided minimum' as a member of the now departed National Board for

Prices and Incomes (NBPI) described it.[2] The Low Pay Unit estimated that a married couple with two children would have needed a gross wage of approximately £55 a week in 1978 to be left with a net income (after taking into account direct taxes, child benefits and average housing costs) equivalent to what they would receive if dependent on the inadequate subsistence standard of SB.

The NBPI rejected this definition of low pay not on the obvious grounds of its inadequacy for subsistence but because assumptions had to be made about family composition and housing costs which made it impossible to apply such a definition to individual earnings.[3] They, together with the later Royal Commission on the Distribution of Income and Wealth, therefore adopted a relative definition of low pay, taking the earnings of the lowest decile of workers in each group as their yardstick.[4] The lowest decile is the point on the earnings distribution below which 10 per cent of individuals fall; this would have given a figure for 1978 which was very close to £55 a week (taking all adult men as the reference group). The TUC adopted an alternative, although still relative, measure of low pay in setting its minimum wage targets, defining the low paid as those with earnings of less than two-thirds the average (median) wage. Again, with a reference point of all adult men, this yields a figure very close to £55 for 1978. So while much of the government's reluctance to specify what it meant by 'low pay' was justified by the arbitrary nature of any one definition, each of the main criteria used yielded the same result. When the government did finally commit itself to a figure in 1978 it was very much lower than that derived from any of these methods and it excluded the bulk of the public sector low paid.

Low pay and poverty
We still need to ask whether the eradication of low pay was a suitable objective for the Labour Government. This may seem a strange question but during the period under review there was a growing belief that the old link between poverty and low wages had been broken. This view (manifest in the deliberations of the NBPI throughout the 1960s) reasserted itself with renewed vigour after 1974. The Diamond Commission (established in 1974 'to help secure a fairer distribution of income and wealth') saw little role for improvements in low wages as a means of bringing about such an outcome:

Low earnings and low incomes are not coextensive.... The men and women with low earnings are not highly concentrated in the families with lower incomes because many low earners do not have large families to support or have other earners in the family; conversely the majority of lower income families do not contain members with low earnings; indeed over 60 per cent of the lower income families as defined do not contain any earners.[5]

The Commission's conclusions were based on an analysis of the General Household Survey carried out by researchers at the London School of Economics. While the study found a correlation between the level of *male* earnings and family income, it also found that the proportion of the lowest paid men *and* women together who found themselves in the lowest income households was not large. The association between the two was strongest in families with children and became stronger still if the definition of low pay was raised closer to the definition specified above.[6]

Such findings had the effect of reducing further the government's determination to act decisively on low pay. The difficulty is that such a snapshot picture of the low wage problem cannot take account of the life cycle effects of low pay. Unable to accumulate savings or occupational pension rights, the low paid are more likely to find themselves in poverty in old age, they are more vulnerable to unemployment or sickness and their children are less likely to enjoy the financial security necessary to undertake extended education or training. The effect of low pay has the habit of reasserting itself at other points in the life cycle. As A. B. Atkinson has argued, 'low pay is a thread which runs throughout people's lives and beyond into retirement and what may at first sight appear to be "bad luck" is likely to be related to labour market disadvantages'.[7] Moreover, evidence from official sources suggested that low pay *was* becoming an increasingly more important cause of family poverty after 1974.

Despite the increasing importance of low pay as a cause of family poverty, the number of households involved is very much less than the number of individuals who are low paid, as will become clear when we consider estimates of the total numbers of low wage earners. This should not surprise us: most of the low paid are women and most women earners are not sole breadwinners – largely because of their levels of pay. The LSE study showed that the number of poor households would have trebled were it not for working wives contributing to household incomes. Amongst those men earning less than 80p per hour in 1975, three-quarters would have been in households where the family income was less than 40 per cent above SB were it not for their wives working (no doubt also in poorly paid jobs).[6] The question we need to ask is whether this low pay can be disregarded because the earnings of two or more people amount to a total joint income which is above some specified poverty line.

The lack of a consistent answer to this question within the Labour movement reflects the absence of a consistent conception of the inequalities produced by low pay. While, for some, low wages were a matter of concern only if they led demonstrably to family poverty, for others they were 'one of the major manifestations of the inequalities of a competitive and acquisitive society'.[8] For the former, solutions to low pay itself may be unnecessary so long as hardship can be alleviated through the payment of cash benefits to the families of low wage earners – a strategy which had become increasingly popular from the late 1960s onwards with governments of both persuasions.

The failure to place the problem of low pay within the framework of wider inequalities was also manifest in a confusion between differentials (differences in earnings *within* a bargaining group) and relativities (*between* groups). The trade union movement faces a long standing dilemma of trying to tackle low pay whilst dealing with the resulting disruption to differentials. The dilemma is, however, less pressing than appears at first sight. Since the low paid tend to be concentrated in industries where earnings generally are relatively low, raising their earnings involves not so much the collapse of differentials as the disturbance of relativities between groups. In other words, it involves the disturbance of more fundamental inequalities in earned income which the Labour Government in any case had promised to tackle. The failure to distinguish between the two led both the unions and the government to resist changes in established relativities (in effect accepting the existing distribution of earned incomes) as a means of preventing the erosion of differentials.

The historical backdrop
The problem of low pay has proved remarkably resilient. In April 1974, the lowest decile of male manual workers earned 68.6 per cent of the average (median) wage, the same proportion – exactly – as that earned by the lowest decile in 1886. Against this, what happened to the distribution of pay since 1974? The answer is 'very little', as Table 5.1 illustrates.

Table 5.1 *Dispersion of gross weekly earnings, 1974–1978: full-time manual men aged 21 years and over (% of medium earnings)*

	Lowest percentile	Lowest decile	Lower quartile	Upper quartile	Highest quartile
1974	49.3	68.6	82.2	121.0	144.1
1975	48.1	69.2	82.8	121.3	144.4
1976	49.4	70.2	83.4	120.8	144.9
1977	50.6	70.6	83.1	120.3	144.4
1978	50.0	69.4	82.4	121.2	146.0

Source: Department of Employment, *New Earnings Survey*, 1978.

In one respect, Table 5.1 is incomplete since it presents data only for full-time manual men over 21. Their earnings, relative to all full-time adult men, remained fairly stable over the period but there were some changes for various groups *within* the low paid as a whole. Juvenile males (under 21) seem to have improved their relative earnings while juvenile females (under 18) apparently did even better. Largely because of the effects of Equal Pay, women in general improved their position relative to men.[4] What remains to be explained is that *within each group* the relative earnings of the lowest paid remained virtually unchanged; this is true throughout the period from 1970. We now turn to the extent of the low pay problem in 1978 – the last full year of the Labour Government's office.

Low pay in 1978

Using the definition of £55 a week as our benchmark, in April 1978 there was an estimated 1 million men (700,000 of them manual workers) and 2.6 million women (1.7m of them non-manual) who worked a full week plus overtime for less than this amount. This represents a substantial proportion of the total working population – some 25 million people – but it by no means includes all those who we would define as low paid. It excludes, for instance, men aged 18, 19 and 20 who were not treated as 'adults' in the survey but almost half of whom were low paid in 1978. Nor do the figures take account of the effects of overtime working which, if excluded, would result in an increase in the number of low paid adult workers from 3.6 million to 4.4 million (1.7 million men and 2.7 million women). While overtime earnings are relatively unimportant to women or non-manual men, the numbers of manual men who would be low paid if they worked only a basic week without overtime rises by 60 per cent.[9] The Low Pay Unit has shown that the total number of low paid would rise again if shift premia were also excluded: 'if manual workers were to rely on their basic rates of pay (as most salaried employees do), a great many more would find themselves in poverty.'[10]

Nor do these summary figures take account of interruptions to earnings (through lay offs, sickness or other causes of absence) which tend to afflict the low paid more than other groups. Nor have we considered the several million young people and part time workers who are low paid. The NES figures suggest that the number of part time women earning less than £1.40 per hour (roughly equivalent to the £55 weekly definition) was just under 1.8 million, with just 145,000 low paid part time men.[9] Jennifer Hurstfield has warned, in her major study of part time workers, that the NES results seriously underestimate the extent of low pay amongst part timers. Nevertheless, using data from that survey, she found that 'nearly one in five part time women workers – an estimated 633,500 women – had earnings which fell 30 per cent or more below the SB level'.[11]

Low pay affects mainly women, manual men and young people. but is not confined to the lower end of the age spectrum; amongst those over 60, the chances of being low paid are almost double that of the adult population as a whole. Those at the beginning and the end of their working lives are joined by other demographic groups sharing a higher risk of low pay – the sick and disabled and ethnic minorities.[10]

The concentration of low pay has led some observers to suggest that it can be 'explained' by reference to individual characteristics. Whilst these may determine whether an individual finds himself in a low paid job, it does *not* explain why the job itself is low paid. As the Low Pay Unit has argued 'in each industry there is a structure of jobs, each with a different wage rate "label". This job/wage structure exists independently from the individuals that happen to fill it at any particular moment in time'.[12]

Low pay is markedly concentrated in certain industries. Distribution and 'miscellaneous services' (including hotels and catering, hairdressing and laundries) between them account for about one-third of all low paid. A high proportion of men in agriculture are low paid as are a high proportion of men and women in clothing and footwear. Employing relatively few people, neither of these industries contribute substantially to the total *numbers* of low paid. A distinction should therefore be drawn between industries where the *concentration* of low pay is high and those which employ large *numbers* of low paid. If policies are directed on a selective basis to industries with high concentrations, then very large numbers of low paid workers will remain unaffected. The distinction is particularly important when considering the role of the state in low pay. Despite some improvements in the relative earnings of the public sector as a whole, large numbers of the low paid are still on the government payroll – in local authorities, the health service, nationalised industries, the civil service and education. About one-fifth of manual men and a half of all women employed in 'public administration' (central and local government) are low paid, although they represent relatively small proportions of all low paid workers. The same is true for 'professional and scientific services' (which includes education and the NHS) in which a quarter of manual men and non-manual women were low paid, together with three quarters of manual women. While this sector accounted for almost one fifth of all low paid women, it represented only 7 per cent of all low paid manual men. By contrast, only 5 per cent of non-manual men in this industry were low paid, but they represented one eighth of all low-paid non-manual workers.[5]

While the public sector as a whole does not therefore account for a disproportionately large number of the low paid, there remain size-able concentrations in that sector. This applies to local authority manual workers, industrial and clerical civil servants, NHS ancillary staff and nurses, and British Rail manual workers. Moreover, in comparing the public and private sectors, it is important to look in detail at different parts of each. Much of the apparent improvement in the relative earnings of the public sector in recent years has been due to improvements in coal mining together with a deterioration of wages council earnings in the private sector. Male non-manual earnings vary little between sectors, but for manual men in the private sector earnings stood almost £10 a week higher than their counterparts in central and local government. Meanwhile, those employed in public corporations earned almost £7 a week *above* the private sector average. The gap between the private sector and local government widens to £12 if wages councils are excluded from the figures. So while it appears at first sight that public sector earnings have caught up with – or even overtaken – those in the private sector, more careful analysis presents a more complex picture.[13] The fair conclusion is that from 1974 to 1978 there was a small improvement in the relative position of public sector employees. There is no particular geographical pattern of the low paid. Some regions, such as East Anglia, have high proportions while others, such as the Northwest, have large numbers.

Britain's minimum wage system

The wages councils set legally enforceable minimum rates for almost 3 million of the lowest paid workers in retailing, clothing, catering and other miscellaneous services such as hairdressing and laundries. Paradoxically, it is in this, the only sector of British industry covered by legal minimum wages, that the problem of low pay is concentrated. The wages councils have failed lamentably to fulfil the original purpose for which they were established at the beginning of the century: to protect those in the 'sweated trades' where wages were exceptionally low and collective bargaining weak.[14] This failure is evident in the level of minimum rates set. In November 1978, the minimum rates for typical adult grades ranged from £27.50 a week (in the Fur Wages Council) to £42.50 (in Retail Bookselling). Only four of the 42 councils then operating set rates exceeding £40 a week, while over half of them (24) had adult minimum rates of less than £35 a week. These wage levels must be compared with the supplementary benefit level (plus average rent) for a two child family of £43.60 and with average male earnings (excluding overtime, shift payments and piecework earnings) of almost £75 a week.[9]

Evidence also suggests that the problem of low pay has been worsening in the wages council sector since the early 1970s. In 1977, the major industrial sectors covered by the councils (miscellaneous services, distribution, agriculture and clothing manufacture) accounted for 42.2 per cent of all low paid manual men and 44.5 per cent of low paid non-manual men. In 1970, the proportions had been 33 and 34.2 per cent respectively.[4] The same wages council industries (excluding agriculture) also employed a third of all low paid women – again suggesting a deterioration compared with 1970.

Policies towards the low paid in wages councils after 1974 were affected by wider developments in industrial relations. Disillusionment with the final stages of the 1964–70 Labour Government's pay policies together with the three phases of Conservative statutory pay policy and the Industrial Relations Act had made the labour movement more sensitive to *any* government intervention in the wage determination process. As part of its Social Contract commitment, the government therefore agreed to withdraw as far as possible from that process; nowhere was this policy of *laissez faire* in industrial relations more evident than in the wages council sector.

It was almost universally accepted that the wages councils had failed to meet their objectives and the general policy was to abolish, wherever possible, this minimum wage machinery. This, it was hoped, would stimulate the development of voluntary collective bargaining. The Employment Protection Act, 1975, allowed for the abolition of a wages council where it was 'no longer necessary to maintain a reasonable standard of remuneration for the workers concerned'. Alternatively, the councils could be converted into 'statutory joint industrial councils' – a half way house en route to abolition. In the five years following Labour's accession in 1974, eleven councils were abolished compared with a total of 14 in the previous 30 years.

This policy was cause for some concern for, although the councils had performed abysmally, they at least afforded some minimum protection for the most vulnerable workers. It is a characteristic of wages council industries that they are dominated by small firms employing large proportions of female, part time and juvenile labour with high rates of staff turnover. This makes it extremely difficult for trade unions to gain a foothold. And, as the Department of Employment subsequently acknowledged, even in those industries where voluntary collective bargaining machinery had developed, 'abolition of a wages council is always likely to leave some workers without immediate protection.'[15]

The Employment Protection Act also contained a mechanism designed to make wages council rates redundant. This allowed a trade union (or employers association) to claim that the wages paid were less favourable than 'general' or 'recognised' pay and conditions operating for the same work elsewhere. If a union succeeded in negotiating rates more favourable than those of the wages council in the same trade, employers in that industry could be obliged to pay the higher rate. In principle, the new 'Fair Wages' law should have represented a major step forward for the low paid, as should the Equal Pay Act for women. The outcome was disappointing, largely because of difficulties in enforcement. Claims could only be pursued through ACAS by a recognised trade union (individuals could not act on their own) and the majority of wages council employees are not union members. Even if they were encouraged to join solely to take advantage of the new law, trade unions might understandably be reluctant to commit resources to the pursuit of claims on behalf of a handful of workers in a shop or hotel. In the event, therefore, this provision proved of less help to the underpaid than to better organised groups as a means of circumnavigating pay policy.

Finally, the government's retreat from the industrial relations scene led it to award the wages councils an independent status. No longer could the Secretary of State instruct councils to act in a certain way, for instance to observe minimum wage targets. Given the poor record of the councils, this abdication of influence was a rash step to take, as became evident when the government introduced its £6 flat rate pay policy, intended to be of most benefit to the low paid. Many councils failed to award the full amount specified under this and the subsequent stage of the policy. Yet the government now had no power to instruct them to do so.

Despite the low level of the minimum rates set by the councils, a large and increasing proportion of employers illegally pay below them. The Department of Employment found that between a quarter and a third of employers inspected in 1976 and 1977 were underpaying at least some of their staff – about double the rate in 1974 and three and a half times that of 1970.[4] By 1978, the Low Pay Unit estimated that illegal underpayment amounted to some £18 million a year.

The government response to this growing infringement was disappointing, based on the belief that most underpayment was unintentional. The Wage Orders setting out the minimum rates are complex, as is the structure of the rates themselves.[16] The government took steps to rationalise the wages councils and encouraged the councils to simplify their Orders. The DE even experimented by producing simplified guides to one or two of the Orders. But if the inability of employers to understand the minimum rates helped to explain the high level of underpayment, it could hardly explain a doubling in the *rate* (short of a rapid decline in employer literacy!).

Part of the explanation is that employers have every incentive to disregard this particular aspect of the law. The likelihood of being caught is remote. Just 150 inspectors are employed throughout the country to oversee the wages paid to 3 million workers in almost half a million establishments. The proportion of firms visited on a routine basis is low: in 1955 the government and unions agreed on a routine inspection rate of $7\frac{1}{2}$ per cent of firms a year.[17] This implied that a firm would be visited on average once every 43

years. Given the high turnover of staff and firms, many people
would never see a wages inspector. In the late 1960s and early 1970s,
the inspectorate achieved a routine inspection rate of up to 10 per
cent.[18] But in 1973 the DE announced its intention to cut the
number of inspectors subject to a guarantee that the numbers
would be increased again should the inspection rate fall below $7\frac{1}{2}$
per cent. It did. By 1975 the inspection rate was down to 6.8 per
cent. By 1977 only 5.5 per cent of establishments were visited on
a routine basis. Yet the DE now argued that 'public expenditure
and manpower constraints rule out any significant increase in the
number of wages inspectors'.[19]

The likelihood of an employer being caught is therefore small;
that of being prosecuted is smaller still. In 1977, out of approximately
11,000 employers found underpaying, just 11 (one in a thousand)
were prosecuted. After a thorough review of prosecution policy, the
DE announced that they were satisfied with their policy 'to
consider offences disclosed at second or subsequent inspections as
potential prosecution cases. *First offenders are not considered for
prosecution* unless the offence is flagrant'[19] (emphasis added). It is
interesting to compare this approach with that of the DHSS whose
policy on social security abuse is 'to prosecute in each and every
case'. Since 1974, it is true, the number of prosecutions increased
significantly: between 1971 and 1973 there were no criminal proceedings whatsoever against underpaying employers; between 1974 and
1977 there were 11 such prosecutions, seven of them in 1977. The
number of prosecutions has increased less, however, than the rate of
detected underpayment itself.[20]

Even for those employers unlucky enough to be caught *and* prosecuted, the maximum penalty is less than harsh. The maximum fine
was set at £20 in 1909, at which level it remained until 1975 when it
was raised to £100. This is still half the maximum penalty currently
applicable for travelling on London Transport without paying the
correct fare or for having a TV without a licence. And this is
the *maximum* penalty, which courts have been reluctant to impose.[21]

The Labour Government's response to illegal underpayment was
therefore disappointing, reflecting an unwillingness to commit
additional resources to protect the lowest paid. But pressure
following the announcement of a 24.6 per cent underpayment rate
uncovered in routine inspections in 1976 made some action essential.
The policy adopted was to initiate 'saturation' or 'blitz' inspections
concentrated on certain trades in certain towns. This blitz, carried out

in autumn 1976, revealed an even higher level of underpayment (rising as high as 63 per cent of employers inspected in Northwich and 55 per cent in Warrington). Equally alarming results emerged from similar exercises carried out in 1977. As a publicity stunt, the policy was an undoubted success, increasing awareness of the existence of minimum wages and raising the level of self enforcement. But there were costs involved in the blitz strategy: the rate of routine inspections in towns not covered by the blitz fell further still and employers soon adapted to the new threat.[20] The blitz was no substitute for a commitment of additional resources aimed at eradicating illegal underpayment.

Pay policies

Socialists have long believed that a consistent policy on incomes is the only long term solution to economic inequalities. But, as Barbara Wootton has warned, 'An incomes policy must be what its name implies and not just a policy for the control of wages'.[22] We should therefore not confuse the policies of wage restraint applied after 1974 with an incomes policy which would apply to all wage and non-wage incomes. Such confusion is encouraged by the packaging with which pay policies are usually presented. Although each stage of pay policy since 1974 has professed to be of some additional benefit to the low paid, this period is characterised by a marked shift in priorities, from a desire to improve the relative position of the low paid to that of restoring established relativities and differentials.

The period begins with the establishment of the social contract; no formal pay restraint existed but negotiators were instructed by the TUC to aim at wage increases sufficient to offset the rise in the cost of living. The TUC also established a minimum wage target of £25 a week, subsequently raised to £30. Those earning less than the target, and women moving towards Equal Pay, were exempt from the guidelines. At the time, there was concern that the low paid would be left behind in the 'free for all'. In retrospect, they probably achieved more during this period than during subsequent periods of formal wage restraint. The existence of the minimum wage target (subsequently abandoned) probably helped in this; several low paid public sector groups such as the local authority manual workers and NHS ancilliaries achieved the target, as did some food manufacturing workers and a handful of shop workers. Paradoxically the improvement for the low paid was also in part due to the existence of the cost of living threshold payments – a hangover from Ted Heath's Phase

3 policy. Amounting to £4.40 a week, these represented a substantial percentage increase for some of the low paid. It was the better organised groups in the public sector which gained most from these arrangements.

For those in the private sector, and especially in wages councils, the social contract provided fewer gains. By the end of the summer of 1975, not one of the wages councils had established a minimum adult rate equivalent to the £30 target set almost a year before. Indeed, all but three councils still had minimum adult rates below £25, while nine had not yet reached £20.[23]

The first stage of the social contract ended abruptly in July 1975 amidst concern that Britain was in the grip of a 'wage explosion'. Earnings rose by 27 per cent in the year to July 1975; prices, meanwhile, had risen by 26 per cent. So, even allowing for the larger increases permitted for women and the low paid, earnings only rose by 1 per cent more than the guidelines permitted. Although money wage costs were rising fast, wage-earner living standards probably fell.[24]

The £6 pay policy was therefore ushered in as a more formal (though still 'voluntary') form of pay restraint. Again the policy was presented as being of benefit to the low paid who would gain larger percentage increases through the flat rate formula. Those earning in excess of £8,500 a year were to receive no increase at all. Given this highly egalitarian presentation, it is surprising that the policy did not secure an improvement in the relative position of the low paid. On the contrary, the largest percentage increases were achieved by higher paid professional and managerial groups.[25]

This result demands some explanation, part of which is to be found in the nature of the £6 policy. First, it was a maximum increase to be achieved through collective bargaining rather than an entitlement. The low paid do not generally enjoy significant bargaining strength (why else are they low paid?) and many did not therefore receive the full £6 payment. In particular, wages councils covering some quarter of a million workers refused to pay the full amount allowable, and the government was now powerless to instruct them to do so.[26] Secondly, the £6 increase could not be added to basic rates in calculating overtime pay, so that many workers found themselves working overtime at an hourly rate lower than their normal basic pay. This helped to depress the earnings of lower paid manual workers, more dependent on overtime pay than their white collar counterparts. At the other end of the spectrum, the policy did not prevent higher paid professional groups from receiving their incremental increases in addition to the £6. Through these mechanisms, together with job promotions (both real and artificial) and job changes – not to mention flourishing fringe benefits – managerial salary surveys covering the period reveal substantial percentage increases for the higher paid groups.[27] Meanwhile, the bulk of manual and lower grade clerical workers faced the pay policy in its full rigour.

The impact of the £6 policy was to maintain cash differentials while compressing them in percentage terms. Meanwhile, relativities appear to have been unaffected by the policy. The widespread belief was that both had been disrupted and when the next stage of formal pay restraint was unveiled in the summer of 1976 it allowed for an increase of 5 per cent. Again the low paid would benefit, it was argued, by the implementation of a flat rate limit of £2.50 for those earning less than £50 a week, and £4 for those earning more than £80. We need not rehearse the repeated drawbacks of this stage: again the increases were a maximum, again a number of wages councils refused to pay them in full, again manual workers found their overtime earnings depressed and again better paid managerial groups passed through the pay limits undeterred.[28]

The final stage in the transition from concern for the low paid to a desire (bordering on panic) to re-establish differentials came with stage three of formal pay restraint, with its limit expressed wholly in percentage terms. This preoccupation with differentials was not confined to the government. Throughout the period, the TUC minimum wage target had remained at the £30 set in 1974. Yet when NUPE proposed, at the 1977 Trades Union Congress, that the target be updated to £50 a week, fellow unions rejected the suggestion. Trade unions apparently believed that improvements for the low paid had progressed sufficiently for this no longer to be a priority.[29]

The adoption of an updated target of £50 would indeed have proved something of an embarrassment for the wages councils, many of which still had not achieved the three year old £30 target. For this section of industry, the 10 per cent policy was embarrassment enough: so low were most of the basic rates that the cash value of 10 per cent would have been derisory. Many of the councils therefore proposed cash increases which, although low, exceeded the maximum 10 per cent. But whereas the government was unable to trespass on the newly acquired independence of the councils to ensure that they paid the full £6 and 5 per cent under previous stages of the policy, it now submitted a formal objection to each council proposal which exceeded the pay limit, even to councils whose increase would have done no more than bring minimum rates up to the 1974 TUC target of £30. The government's embarrassment in being seen to oppose increases for the poorest workers must have been compounded by the fact that the wages councils could now ignore such protestations anyway.

The government were not to fall into this trap in the fourth phase of pay policy in which the limit was 5 per cent. To avoid the inevitable confrontations with wages councils over tiny cash increases, the government established a minimum earnings level of £44.50 below which workers would be exempt from the 5 per cent limit (as long as their resulting earnings did not exceed £44.50). The choice of such an arbitrary amount appeared puzzling; it excluded the wages councils, none of which had achieved rates approaching such a generous figure; on the other hand, it bore no relation to the £30 target which – if updated as NUPE once more unsuccessfully suggested – would have stood at £60 a week. The government argued that it represented the TUC target plus subsequent pay policy supplements. However calculated, the effect was to exclude the low paid in local authorities and the NHS from the pay policy escape clause. The basic wage of these groups stood at £42.40 which, with 5 per cent added, rises to £44.52 – just 2p above the lower earnings limit. This was taken as an explicit challenge by public sector low paid workers and, together with the choice of an unrealistically low 5 per cent limit, proved to be the misjudgement that spelt the end of formal pay restraint[30] and, it has been suggested, of the government.

Tax policy and the low paid

No discussion of pay policies is complete without an examination of the accompanying tax policy; in the period after 1974 the two became inextricably linked. Taxation has long been used as an alternative, or reinforcement, to pay restraint and the Labour Government was exceptional only in its decision to make this link explicit. This relationship is especially important in the discussion of low pay for, while pay policies were intended to benefit the poorest families most, taxation was working in the opposite direction.

Wilkinson and Turner, examining the period 1948 to 1970, found that (with the exception of years preceeding an election) the rise in

real wages was restrained by the use of either pay policies or taxation.[31] This argument applies equally to the period after 1974. In the
year to April 1975 (covering most of the first stage of the social
contract), gross earnings rose by 27.7 per cent, while prices rose by
21.7 per cent. But tax receipts were allowed to rise to mop up the gains
in real incomes, leaving wage earners with an increase in living
standards of little more than 1 per cent.[24] The introduction of the first
stage of formal pay restraint (the £6) together with continuing high
inflation and a rising tax burden resulted in a fall in living standards
which accelerated in stage two. The link between taxation and pay
policy was made explicit in April 1976 when the Chancellor offered
the TUC a trade-off between wage restraint and tax concessions.
Unfortunately the terms of the trade-off were less than favourable for
working people. Real net incomes fell by over £4 a week in the
following 12 months. The following year, further tax concessions
were paid which helped a partial recovery in living standards, although these were not part of the government's policy, being the
result of the back bench revolt of Jeff Rooker and Audrey Wise. By
April 1978, real net incomes were still £2.25 lower than in April
1974.[32]

It appears surprising that the union movement was prepared to
accept pay restraint for tax 'concessions' which never materialised.
The reason is that Denis Healey was able to offer tax concessions
while allowing inflation and fiscal drag to increase tax receipts for
him. The procedure merely involved raising tax allowances by less
than was sufficient to maintain their real value against inflation. As a
result of the backbench revolt of Jeff Rooker and Audrey Wise. By
payable) was allowed to fall, and wage earners found an increasing
proportion of their income becoming taxable. In his April 1976
budget, for instance, the Chancellor offered tax concessions worth
over £1,000 million in exchange for wage restraint. Yet in the 12
months leading up to that budget, inflation had increased the revenue
from income tax by almost £3,000 million. The budget did no more
than give back to wage earners about one-third of the additional
revenue which had been collected from them during the preceding
year. This was an old strategy beloved by Chancellors for thirty years,
but ended by the Rooker–Wise amendment requiring personal allowances to be index linked from 1977 onwards.[33]

The Chancellor's willingness to use this covert means of raising
revenue is in itself surprising, given his statement in his first budget
of March 1974 that 'one of the worst consequences of inflation has

been to force more and more of the worst off into paying higher tax'.[34] The truth of Healey's statement is illustrated in Table 5.2, which shows the real value of the tax threshold – or tax-free income – for each year since 1974.

Table 5.2   Tax-free income, 1974 to 1979

								(£ per year)	
	Single person		Married couple		Married 1 child		couple with 2 children		4 children
April	(a)	(b)	(a)	(b)	(a)	(b)	(a)	(b)	(a)	(b)
1974	625	625	865	865	1105	1105	1293	1293	1704	1704
1975	675	555	955	785	1195	982	1383	1136	1794	1474
1976	735	508	1085	750	1385	957	1633	1129	2164	1496
1977	945	556	1455	856	1703	1001	1951	1148	2482	1460
1978	985	537	1535	837	1755	957	1974	1106	2448	1335
1979	1075	532	1675	829	1883	932	2091	1035	2507	1241

(a) is money amount; (b) is real amount at April 1974 prices.

By 1978, single people were paying tax on a real income (at April 1974 prices) £1.69 a week lower than in 1974, while the tax threshold for a married couple fell by 54p a week. The real losers were families with children, whose tax free income (including child benefit) fell by £2.85, £4.17 or £7.10 a week depending on whether they had one, two or four children. In Healey's 13 budgets between March 1974 and April 1978, he claimed to have lifted several million low paid workers out of the tax net altogether. But by 1978/9 there were 1.2 million *more* taxpayers than there had been five years earlier – without a substantial increase in the size of the working population. The distributional consequences of this strategy were well known to the government. Joel Barnett, Chief Secretary to the Treasury, explained in one candid interview that 'when we refrain from increasing the personal allowances in line with inflation, we are taking more in taxation in that way. We have said so straightforwardly; what we are doing is redistributing the tax burden.'[35]

We can see in Table 5.3 how the government's tax and child benefit policies affected households of various kinds. By 1975/6 real incomes had fallen reflecting both inflation and the lack of indexation in the tax allowances. There had been a sharp increase in the taxes paid by the poorest as the tax threshold fell; this fall in the tax threshold was to be repeated in 1976/7. In 1974/5 the number of taxpayers increased by 700,000 as a result of the fall in the tax threshold. In 1976/7 poor families gained little from the trade-off between tax concessions and pay restraint.

Table 5.3 Index of real weekly net income (1973/74 = 100)
selected households (1970/71 prices)

	Single	Married	Married with two children under 11	Married with four children, two under 11 and two 11-16 years
1974/5				
Lower quartile	98.4	99.5	100.5	100.8
Median	98.3	99.1	99.6	99.6
Upper quartile	97.9	98.6	100.6	99.7
1975/6				
Lower quartile	94.2	95.4	95.9	96.3
Median	93.5	94.1	95.0	95.1
Upper quartile	93.6	95.8	95.2	95.5
1976/7				
Lower quartile	92.1	93.4	94.9	96.3
Median	90.9	92.4	95.0	95.1
Upper quartile	90.8	92.1	92.9	93.8
1977/8				
Lower quartile	92.6	95.4	95.9	94.7
Median	91.7	94.1	94.6	93.2
Upper quartile	91.2	93.5	93.6	93.2
1978/9				
Lower quartile	96.8	99.5	101.4	100.8
Median	96.5	98.7	100.4	99.6
Upper quartile	95.8	97.6	99.0	98.8

Note: Net income is earnings (from new earnings survey) less tax and national insurance contributions plus family allowance or child benefit where approriate.

Source: Hansard 26 July 1979.

In 1976/7 there was a further fall in real incomes. The continued fall in the real incomes of the very well-off was perhaps less harshly felt than the fall in the real incomes of the poorest families. In 1977/8 the position improved somewhat largely as a result of the Rooker–Wise amendment which indexed the tax allowances. There was further improvement after the April 1978 budget which introduced a reduced rate band together with substantial increases in child benefit. But the position of higher rate taxpayers was also improved. Mr Healey had pledged in his first budget of March 1974 'to use the tax system to promote greater equality'. By 1976 he was saying that 'there must be some reduction in the tax burden, particularly on middle managers in industry who have seen their net pay reduced

Table 5.4   The tax threshold and the poverty line
for a two-child family (£ per week)

	Tax threshold[a]	SB level[b]	FIS level
1973	22.69	20.86	22.00
1978	38.87	46.50	47.80

[a] Including child benefit in 1978.
[b] Ordinary scale rate plus average rent.
Source: Hansard, 24 January 1978, written answer to R. Howell M.P.

in real terms over recent years by inflation and incomes policies of successive governments'.[36] In 1977 he cut the number of higher rate tax payers by one-quarter and there was a further reduction in 1978 following amendments by the Conservative opposition supported by the Liberal Party. By 1978/9 only 808,000 taxpayers – about 4 per cent of the total – were subject to the higher rate. The net effect of all these changes was however very slight if we compare all levels of net income except the highest from 1974/5 to 1978/9. At least, however, from 1977/8 onwards the government (with a large amount of help from backbenchers) did stop further deterioration in the position of families.

The fall in the tax threshold after 1974 had other implications. These are illustrated in Table 5.4 which shows how the tax threshold has changed in relation to official criteria of poverty, the supplementary benefit level and the eligibility limits for family income supplement (FIS).

In 1973, a two-child family started to pay tax once their income exceeded (marginally) the supplementary benefit poverty line. But by 1978 a gap of more than £7.50 a week had opened between the two: families now pay tax when in full time work on an income which is substantially below that which they would receive if unemployed and dependent on supplementary benefit. This helps explain the dramatic increase in the number of wage earning families living below the poverty line. Nor is this due to generosity with supplementary benefit levels. While SB rates have increased relative to net earnings (that is, after taking account of increasing tax payments), they have remained stable when compared with gross pay.

A second consequence of the fall in the tax threshold is that families in receipt of Family Income Supplement (FIS) can at the same time find themselves paying all or part of it back in income tax. Indeed, by 1977, no less than two thirds of all those families receiving FIS were in this position. On the government's £44.50 lower earnings limit for stage four pay policy, a two-child family would pay as much in income tax and national insurance as they received in FIS. As a result of this widening gap between the tax threshold and the FIS limit, increasing numbers of families have found themselves in the poverty trap whereby a pay rise results in a greater loss of tax and means tested benefits. The number of families in this position is estimated to have increased from 17,600 in 1974 to 86,000 in 1978.[38]

Conclusion – a way forward
The conclusion must be that little was achieved for the low paid between 1974 and 1979. This chapter began by suggesting some of the reasons for this. We should end by proposing ways in which the next Labour Government might build a constructive policy on low pay. Government responses to the problem depend largely on what they see as its most important cause. The Royal Commission on the Distribution of Income and Wealth leaned heavily towards explanations based on the attributes and abilities of the individuals involved – their education, qualifications and experience, family background, race, health and genetic endowment.[4] Others have argued that the stability of the earnings distribution can be explained by the 'physical, mental, motivational or other differences of a kind which may plausibly be expected to remain reasonably stable from one generation to the next'.[39] In their search for the causes of poverty, Layard *et al.* take

this type of explanation one step further by arguing that personal characteristics are important, but so are the prices which the labour market places on these characteristics.[6]

These explanations would suggest that government attempts to influence wage levels by institutional (non-market) measures such as a minimum wage or incomes policies are mistaken. The underlying inequalities determined by personal attributes and market forces are always likely to reassert themselves.[6] A logical conclusion might be that, as well as trying to improve the labour supply through education and training, regional policy and industrial subsidies should aim to increase the demand for certain types of labour to pull wages up. Meanwhile, cash transfers represent a more efficient way of alleviating hardship caused by low pay than direct influence on wages.

There can be little doubt that these views enjoy an element of truth; skills, education and qualifications are clearly associated with earnings levels and those who have been able to acquire them are less vulnerable both to low pay and unemployment. But there is always a danger of confusing association with causation. Britain, is not a meritocracy in which earnings are closely correlated with ability. Little has changed since Cannan observed in 1914 that 'even if road sweeping were paid by the piece in strict proportion to the amount of service rendered, the most industrious and able man in the world would not earn £1,000 by it', and asked why 'the value of the work of an average person is less in some occupations than in others'.[40] Some might answer by explaining that only those of low ability find themselves in low paying occupations. But that is to ignore the factors other than ability which restrict occupational mobility – including social class restrictions on entry to certain occupations and to the education that might act as a passport. Cannan's point remains that certain jobs pay low wages regardless of the incumbent and although the shape of the earnings distribution had remained stable, the position of individuals within the distribution changed quite considerably. His mistake was to identify the problem as an *occupational one*. Earnings vary quite widely within occupations except – and this is the important point – where they are restricted to a single or relatively few industries. Individuals with the same personal characteristics and occupation are likely to receive earnings which vary widely between industries. For this reason, we share Tawney's view that 'The problem of poverty is not a problem of individual character and its waywardness, but a problem of economic and industrial organisation ... to be studied first at its source, and only secondly in its manifestations'.[41]

The conclusion that emerges from this is that governments do have a significant role, through minimum wage policies or incomes policies, in improving the relative position of the low paid. That such policies have failed results more from the way in which they have been implemented than from their nature. One policy which has yet to be tried is that of a national minimum wage. Disillusionment with the effect on the low paid of pay policies between 1964 and 1968 led to considerable interest in this idea. The 1969 TUC *Economic Review* outlined a range of policies intended to tackle low pay 'extending if necessary to the establishment of a national minimum wage backed by statutory action'. A governmental working party on the issue followed, but neither the Green Paper that emerged from the exercise, nor the TUC's subsequent deliberations on low pay were enthusiastic about the idea of a statutory minimum wage.[8] As a result, the proposal was never even on the agenda for discussion after 1974.

Trade union opposition to the idea springs from a mistrust of *any* government intervention in the wage bargaining process. For many, the only effective solution to low pay must come through trade unions and collective bargaining. We are inclined to agree. But the mistake is to view the trade union role as purely local. The structure of many industries (retailing and catering among them) present considerable recruitment difficulties which will not disappear overnight. Moreover, in areas where membership is high (as in agriculture and local authorities) pay levels remain low. If British trade unions are to extend their bargaining function they would do well to follow their French counterparts who determine the level of the minimum wage through a national bargain with the government. This process would also help guard against the very real objection that the minimum would be set so low as to be worthless.

Other objections to a national minimum wage – its effect on differentials, prices and employment – are of a rather different nature. These are important issues but they would arise if *any* effective solution to low pay were implemented; they are not the preserve of this particular type of solution. The costs of a national minimum wage would depend on whether both differentials and relativities were to be preserved (in which case there seems little point) and there can be little doubt that this increase in wage costs could once and for all have an effect on the price level. This should be distinguished from an 'inflationary effect' which implies a continuing process. If an improvement in *real* wages were to be achieved, these price level effects would have to be offset by policies on indirect taxation and price subsidies. The evidence on the likely employment effects is inconclusive, many of the worst fears emanating from an oversimplified view of the labour market. To the extent that the increase in wage costs did result in job losses, the effect on aggregate demand would work in the opposite direction. Decline in female employment following the introduction of the Equal Pay Act appears to have been small, partly no doubt due to phasing in the change over a number of years. The employment, price level and differentials effects of a minimum wage might be minimised if the same type of staged introduction were adopted. An obvious starting point would be the wages councils where minimum wage machinery already exists. A common rate across the councils, set at an adequate level and enforced, would be a significant first step along the road.

A national minimum wage has much to commend it, but it could not be implemented in isolation. Policies on prices and taxation would be essential complements. Yet the achievement of any of these objectives is unlikely in an environment of restrictive macro-economic policies. A policy for economic growth is important not only because it would ease the transitional problems of a minimum wage. We warned at the outset that a definition of low pay expressed in weekly or hourly terms was too restrictive. Taking account of the higher incidence of unemployment amongst the low paid, the problem viewed on an annual or life time basis appears more formidable still. This is why, if we are really committed to an improvement in the living standards of the low paid, action on wages must be accompanied by a policy for a return to full employment.

6 Inequality at Work

by Robert Taylor

The time is long overdue for a radical programme to bring about social justice for Britain's 12,400,000 manual workers through both political action and more effective trade union bargaining. Yet these vital questions have never attracted much concern from the Labour movement, although the inequalities of status and treatment between blue and white collar workers remain far more widespread and intractable in this country than in most of the rest of democratic Western Europe.

In her contribution to this book's predecessor, *Labour and Inequality* (Fabian Society, 1972) Dorothy Wedderburn argued that the Labour Governments between 1964 and 1970 'did nothing to interfere with those fundamental ideological and market mechanisms which serve' to perpetuate workplace inequalities. The record of Labour rule between March 1974 and May 1979 was hardly much better. Under almost continual economic crisis and faced with a severe cutback in many of Britain's major manufacturing industries, the Wilson and Callaghan Governments appeared to have neither the time nor perhaps the will to make any direct attempt to remove the causes of workplace inequality in our class divided society. To be fair, neither Labour's programmes of 1973 and 1976, nor the innumerable policy statements issued during the period by the TUC–Labour Party Liaison Committee took up the crucial issue either. And the unions with large manual worker memberships failed to put the demand for staff status and equality at the forefront of their agenda.

First, this chapter will review in outline some major legislative steps or proposals (other than wage agreements or incomes' policy) which were intended to improve the position of wage earners in industry. It will then discuss in some detail the problem of workplace inequality which remains. Finally, it will draw out some of the lessons which the Labour movement should learn.

Progress made

Labour's years in office from March 1974 to May 1979 were not entirely barren of achievement in the area of workplace inequalities. The 1975 Employment Protection Act, described by Jack Jones of the Transport and General Workers as the 'workers' charter', extended a wide range of basic rights to all workers, but they were of particular value to the manual grades. The provisions of the measure have not yet made a big impact on the shopfloor but they challenge some of the assumptions of employer power in crucial parts of workplace organisation. The most effective change has enabled workers to seek redress from their employers through industrial tribunals for unfair dismissal, a legacy from the 1971 Industrial Relations Act. A study on the impact of the employment legislation suggests that the unfair dismissal provisions made far more difference to the behaviour of employers than other parts of the 1975 Act[1] though Linda Dickens has questioned the widely held assumption that industrial tribunals have been inundated with cases by dismissed workers seeking redress from wronged employers.[2] The median sum of compensation for workers dismissed unfairly is under £600, hardly a punitive sum. It is too early to judge the help provided for manual workers, in particular, by the provisions to ensure maternity leave, entitlement to normal pay while under medical supervision, time off with pay for carrying out union or public duties and job seeking after notification of three months of being made redundant, and clearer procedures on how a redundancy takes place. Many employers and Conservative politicians have argued that the 1975 Act has tilted the balance of power away from capital and towards organised labour. But the ultimate authority of the employers has hardly been challenged in practice and in its manifesto the Conservative Party did not find it necessary to call for its repeal. Certainly the PSI study found little evidence among larger and medium sized firms employing 50 workers or more that the measure was creating genuine difficulties for employers. The individual rights enshrined in that law only establish certain minimum conditions at work.

Schedule eleven of the 1975 Act was designed to help workers whose rates of pay were below the agreed rates in an area for doing broadly similar work in the same industry. The Central Arbitration Committee has been inundated with cases from unions seeking pay increases for their members on these grounds of comparability. It looks, however, as if it is non-manual workers who have enjoyed the largest benefits from this controversial provision. It is unions like ASTMS and TASS with exclusively white collar memberships who have been the most effective in winning schedule eleven cases, not unions with manual worker members.

The 1974 Health and Safety at Work Act was also of direct relevance to manual workers. The introduction of safety representatives on the shopfloor from September 1978, with power to keep a close scrutiny of safety standards in the workplace, is potentially a great step forward, although it will take some years to discover whether their presence will reduce accidents at work. The new emphasis on prevention of accidents rather than on compensation only after injury represents an encouraging step and manual workers should benefit from this. But while the Act will help reduce safety risks, it does not positively promote improvements in the wider range of working conditions.

The achievement of some form of industrial democracy could be of immense benefit to equality of treatment for manual workers, but although the Labour Party was committed to action on this controversial issue in both the 1974 election manifestos, no legislation emerged during the lifetime of the 1974–79 government.

The Bullock Committee of Inquiry, which reported in February 1977, produced a divided report.[3] The majority favoured the proposal of worker representatives sitting on the top board of their companies in equal number with shareholder representatives, and a small group of appointed independents (the '2x plus y' formula). This was bitterly denounced by the Confederation of British Industry as a threat to business enterprise. The majority on the Bullock Committee wanted the new system to be based on recognised trade union machinery through the formation of joint representation committees of shop stewards at the workplace. This brought the charge that industrial democracy was simply going to mean the unacceptable growth in the power of the trade unions, not a genuinely democratic form of participation for shopfloor workers. Edmund Dell, the Trade Secretary and the man responsible for formulating industrial democracy legislation, never disguised his scepticism about Bullock. Moreover the unions themselves were divided about what they sought and few union leaders showed much enthusiasm for making industrial democracy an urgent priority. It is doubtful whether there was much pressure for any move in that direction during the seventies from the shopfloor. The Cabinet was uncertain of how to proceed. The July 1978 White Paper on industrial democracy left many thorny questions unresolved, such as methods of electing worker representatives, the rights of workers who were not members of unions and the role of management in an industrial democracy system. The outline of the proposed legislation with an emphasis on a two tier board system and a third representation for worker representatives showed a clear retreat from the more full blooded Bullock majority proposals.

Too much concentration on the intricate details of company law diverted attention away from a debate on general principles. It is possible – but by no means certain – that any involvement by workers in the running of their companies would transform industrial life for the better and bring a major advance towards equality of treatment between manual and non-manual. However, industrial democracy as workers on the board would inevitably mean a blurring of function between collective bargaining and managerial decision making, with a resulting threat to trade union autonomy. Can workers be bargainers and managers? We need to resolve this in the 80s.

Inequalities at work
What are the inequalities that remain? The most obvious and painful that persists between manual and non-manual workers lies in the size and composition of their wage packets. While low pay is the subject of a separate chapter, pay is so closely linked with other work inequalities that some account of its form and implications needs to be given here. In April 1978, male full time manual workers aged 21 and over averaged a gross weekly wage of £80.70 compared with an average £100.70 for male white collar workers.[4] The disparity in earning power is more startling in terms of particular occupations.

In April 1978, marketing sales managers and executives averaged £131.40 a week, office managers £116.10 and senior civil servants £113.70, while draughtsmen earned £92.00, steel workers £91.70 and toolmakers £89.80. Catering workers earned £57.00 a week and farm workers £57.70. As much as 26 per cent of the male manual worker's weekly pay packet derived from supplements on top of the basic rate. Overtime pay accounted for 14 per cent (£11.60), payment by results, bonuses and commissions a further 9 per cent (£7.20) and shift premia 3 per cent (£2.40).[4] Without these additions to their basic pay, most manual workers would simply be unable to enjoy a tolerable standard of living, particularly after the crushing extra burden of direct taxation imposed on low paid workers over the past ten years.

By contrast, a mere 6.4 per cent of white collars' gross weekly earnings came from additions to basic pay. They receive the same sum of money week after week, month after month between pay settlement dates for the work they do, whereas the wage packets of manual workers fluctuate, often wildly, because they are paid by the hour and the maximisation of those earnings must depend on the ups and downs of production. Lay-offs, whatever their cause, are fairly commonplace in manufacturing industry. Under provisions of the 1975 Employment Protection Act, employers are obliged to pay their workers a minimum guaranteed payment if they are laid off through no fault of their own. Many larger and medium sized private firms with enlightened management and the nationalised industries tend to provide more generous safeguards to manual workers, but this does not mean the same stability of earnings throughout the year as that experienced by those in office jobs. A NEDO study on the car industry discovered that, on average, manual workers only received the full rate of pay for their work for a quarter of all working days.[5] No doubt the relative strike proneness of motor manufacture may make this atypical, but many manual workers are rightly incensed by the view that their level of earnings are adequate. The constant uncertainty of pay expectations for manual workers makes it very hard for them to plan a family budget without anxieties about making ends meet. In some cases, it encourages a live-for-today attitude and confirms the cynical view held by many manual workers that life is just a lottery in an economic and social system which thrives on greed and the pursuit of material ends and which scorns the ideals of social justice and collective solidarity.

White collar workers with a monthly pay cheque usually going straight into their bank accounts suffer none of the indignities and frustrations that face the manuals in the method by which they are paid. During the seventies elsewhere in Western Europe, substantial strides have been made towards the equality of treatment between manual and non-manual, especially in France (perhaps under the stimulus of the shocks of May 1968). In this country, the movement away from paying manual workers cash in the hand at the end of the week has still a long way to go. The banks remain middle class preserves of privilege, and the Giro system has so far failed to make any major impact. It is true that the overwhelming majority of male manual workers prefer weekly pay packets and, as a consequence, over half the wives of manual workers still do not know the true amount of what their husbands earn. Unions need to stress the advantages to manual workers of monthly payment, in particular the access this provides for the divèrse range of credit facilities now offered by banks to their customers. Ironically the opening hours of banks work against this reform, and the white collar union (BIFU) has been a major obstacle to more flexible use of office time, a necessity if manual workers are going to see the wisdom of changing the method by which they are paid.

Another severe inequality between manual and non-manual workers lies in the size and pattern of working hours. Manual workers worked an average of 46.0 hours a week in April 1978, 6.1 per cent of which was in overtime. As many as 29.2 per cent of male manuals actually clocked in over 48 hours. Railway employees worked 13.6 hours overtime or 53.5 hours in all for £79.00 gross a week (of which £23.60 was for overtime). Lorry and bus drivers also worked on average more than 10 hours of overtime a week to provide £18.70 and £18.90 respectively of their gross earnings of £87.30 and £84.20. By contrast, the white collar man only worked a 38.7 hour week of which on average a mere 1.4 hours was overtime.[4] In fact, our white collar staff enjoy the same length of working weeks as their contemporaries in the rest of Western Europe; but, with the main exception of France, our manual workers work longer hours than any others in the western industrialised world. The modest growth in flexitime is almost wholly confined to office employment. So much for the glib myth of the work-shy British worker.

A growing number of manual workers are having to work more unsocial hours on shifts in continuous production processes. There are no precise statistics on the extent of shiftworking but the April 1978 New Earnings Survey revealed that 23.4 per cent of male manual workers (compared with only 5.5 per cent of non-manual workers) were in receipt of shift payments. The percentage of male manual workers in receipt of shift work premia rose from 19.3 per cent to 23.2 per cent in 1976, while for women the proportion rose from 7.3 per cent to 11.2 per cent.[4]

The medical evidence on shift working is rather divided as to whether it has any long term consequences. There does appear to be a process of self-selection, which must qualify any overall gloomy view that shiftworking is injurious. Yet the disruption of sleep patterns and the strain imposed on normal social life can prove severe for many shift workers. There are signs of employers in some areas finding it difficult to recruit workers for jobs on double day shifts, especially in those parts of the London area where the labour market is tight. Immigrant workers predominate on night shifts in the foundries and manufacturing plants of the Northwest and Midlands. To date, our society (unlike, for example, the United States) has failed to adapt to the needs of round the clock working in a wide range of services, notably public transport, entertainment and opening hours for shops.

The issue of working hours has become more urgent in the past few years, with the growing demand among some unions for the negotiation of a new basic 35 hour week without loss of earnings. This is seen by many in the Labour movement as a major contribution to help cut the dole queues, although the Treasury believes the cost of such a move would be prohibitively expensive for the country in its present economic condition. But the 35 hour week demand is also a belated recognition of the need for a move towards equality of working time between the worker on the shopfloor and the worker in the office. The Post Office workers made a breakthrough to a 37.5 hour week in 1978, but other workers can be expected to push the claim over the next few years.

A further inequality at work stems from the lack of regular increments and promotion prospects for manual workers. In 1973, a mere 3 per cent of all manual workers were paid any increments, compared with 90 per cent of non-manuals.[6] The prospects for promotion are much more restricted for many workers today than they were a decade ago because opportunities for supervisors and foremen or first line management are now being taken up by young men and women with reasonably high formal education qualifications.

Most full time male manuals reach the height of their earning capacity at a relatively young age – between 30 and 39 (an average £85.60 a week in April 1978). This is usually the time of a workers' life when families are being brought up and there are mortgage and hire purchase commitments to meet. The longer hours worked (6.9 hours on top of the basic week for the thirties age bracket) provide the extra money needed to compensate perhaps for the loss of take home earnings from a working wife who has left the labour market to rear a family. Moreover, this is also the time when manual workers are at their most physically agile.

By the time manual workers reach their fifties, their average gross weekly wage has dropped to £79.10 a week and it falls even more to £72.10 for the 60 to 64 year old age bracket. In contrast, the male white collar worker reaches his earnings prime during his forties

(£112.60 a week in April 1978) with only a slight dip to £108.00 in his fifties.

The age for retirement is 60 for some male non-manual workers and for women, whereas the male manual workers must work on until 65, even though their life expectancy is much lower than for white collar males (68.2 years compared with 71.3).[7] The early retirement scheme negotiated by the miners in 1977 was a long overdue move in the right direction but we need some similar movements in manufacturing. In other Western European countries, workers in physically arduous jobs can retire after a specific length of service, often as young as 55. Under the regime of industrial company paternalism in Japan, this is a common age for workers to finish work. However, in Britain the sheer cost of such a step is prohibitive. If pensions were brought up for married couples to half of average earnings, it would cost £8,000 million to bring the retirement age for manuals down to 60. At present pension levels, the burden would amount to £2,000 million. There is something morally offensive about the contrast between the relatively secure white collar worker retiring at 60 on a usually superior pension (often index linked in the public sector) to live a longer old age than the unskilled and semi-skilled manuals, in particular, who must struggle on to 65 when for most of them their lives are drawing rapidly to a close.

The four-week holiday has grown more widespread among manual as well as non-manual workers since the early seventies. The average holiday entitlement for manuals is between 16 and 19 days, compared with 25 or more for directors and 20 to 25 for senior management. But few manual workers enjoy full weekly earnings for their time on holiday, hence the need to save up during the rest of the year. A BIM survey showed that just under half of manual workers only received the basic rate of pay for holidays, with just under a third enjoying average hourly or weekly earnings.[8] This is in stark contrast to the substantial progress made in the rest of Western Europe, where a full extra month's pay (the so-called 13th-month bonus) is now commonplace for all workers.

Manual workers have been to a very great extent the main victims of the new recession. In December 1978, as many as 862,822 of the 1,219,195 registered unemployed were manual workers. A total of 444,337 were classified as general labourers for which there were only 10,242 job vacancies. Figures published in 1978 show that over 80 per cent of men unemployed since June 1974 were manual workers and between 51 and 45 per cent of the women (this lower

Table 6.1   Sick pay and social class (full-time employees aged
15 or over (1971), 16 or over (1976), Great Britain)

	% who get paid when sick	
	1971	1976
Managers in large establishments	99	99
Managers in small establishments	94	95
Professional workers – employees	100	98
Intermediate non-manual workers	95	97
Junior non-manual workers	90	93
Personal service workers	71	75
Foremen and supervisors	78	87
Skilled manual workers	48	60
Semi-skilled manual workers	50	60
Unskilled manual workers	57	63
Agricultural workers	66	[67]

Farmers have been excluded on account of small base numbers.
Source: *The General Household Survey 1976*, HMSO, 1978.

figure hides the fact that many women have left the labour market
in the recession altogether but not registered).[9] While 3.9 per cent
of all male manual workers were unemployed in June 1974, the figure
had risen to 8.3 per cent by June 1977 (compared with figures of 2.0
per cent and 3.4 per cent respectively for the non-manual men).

In regions such as Merseyside, Northern Ireland, Clydeside and
the north east of England, older and middle aged male manual
workers are particularly likely to be unemployed for long periods
and thus dependent on supplementary benefit. The annual reports
of the Supplementary Benefits Commission since 1975 testify to the
human misery and degradation inflicted on manual workers as a
result of rising unemployment. The increase in the number of redundancies during the 1970s affected manual workers in industries like
shipbuilding, steel, textiles and car production. Surveys on the redundancies at Upper Clyde Shipbuilders underline the inadequacies of
labour market policy.[10] The 1965 Redundancy Payments Act is now
a permanent system of severance payments but the lack of retraining
and support for mobility makes this crude money incentive an unsatisfactory 'once for all' response. The British Steel plant closures

of 1977–78 set high figures for severance payments but the average level is no more than £600. The Manpower Services Commission has made some improvement in the provision of training places and increased job replacement through state agencies, yet too often the training opportunities programme has helped middle aged women to learn clerical skills rather than aid manual workers. The Labour Party proposed, rather belatedly, in their May 1979 election manifesto to provide a worker unemployed for more than a year with training or the offer of a job.

The recession and structural decline in industry had harsh effects on opportunities for manual workers. The Manpower Research Group at Warwick University estimated that there will be a 4.2 per cent drop in the numbers employed in manual occupations between 1976 and 1982.[11] This amounts to a net loss of 536,000 jobs compared with a projected increase of 380,000 non-manual jobs. The government's Unit for Manpower Studies estimated a net increase of 1.09 million jobs between 1971 and 1981 with the big annual growth being among employers, managers, professional workers and other non-manual groups and with a net decline in all manual grades.[12] Between 1971 and 1976, there was a growth of 314,000 in clerical and secretarial workers but a drop of 740,000 in manul occupations.

A sense of insecurity affects many manual workers, as was noticeable among skilled craftsmen who left their former trades in large numbers in the 1970s for higher pay and status outside manufacturing. This exodus precipitated serious skill shortages even at the height of the slump.

A number of surveys carried out by the National Economic Development Office in 1976 and 1977 confirmed the malaise among skilled workers. A survey of former engineering workers in 37 companies found 37 per cent were made redundant by their employers and left the industry in disgust, while a further 28 per cent found other work because of the 'poor prospects for advancement' in engineering.[13] Many complained that the work they had to do was boring and monotonous and, even if it meant a wage cut, they preferred to work in employment with more social prestige and a sense of pride. A man with thirty years' experience complained that he was thought less of than 'an unskilled man of one year standing. I still have to clock on – no full pay when sick – no pay for time off for domestic reasons'. Another said that skilled manual workers were 'looked upon as the poor relations of the office boys'. One worker argued: 'Men who at the age of 15 were lucky enough to get an apprenticeship, stuck it out on low wages only to find in the end how much better they would have been in a clean office type job – short hours, all the perks, low interest loans'.[13] A study of machine tool workers found deep bitterness at their treatment by management, especially because of the readiness by their employers to sack them in a recession.[14] As the survey argued: 'A number of manual employee groups said it always seemed to be the manual workers who were most seriously affected by redundancies. This was seen as being extremely unjust. The view was expressed in several plants that there were "too many people walking around in white coats and not working on machines".' It added: 'Many employees felt it was unfair that skilled men, many of whom had long periods of service, should have lower status in some respects than a young girl clerk.'[14]

A major inequality for manual workers lies in the nature of the jobs they do. At work, they face greater health hazards. The reports of the General Household Survey show that absence because of sickness is strikingly higher among manuals than non-manuals.[15] Mortality rates for manual workers are also much higher than for non-manual workers.[7] The 1976 accident statistics reveal that there were 569 deaths in that year, virtually all of them manual workers. As many as 324,034 accidents were officially reported to the Health and Safety Commission. These overall figures do represent a slight improvement on the record for the early seventies, but they leave no room for complacency. Many manual workers are exposed to excessive noise, heat and danger in their jobs as well as substances that carry with them the dangers of infection and disease. The annual debates of the TUC on health and safety during the past decade do not suggest that concepts like 'humanisation of work' or 'job enrichment' have made much of an impact in manufacturing industry. Sick pay is yet another source of inequality (see Table 6.1).

Recent evidence indicates that the relative position of manual workers has deteriorated *vis à vis* higher paid non-manuals, mainly because of the mushrooming growth in perkery and fringe benefits for white collar staff which took place during the years of national pay restraint.[16] Helen Murlis discovered substantial improvements for all workers, but more senior white collar staff enjoyed much more than the rest of the labour force.[17] While a mere 8 per cent of manual workers enjoyed any bonus based on the profit performance of the company they worked for, 28 per cent of the clerical staff did so and 66 per cent of directors. Bonus schemes introduced before 1975 were exempt from incomes policy and while the average bonus for all workers was 5 per cent of annual salary or less, the bonus averaged as much as 11 to 20 per cent of substantially higher pay for senior management. The provision of loans to help in car purchase, season tickets and other fringe extras is far more common among non-manuals than the manuals. The growth of the use of a free company car into the ranks of junior management and even expansion into the clerical grades in many companies since 1975 merely highlights a widening inequality of treatment between manual and non-manual.

Until now, it has been the white collar unions which have been the militants on workplace inequalities, anxious to defend their staff privileges or widen the status gap between their members and the shopfloor. As Dorothy Wedderburn has argued, 'Manual worker trade unions have been concerned to defend their members within managements' own rules rather than to question the assumptions upon which those rules are based'.[18] Recent sociological research illustrates the uncomfortable fact that most manual workers do not feel a deep sense of moral outrage at the way they are treated by the economic system, in comparison with white collar staff.[19] The results of the job satisfaction polls for the General Household Surveys reveal that a vast majority are content with their work, though the proportion of skilled men who are critical has grown during the seventies. The fact is that the terms of reference on pay, fringe benefits and working conditions remain surprisingly narrow for manual workers. They look to others performing similar kinds of work to see whether they have stolen a march, not to those working in offices in relative comfort and security.

The absence of any coherent or systematic pressure from the manual unions is one obvious explanation of why staff status for manual workers has failed to become a burning issue. Sensible demands have often been bought off with extra cash in the pay packet. But there are some signs that the trading of benefits for money may be starting to change. The 1977 and 1978 Ford Company manual worker pay claims gave a welcome recognition for the justice of staff status. The contestants for the presidency of the Amalgamated Union of Engineering Workers in 1978 laid stress on workplace equality. But it may require a much more sympathetic attitude by the unions to ideas like profit sharing and share ownership. A

1978 survey found that 48 per cent of companies confined profit sharing to their management grades or senior staff,[20] but there is widespread support for the idea that workers should benefit directly from the profitability of the companies they work for. Only a small minority of enterprises reward their workers through improved company performance. Only between 17 per cent and 22 per cent of companies in Britain have any schemes based on principles of profit sharing. The unions may be putting vague feelings of distaste before the possibility of real gains for their members.

The British Labour movement has simply failed to make equality at work an important priority. Social democracy in Scandinavia and West Germany under union pressure has emphasised the rights of manual workers. The growth in new methods of manual work organisation and the introduction of technological changes to reduce stress and boredom at work owe much to the alliance between the unions and social democracy. A new deal for manual workers would be concerned with the distribution of power and privilege in society and inevitably involve a fresh emphasis on the politics of class. Yet a shrewd appeal to the idealism as well as the self-interest of manual workers is long overdue in the Labour movement, which too often appears to have lost touch with the needs and aspirations of working people on the shopfloor – especially in the inner areas of many big cities where local Labour Parties are too often dominated by middle class activists with no direct concern or interest in the harsh realities of shopfloor life.

What we need to see in the 1980s is a new revived alliance between the Labour Party and the trade union movement at local as well as national level, which will place the cause of workplace inequalities near the centre of the programme. If democratic socialism is going to mean anything to working people, it must begin to make sense in the factories and workshops. The interests of manual and non-manual do not have to be antagonistic. A new harmony in industry based on realism and social justice is long overdue. The removal of workplace inequalities in other countries has not produced obvious tensions between workers on the shopfloor and in offices. Certainly the overwhelming evidence from Britain at the end of the seventies is that the relative position of the manual worker has hardly improved, despite the existence of Labour Governments for 11 out of the past 16 years.

7 Wealth

by Michael Meacher

Since much of both social and economic policy can be regarded as consequential on marked inequalities in the distribution of income and wealth, direct action to reduce these inequalities within acceptable limits might be expected to provide the cornerstone of redistributive Labour policy. In fact, if policy on wealth was Labour's Achilles heel in 1972, it remains so today.

What is meant by 'equality' in ownership of wealth?
According to the latest official figures,[1] aggregate personal wealth in the UK in 1975 was valued by the estate multiplier method at £190,290 million. This total was divided among 21 million identified wealth-holders representing just over half the total adult population. This means that if total personal wealth were equally distributed among all individuals aged 18 and over, each individual would possess approximately £5,000. In fact, the Inland Revenue calculates on the assumption that persons not covered by their estimates have no wealth (a crude but not too inaccurate assumption as is shown below), that the least rich individual of the richest 1 per cent in the UK had £46,000[2] while the member of this group with the average (i.e. mean) wealth-holding had about £109,000. In other words, the average wealth-holding of the richest 1 per cent was around 22 times a theoretically equal portion for the whole community.

'Equality', or to put it more realistically – minimally acceptable inequality – must therefore, first of all, by any reasonable canons of social equity, reflect a substantially lesser span of inequality than actually exists. But how much less? What should be the target for a positive policy on wealth distribution?

Absolute equality would presumably mean the possession by each adult citizen of a sum representing the mean amount of personal wealth in society, currently around £5,000 in Britain. But no doubt such a distribution is unobtainable; it is certainly politically unrealistic, and perhaps it is undesirable anyway. A more relevant political concept therefore in this context is rather equality of opportunity. What disparity in ownership would invalidate this goal?

There is here a fundamental conflict between the view, strongly held by some especially on the Right, that a father (or mother) should be entitled to pass on the bulk of their possessions to their children, and the view, equally strongly held by most people but especially on the Left, that persons should start life with at least reasonable equality of opportunity. Clearly there has to be some reconciliation between these opposing standpoints, though the tension between them may lead to changing compromises at different political periods according to the strength of one or other set of values at any given time. Clearly the gift, whether by inheritance or by lifetime transfer, of a certain limited amount of capital or property is unlikely to interefere much with the aim of equality of opportunity. Setting the limit can never of course be a scientific exercise. But a reasonable political compromise might perhaps be put at around £20,000; this is the proposal adopted in this chapter as a realistic target.

The present position on the distribution of wealth

If this analysis offers a framework for what might be meant by reasonable equality in wealth ownership, it contrasts starkly with the picture of huge inequality that actually exists in Britain. According to early reports of 1979 official estimates, the position in 1975 was that the wealthiest 1 per cent of the population owned 23.2 per cent of total personal wealth, the top 5 per cent had a share of 46.5 per cent, the top 10 per cent a share of 62.4 per cent and top 20 per cent a share of 81.8 per cent. This left four-fifths of the population holding only 18 per cent of total personal wealth. However this is based on the assumption that those not identified as wealth-holders by the estate multiplier method (in fact 52 per cent of the total adult population in 1975) had no wealth. Now the Inland Revenue has sought to refine the crudity of this assumption by using independent information on aggregate personal holdings of assets and liabilities presented in the form of a personal sector balance sheet. This adjusted distribution includes an allowance for the wealth holdings of the excluded population, and also for the under-statement of holdings among the included population, arising, for example, from the exclusion of exempt settled property from the Inland Revenue estimates. On this basis, total personal wealth in mid-1975 was valued at £238,927 million, or almost £49 billion more than the unadjusted total. Of this, 24.3 per cent was held by the richest 1 per cent of the adult population, slightly more than that estimated by the unadjusted method, though the shares of all other groups making up the wealthiest 20 per cent were slightly lower. Still, the proportion of total personal wealth held by the other four-fifths of the population amounted only to 23.8 per cent.

Now even these adjustments can be amended on the basis of further, far-reaching assumptions. It has been claimed, for example, by Polanyi and Wood[3] that, because of the growth of small savings and acquisition of consumer durables, the average wealth of the missing 20 million could be as high as £5,000, adding £100 billion in all, which is no less than half the total Inland Revenue unadjusted estimate for 1975. But using external checks from the known total holdings of individual assets likely to be held by small savers (such as deposits in National Savings Banks, and building societies, plus total purchases of consumer durables suitably depreciated) Atkinson concludes that allowing for the wealth of 'missing' persons on a market realisation basis would decrease the share of the richest groups by only some 3 per cent from 24 per cent to perhaps 21 per cent.

On the other hand, it can be argued (as we did in a previous book) that a very high degree of estate duty avoidance severely understates the true potential yield and therefore the estimates of total personal wealth based on it.[5] Evidence for this is that it is known that in the immediate pre-First World War period the estate duty yield represented some 1.1 per cent of net national income. Yet by 1970, despite in the meantime a 5-fold increase in the duty rate on estates over £50,000 and a 6-fold increase on estates over £1 million, the estate duty yield still stood at only 1.0 per cent of net national income, no higher than 60 years earlier and half its level relative to net national income immediately pre-Second World War (2.0 per cent in 1938), despite the fact that since then the duty rate has not halved, but doubled (to 80 per cent). However, using such estimates as have been made about the likely total of missing wealth (such as the Inland Revenue's special inquiries into the extent of trusts) and incorporating this estimated missing wealth on a range of different assumptions about its ownership, Atkinson and Harrison calculate that the share of the richest groups would rise because they own a disproportionate amount of settled and other property.[6] But on their assumptions the effect is measured in terms of only a few per cent.

For example, in 1968 the share of the richest 1 per cent was increased by 2.2 percentage points. Nevertheless, the extent of total personal wealth is seen as very considerably greater than that implied by the Inland Revenue estimates; for 1969, the latter figure amounted to £88 billion, while the balance sheet estimate for that year was £134 billion.

The other central question about the present picture of wealth ownership in Britain is the rate and direction of change over time. Here Atkinson and Harrison, having produced estimates for all available years over the period 1923–72, conclude that the evidence suggests an annual 0.4 per cent drop in the share of the top 1 per cent but no apparent acceleration in the arithmetic rate of decline in their share. However, they found no apparent downward trend in the share of the next 4 per cent richest group, but rather a slight *increase* since the 1920s. This may perhaps simply indicate redistribution *within* the family, since one of the principal methods of avoidance has been that of passing on wealth before death in the form of gifts to heirs.

Changes in philosophy
For all the refinements of data that have been made in the 1970s, the picture remains one of huge inequalities, indeed considerably greater than in the USA. Yet despite the emphasis on fairness and social justice that has accompanied the successive incomes policies throughout the 1960s and 1970s, there has been remarkably little public outcry about disparities of wealth. Thus Inland Revenue figures based on the 1968 special charge on investment incomes show that at that time the richest 92 individuals had an average investment income of £196,000 per year, implying an *average* wealth-holding of £2½ to £4 million each. The highest earning 92 managing directors probably then earned gross some 40 times the earnings of the average worker. But the richest 92 wealth-holders own over 1,000 times the wealth of the average man. In view of this staggering differential, why is there not much more public feeling about this issue?

There are probably several reasons for this. A main one is massive public ignorance about the whole subject. Large-scale holdings of wealth are outside the everyday experience of the vast mass of ordinary people, and constitute if anything a source of awe (for example, country houses and estates open to the public on Sundays) rather than resentment. Secondly, there is very little discussion on wealth distribution in the newspapers or on television – if mentioned at all, it is normally in terms of preservation of the national heritage. Since the media are owned by wealthy tycoons or form part of large conglomerate corporations, this selective omission is perhaps scarcely surprising, but it does mean that the issue is prevented from emerging by suppression of the information on which it is based. Thirdly, the political force behind grievances is well known to be based on experience of reference groups. Comparisons based on inter-personal experiences are the operative ones; in a class ridden society these tend overwhelmingly to be limited to those persons in a closely proximate class position – which in almost every case excludes those with substantial wealth.

For these reasons, whilst certainly the interest of academics and politicians has been focused on the issue of a wealth tax since 1974 more than ever before, in the absence of much wider discussion in the media or much more deliberate and sustained campaigning by the political or trade union leadership, public opinion never gets to the point where philosophies or values on this matter are clarified in the minds of most people.

The political and economic climate

In the absence of any clear, let alone changing, broad public philosophy, the political and economic climate has been set, on the one side by market factors and on the other by several official reports. In the market, the relevant happenings have been the 1972 Stock Exchange boom and the subsequent fallback and then recovery, the steep rise in inflation up to 26 per cent in 1975 eroding the real value of most capital assets, and then the decline in inflation to an annual rate of 8 per cent in 1978 with the sub-sequent rise again, which left many traditional investment sectors as ineffective hedges against continuing capital loss. The timing of these factors does not immediately seem consistent with the trend traced by the Inland Revenue figures which show a fall in the share of the richest 1 per cent from 30.5 per cent in 1971 to 22.5 per cent in 1974, followed by a rise to 24.9 per cent in 1976.[7] Probably this trend largely but not wholly reflects changes in the prices and assets relative to one another especially the rapid and continuing rise in prices of residential property while share prices which peaked in 1972 fell to a low level and partially recovered in 1975/6.

On the political side, the climate was set by a succession of reports. The 1974 government Green Paper, *Wealth Tax*,[8] stated that 'it is the government's intention to introduce a wealth tax', stressing particularly the argument on horizontal equity. It followed the Labour Party manifesto commitment of February 1974 to 'introduce an annual tax on wealth above £100,000. However, the lack of wider agreement on this issue was starkly exposed by the Jay Select Committee on a Wealth Tax, reporting in November 1975, which split four ways.[9] The Chairman's own report stated that 'in addition to raising a modest revenue, a wealth tax has some part to play in reducing inequality, but a major purpose must be to promote horizontal equity. This is its purpose in the European countries whose wealth taxes are summarised in the Green Paper'. The Liberal draft stressed that 'a wealth tax may serve to counteract an investment distortion towards nil or low yield which arises from the existence of high marginal rates of income tax. Also the introduction of a wealth tax may be used as the occasion for a partial substitution of wealth tax for income tax.' The Tory draft took the view that no final judgement should be made about a wealth tax until new information on inequalities of wealth distribution had been unearthed by the Diamond Commission (a postponement, no doubt, to the Greek Kalends). It also used the horizontal equity argument to repudiate an investment income surcharge. The Committee proceedings clearly manifested the persisting fundamental chasm between the political parties over wealth ownership.

A further important contribution to the political debate was the publication in January 1978 of the Meade Committee Report on Direct Taxation. Its two principal alternative proposals in the field of capital taxation are both significant. The first is a progressive tax on accessions (PAWAT) based upon the age of the recipient as well as the size of his accumulated accessions. The tax would provide a maximum incentive for the redistribution of wealth but would involve a number of serious administrative problems. The second alternative, a non-progressive accession tax (LAWAT) combined with an annual wealth tax, would avoid some of the administrative problems of PAWAT and would impose an effective tax differential between wealth saved out of earnings and wealth which is inherited. The advantage of both the Meade proposals over the existing CTT would be the imposition of a tax upon the *receipt* of wealth by bequest or gift, thus encouraging the distribution of wealth to small wealth holders.

In addition, throughout the period 1975–78 the body set up by the Labour Government to elucidate the facts in this area in greater depth and range than were yet available, the Diamond Royal Commission on the Distribution of Income and Wealth, produced six reports and a whole mass of new data. But the fundamental political task which the Government set the Commission – to seek information 'to help to secure a fairer distribution of income and wealth in the community' – was neutralised by being suspended on a premise that was never clarified. What is meant by 'a fairer distribution'? Never at any stage during this period has the opportunity been taken by the publication of these reports to set up a major public debate on what the distribution of wealth *should* be in a socialist society.

The record

1964–74
Examination of the trend in the taxation of wealth since the Wilson Government first came to power in 1964 (Table 7.1) reveals clearly that capital, compared with income, has been relatively under-taxed, particularly during the end of the period. The picture that emerges is a bleak one as far as equity is concerned. Taxes on wealth fell steadily as a proportion of total Inland Revenue duties from a level of 7.3 per cent in 1964–65 to 6.0 per cent in 1967–68, and only the special investment surcharges imposed in the 1968 economic crisis raised the level again to 7.6 per cent in 1968–69, the highest point reached in the last 15 years. Thereafter it fell again, only to rise again in the property and Stock Exchange boom of 1972–73. It then declined steadily and sharply each year following, till in 1976/7 taxation on wealth represented only 3.4 per cent of all Inland Revenue duties, less than half the level of only three years previously. There is certainly no suggestion throughout this period of the planning of capital taxation, within the targets set by budget requirements, to meet any canons of equity. On the other hand, by the usual measure, the so-called Gini coefficient, the concentration in the ownership of wealth shows a marked drop in the Labour years (from 72 per cent in 1964 to 65 per cent in 1970), before rising again in the Tory Stock Exchange boom to 66 per cent in 1972, and thereafter declining again in the next Labour period (to 62 per cent in 1975).

The Labour record 1964–70 was essentially confined to blocking some of the main loopholes of tax avoidance and evasion, especially in 1968/9. The estate duty charge on gifts was extended to 7 years,

Table 7.1   Taxation of wealth in the UK, 1964/5 to 1975/6 (£ million)

	Estate duty	Capital gains tax	Capital transfer tax	Special Investment surcharge	Development land tax	Total taxes on wealth	Taxes on wealth as % all Inland Revenue duties
1964/5	296.5	—	—	—	—	296.5	7.3
1965/6	292.9	—	—	—	—	292.9	6.2
1966/7	300.9	7.5	—	—	—	308.4	6.2
1967/8	329.9	15.8	—	—	—	345.7	6.0
1968/9	381.9	46.9	—	67.3	—	496.1	7.6
1969/70	364.8	127.6	—	18.5	—	510.9	6.8
1970/1	356.6	138.9	—	3.4	—	498.9	6.1
1971/2	451.3	155.1	—	1.9	—	608.3	6.7
1972/3	458.6	208.5	—	1.2	—	668.3	7.2
1973/4	412.2	323.6	—	0.9	—	736.7	6.9
1974/5	338.9	381.6	—	0.4	—	720.9	5.1
1975/6	212.3	386.7	117.6	0.3	—	716.9	4.0
1976/7	124.4	323.4	259.2	0.2	1.1	708.3	3.4

Source: Inland Revenue Statistics.

the investment income of unmarried infants was aggregated with parents' income, the use of marriage gifts to avoid estate duty was severely restricted, the use of stock dividend options to avoid schedule F distribution charge was restricted, comprehensive changes were introduced relating to avoidance schemes involving land and land-owning companies, and a charge was imposed on a death of a beneficiary under a discretionary trust. Whilst these anti-avoidance measures were unusually comprehensive, their effect has been inevitably rather limited on the overall pattern of the distribution of wealth, and in particular they have not been complemented by attempts to increase capital ownership at the lower reaches of the income scale.

Policies since 1974
The green paper on a Wealth Tax contained little that was specific, despite several years' gestation. As one commentator has said 'The possibilities outlined ... were so various that any wealth tax resulting from it was compatible both with a reduction in the taxation of the wealthy or with a very substantial increase.'[10] No immediate action

followed the publication of the Jay Select Committee Report on a Wealth Tax. A year later, Denis Healey announced that, after all, he would not introduce a wealth tax during the lifetime of the parliament, though he added that the tax would continue to be an important part of the government's programme. This provoked a strong reaction, particularly from Jack Jones, then General Secretary of the TGWU. Following discussions in the context of stage three of the incomes policy, the TUC–Labour Party Liaison Committee adopted in autumn 1977 a confidential policy paper proposing that 'work should be set in hand immediately on a (wealth tax) White Paper and draft clauses with the clear intention to legislate in the first session of a new Parliament'. *The Times* also stated that Joel Barnett, as Chief Secretary to the Treasury, indicated that a White Paper should appear as soon as possible and that if a general election intervened, the wealth tax would reappear in detailed form in Labour's manifesto.[11] The policy paper proposed a tax of 1 per cent a year on wealth starting at a threshold of £100,000 and rising by stages to 5 per cent on assets above £5 million. It recognised that some of the very rich would have to dispose of part of their estates to pay taxes. It also defined wealth as 'marketable assets', thereby excluding pension rights. By adopting a high initial threshold, it aimed to exclude owner-occupiers, even if they owned their houses outright and had some other forms of wealth. Finally, it recommended that the wealth of husband, wife and children should be aggregated for the purpose of tax, but proposed a concession for small businesses, including working farms, similar to that allowed for capital transfer tax (CTT). In the light no doubt of the Mentmore precedent, it was proposed that owners of country houses could gain full relief if they agreed to reasonable public access. A year later, it was reported that the Labour draft manifesto included a commitment to introduce an annual wealth tax for personal wealth above £150,000.

Apart from the abortive struggle over the wealth tax, the other main event was the introduction of CTT and abolition of estate duty in the Finance Act 1975. The new tax was applied for lifetime gifts, transfers on death and transfers relating to settled property (property held in trust), and was charged on a person's transfers as they occurred throughout his life and on a cumulative basis. The rates of tax were made progressively higher on successive slices of the cumulative total of transfers, with a lower scale of rates for transfers during life than for transfers on death.

CTT was therefore a much more comprehensive tax than estate

duty which was always considered the avoidable tax since so long as property was given away 7 years before death, no duty was charged. Nevertheless, widespread avoidance still remained possible. The annual and other exemptions, the first £15,000 of chargeable gifts on which the tax rate was nil and the lower rates charged on gifts in lifetime, all meant that judicious and early action could achieve the passing on of significant amounts with little or no charge to tax. Thus as much as £150,000 might be passed from parents to their children without there arising any liability to tax if the following devices were systematically used: father's use of the annual exemption of £2,000 for, say, 20 years (age 50 to 70) and mother likewise; mother's 'out of income' exemption at, say, £1,000 per year for 20 years; marriage gifts to the son of £5,000 each from the father and mother, and marriage gifts to the daughter similarly; use of the exemption of the first £15,000 of gifts both by the father and mother.

It was these generous concessions in the treatment of individuals' capital transfer plus the relaxations offered to small businesses in autumn 1977 (especially the raising of the 30 per cent relief on business assets to 50 per cent, up to a maximum of £500,000, in the case of unincorporated businesses) which produced the relatively low yield indicated in Table 7.1.

The impact of these policies
It has already been shown that between 1973/4 and 1976/7 the contribution of capital taxes to total budget receipts, far from increasing as might be expected under Labour, in fact fell dramatically. Estate duty remained chargeable on estates of persons dying up to 13 March 1975, but thereafter it has been increasingly replaced by CTT, embracing gifts *inter vivos* as well as bequests on death. Nevertheless the *combined* effect of these imposts fell from £412 million in 1972/3 to £330 million in 1975/6, though the rise to £384 million in 1976/7 probably reflects the relatively greater bite of CTT as an instrument of capital taxation.

Nor can this relatively low yield be attributed to avoidance via transfer of assets overseas, whether to favoured tax havens or within the EEC. Exchange controls do in fact operate very restrictively on the movement of individuals' funds or property, even within the EEC boundaries. For despite the requirements of the Treaty of Rome, exchange controls were not extensively dismantled by the Labour Government – this only happened later in the first budget of the new Tory Government in June 1979.

What is more remarkable is that even if a wealth tax were operated on the basis of the heavier of the two alternative imposts proposed in the Green Paper[8] (that is, 1 per cent on holdings of £0.1 to 0.3 million, 2 per cent on £0.3 to 0.5 million, 3 per cent on £0.5 to 2.0 million, 4 per cent on £2.0 to 5.0 million and 5 per cent above £5.0 million), the yield would still be only £190 million (though an additional yield from certain kinds of trusts might add another £80 to 230 million). Even if the threshold were cut by half to £50,000 and a 3 per cent rate imposed above this, the yield would again probably not exceed £550 million.[12]

Another pointer to the declining efficacy of capital taxation in the 1970s can be derived from trends in the net yield of these taxes per tax employee over this period. Thus in April 1970, 909 staff employed in capital taxes offices collected £1,060,000 per employee (1978 prices). By November 1978, the number of staff was reduced to 877, but the net yield of estate duty/CTT per employee in 1977/8 had been cut by almost two-thirds (also at 1978 prices) to £395,000.[13]

Proposals for the future
It is first necessary to distinguish between wealth which is inherited and wealth which is built up by individuals over the lifetime. Regarding the former, it might be reasonable, in order to provide for equality of opportunity and to create a fair spread of incentives, to work towards the redistribution of inherited capital or property (other than to the spouse), to some £20,000 per individual. In other words, an accessions tax, or progressive capital transfer tax levied on the donee, would reach 100 per cent at about £20,000. Politically, of course, such an objective could only be achieved over an extended period. But, given that assumption, such a policy would eliminate the fantastic inequalities in opportunity, security and power which derive from very large scale inheritances (or *inter vivos* transfers) which cannot be justified by capitalist meritocratic canons of reasonable equality of opportunity, let alone by socialist canons of equality and social justice.

This would however still leave existing extreme inequalities in wealth holdings in their present hands. For this purpose two further fiscal measures are needed for a socialist policy on wealth and wealth-derived income. One would be an annual wealth tax at, say, 5 per cent on holdings above £½ million (1979 prices). This would have a limited selective impact on the most excessive disparities of wealth, when official figures show that even with a much lower threshold of £0.2 million only 29,000 persons, or 0.07 of the adult population would be liable.

The second requirement, in the form of a tax on the *income* from wealth, is one of 'horizontal equity' – that is, that persons with the same taxable capacity should pay the same amount of tax. In terms of progressive taxable capacity and in the light of relative tax equity between those with low incomes and no wealth (a substantial part of the population) and those with both high incomes and large wealth (a tiny élite), a tax should be imposed on the imputed incomes from wealth-holdings above the threshold (say £20,000 but allowing a generous threshold for housing of perhaps double the national average price of houses in the case of owner occupiers in order to protect pensioners and other low income house-owners) at the wealth-holder's marginal rate on his earned income, or at a minimum 50 per cent where the wealth holder has little or no earned income. A major economic advantage of this latter proposal is that it would compel large wealth-holders to seek high yielding assets, especially in industrial investment, rather than let their capital stagnate in property, land, works of art, and similar assets which offer a high rate of appreciation in capital value, but a low annual yield. Another economic advantage is that the increased tax on unearned income could be used to reduce the standard rate of income tax, so as to produce a direct redistribution from the rich to the average – and low-paid. On the other hand, in order not to penalise the high-paid by an unearned income tax pitched at artificial marginal rates, the structure of income tax should be altered to incorporate the present range of tax allowances (on mortgage interest, life assurance, occupational pension scheme contributions and the like), on the basis of averaging, within the basic rates. This would both avoid the deterrent effect of the false impression of marginal rates at significantly higher levels than they in practice are, and also eliminate a highly anti-progressive element in the tax system.

PART IV
Labour and
Discrimination

8   Racial Equality

by Ian Martin

While socialists may be forgiven for thinking that there is little that is novel in the extent of inequality of wealth and income in Britain or in the failure of Labour Governments to achieve the desired redistribution, the challenge of racial equality in social policy is a newer one. It is also an uncomfortable one, for while the Labour Party is equipped with the principles of racial equality, their translation into practice is liable to encounter the bitter opposition of some of Labour's traditional supporters.

The 1974–79 Labour Government was confronted with an increasing weight of evidence of the extent of racial discrimination and disadvantage. It responded with more powerful anti-discrimination legislation, the effectiveness of which is yet to be seen in practice, and with a recognition of the need for resources to counter racial disadvantage that came too late for them to be delivered in the government's lifetime. It lacked the political courage to reshape racialist immigration law and policy. The Labour Party's response to the growth of racialist parties and the incidence of racial violence left it a party with a more genuine and active anti-racist commitment in 1979 than in 1974, but far short of the day when such a commitment could be relied upon to produce central and local government policies which promised a major advance towards racial equality.

Evidence of discrimination and disadvantage

In the autumn of 1966, when the first Race Relations Act had been on the statute book for less than a year, the Race Relations Board and the National Committee for Commonwealth Immigrants commissioned a survey to assess the extent of racial discrimination in Britain in fields not covered by the 1965 Act. As the introduction to the report, first published by PEP (Political and Economic Planning), concluded, 'after these three surveys all but those with closed minds must accept the fact that in Britain today discrimination against coloured members of the population operates in many fields not covered by the existing legislation and that it operates on a substantial scale'.[1] The first PEP study provided important support for the Labour Government's extension of race relations legislation in 1968 into the fields of housing, employment and financial services.

Between June 1974, soon after the new Labour Government had taken office, and February 1976, the results of a further and more extensive PEP survey were published.[2,3,4,5] These showed that, since 1967, discrimination in the field of housing had decreased to a considerable extent, although discrimination against West Indian and Asian applicants for rented accommodation was still substantial (27 per cent). Discrimination against applicants for unskilled jobs in particular was even more substantial (46 per cent), yet it had probably decreased considerably from 1967 to 1973. The level of discrimination at the first stage of the recruitment process for white collar jobs was roughly of the same order in 1973–74 as it had been 5 years earlier.

The PEP studies in the 1970s were concerned not only to measure the extent of racial discrimination, but to review the disadvantages suffered by racial minority groups compared with the white majority, whether or not these disadvantages were the result of unlawful discrimination against them. Taking these surveys together with other findings, there is now a weight of evidence as to the extent of racial disadvantage, leading to the conclusion that not only are racial minority groups represented relatively heavily in areas of general social deprivation, but that they experience a degree of disadvantage not shared by the indigenous population in the same areas or in the same socio-economic groups.[6]

Housing and urban deprivation

Analysis of the 1971 Census by the Department of the Environment found that 70 per cent of the racial minority population was concentrated in 10 per cent of the enumeration districts, which contained nearly three times the average number of households sharing or without hot water, twice as many sharing or without a bath, nearly three times as many living at a density of over 1.5 persons per room, twice as many lacking exclusive use of all basic amenities, half as many living in local authority accommodation and twice as many in private furnished accommodation.[7]

The PEP study found that whereas a quarter of white households lived at a density of over 1.5 persons per bedroom, 54 per cent of

West Indian households and 65 per cent of Asian households lived at a density of over 2.5 persons per bedroom, compared with 2 per cent of white households. It also found that whereas 18 per cent of the general population did not have the exclusive use of bath, hot water and inside WC, 33 per cent of West Indian, 35 per cent of Indian and 57 per cent of Pakistani/Bangladeshi households shared these amenities.[5]

Further analysis of 1971 Census data by the Runnymede Trust found that racial minorities were unevenly distributed among the different types of estates owned by the Greater London Council, with a high proportion (13.7 per cent) in the pre-war inner London flats, and the lowest proportion (0.6 per cent) in the more attractive London cottage estates: a similar situation was found in the housing stock of a number of London boroughs.[8] The PEP study examined housing policy and practice within ten local authorities and found that Asians and West Indians tended to wait longer before being rehoused, while the nature of the system used to determine priorities between applicants for council housing was the most important source of disadvantage in racial minorities being given accommodation of lower quality.[4] The GLC subsequently undertook its own lettings survey, which confirmed that 'non-white' applicants were disproportionately found in inter-war unmodernised flats or pre-1919 flats, 44.2 per cent being in this kind of accommodation compared with 15.1 per cent of whites. While this was partly because 'non-whites' were concentrated in the homeless and borough general needs categories which normally secured the less attractive vacancies, and a higher proportion expressed a preference for a location in Inner London, where the average quality of accommodation is lower than in Outer London, these two factors even when considered together did not account for all the disadvantages suffered by the 'non-white' sample.[9]

Employment

The Department of Employment's analysis of 1966 and 1971 Census data (see Table 8.1) showed that racial minority workers were less likely to be in non-manual jobs, and more likely to be in unskilled manual work, than the general population, although there had been some progress between 1966 and 1971.[10]

The PEP study found that 15 per cent of white men were working shifts of some kind, compared with 31 per cent of men from racial minorities. Earnings of non-manual workers were substantially

Table 8.1   Employment by job level (%)

Job level	Gen. Population		West Indians		Pakistanis		Indians	
	1966	1971	1966	1971	1966	1971	1966	1971
Non-Manual	32	35	9	11	13	16	38	34
Skilled Manual/ foremen	35	34	40	41	20	21	25	27
Semi-skilled Manual	15	13	26	24	32	33	20	21
Unskilled Manual	8	8	22	16	31	23	12	11

higher among the whites than among the minorities (Table 8.2); in the case of skilled manual workers they were markedly higher; while in the case of semi-skilled and unskilled manual workers, they were exactly the same.[5]

Table 8.2   Earnings of men aged 25–54 by job level (£) *April 1974.*

	Non-manual	Skilled manual	Semi-skilled and unskilled manual
Median gross weekly earnings:			
White men aged 25–54	52.40	39.30	36.30
Minority men aged 25–54	40.50	35.60	36.30

While it might be surmised that disadvantage in employment was related to lack of educational qualifications, the PEP study in fact found that the job levels held by minority men were not equal to those of white men with the same level of educational qualification, even when allowance was made for a possible difference of standard between education in this country and in Asia. In fact, better educated minority men earned wages little higher than less well educated minority men.[5]

At the time of the 1971 Census, the proportion of West Indian men and women who were unemployed (5.8 per cent) was over twice as high as the proportion of the total population (2.5 per cent), while unemployment among Asians closely approximated the rate for the general population. The economic recession particularly affected racial minorities: registered unemployment among minority group workers increased by 302 per cent between August 1973 and August 1976, compared with a 135 per cent increase for the general population.[11]

Young West Indians have been particularly adversely affected. At the time of the 1971 Census, 16.2 per cent of young West Indians age 16–20 were unemployed, compared with 8.1 per cent of the whole age group.[12] Registered unemployment among minority group workers aged 16–24 rose 103 per cent between February 1974 and February 1975, and again by 142 per cent over the following year; and there is good reason to believe that the registered figures are a considerable underestimate of the actual rate of unemployment in this age group. A survey by the OPCS (Office of Population Censuses and Surveys) following the careers of a group of 1971 school leavers found that by the end of 1974 the sample of West Indians who had had at least a full secondary education in Britain had much greater difficulty in obtaining work at all times: 15 per cent of the West Indians had been unemployed whilst actively seeking work for a total of 6 months or more, compared with only 5 per cent of the whites.[13] A more recent study conducted in the London Borough of Lewisham, which covered all young West Indians who left school in 1977 and one fifth of their white contemporaries, found that the West Indians were three times as likely to be unemployed at the time of interview, and that those who had found a job had taken longer to find work, had made more applications, had been to more interviews and were less satisfied with the jobs they had than their white peers.[14]

One of the most depressing survey findings is that the children of immigrants who have grown up in Britain, speak English fluently and have reached the top of the British educational ladder, still experience difficulty in finding the employment appropriate to their qualifications. A study of 22 such students graduating in 1974 with first degrees from Leeds and Manchester Universities and Leeds Polytechnic compared with a group of 54 white students found that 75 out of 110 applications by minority students were turned down without interview, compared with only 31 out of 172 applications by the white students, and 27 out of 41 of the minority students' applications which reached final interview were rejected, compared to 47 out of 144 of the white students' applications. By September 1974, 46 of the 54 white applicants had been offered a total of 97 jobs, while 11 of the 22 minority applicants had been offered 14 jobs.[15]

The responsibility of government itself has been highlighted by the publication of a 1978 report by the Tavistock Institute of Human Relations which showed that minority group workers are considerably less successful than whites in applying for jobs and promotion in the civil service. The departments studied were the Department of Health and Social Security, the Ministry of Defence and HM Dockyard, Portsmouth. In the London North DHSS Region, out of 317 applications for clerical officer grade jobs between June and November 1976, a third came from minority candidates and two thirds from whites. Only 10 minority candidates were offered jobs compared with 78 whites, the relative success rates being 18 per cent as against 54 per cent. More minority than white candidates rejected for interview possessed the minimum educational qualifications, and many minority employees were found to be employed below their level of qualification.[16]

Education
It is not surprising that many first generation immigrants are at a disadvantage in lacking educational qualifications or training which are valued in the job market. Again, the most significant evidence is that which analyses the performance of minority children in the British educational system. An analysis of all pupils in the Inner London Education Authority transferring to secondary schools in autumn 1968 (Table 8.3) showed clearly the gap in performance between minority children and indigenous pupils, with only one in twelve of the former being placed in the upper quartile of achievers, instead of one in four. While Asian pupils fully educated in Britain were performing at a level comparable with the indigenous population, pupils from West Indian backgrounds fully educated here were not doing so (Table 8.4).

Evidence from ILEA also found that West Indians in similar school categories were performing at a lower level than the underprivileged white pupils.[17,18]

Table 8.3 *Performance of pupils on transfer to secondary school*
(percentage of pupils in upper and lower quartiles)

	English		Mathematics		Verbal reasoning	
	Upper	Lower	Upper	Lower	Upper	Lower
Theoretical	25.0	25.0	25.0	25.0	25.0	25.0
Non-immigrant	25.0	23.0	23.0	26.0	20.0	29.0
Immigrant	8.0	53.0	8.0	54.0	7.0	59.0
Immigrants fully educated here	12.4	38.0	12.0	42.0	10.0	46.0
Immigrants partly educated here	5.5	62.0	6.0	61.0	5.0	67.0

Table 8.4 *Percentage of pupils fully educated here placed in upper quartile on transfer to secondary school*

	English	Mathematics	Verbal reasoning
West Indian origin	9.2	7.4	7.2
Asian origin	19.3	20.2	21.1
Indigenous	25.0	22.9	19.8

The response

Anti-discrimination legislation

The new government's priority in 1974 was to introduce promised legislation against sex discrimination, and in its White Paper heralding the Sex Discrimination Bill it stated its ultimate aim was 'to harmonise the powers and procedures for dealing with sex and race discrimination'. The White Paper on Racial Discrimination which followed criticised the 'double disadvantage' of the situation under the 1968 Race Relations Act, whereby all complaints had to be investigated by the Race Relations Board through its conciliation committees, while the victim of racial discrimination had no direct access to legal remedies for a civil wrong. This, it said, 'distracts the statutory agency from playing its crucial strategic role whilst leaving many complainants dissatisfied with what has been done on their behalf by means of procedures which may be cumbersome, ineffective or unduly paternalistic'.[19] The 1976 Act therefore gave the new Commission for Racial Equality, which replaced both the Race Relations Board and the Community Relations Commission, the function of conducting strategic investigations, with the power to compel the disclosure of information, and to issue non-discrimination notices. The individual complainant was given direct access to the county courts or industrial tribunal, while he could be granted assistance and representation by the Commission in appropriate cases. The definition of unlawful discrimination was extended to cover 'indirect discrimination': those practices which have a discriminatory effect upon members of a racial minority, even in the absence of a discriminatory motive.

The new Act came into effect in June 1977, and two years later it is hardly possible to evaluate its effectiveness or the use made of the new powers by the Commission for Racial Equality. In August 1978, the CRE served its first non-discrimination notice on the owners of a Birmingham restaurant and discothèque. This was of no strategic significance, but by early 1979 a total of 29 investigations were under way, 14 of them in the employment category: employers under investigation included British Leyland, the National Bus Company, Phillips Electronic, Prestige Group and Unigate, while other investigations included educational provision in Reading under Berkshire Education Authority, council housing in the London Borough of Hackney, a housing association, an accommodation agency and a working men's club.

While the effectiveness of the CRE's strategic role cannot yet be assessed, fears that the individual complainant would have great difficulty in bringing a successful case have already been borne out. Out of the first 350 cases heard by industrial tribunals, some 33 applicants were successful, with a favourable settlement being reached in a similar number of cases. All but three of the successful complainants were aided by the CRE: the success rate of unaided complainants was less than 5 per cent. The Court of Appeal has already given a restrictive interpretation to the power of discovery of confidential documents, the disparity between the legal representation of complainants and respondents has become apparent, and tribunals have been ready to award costs against applicants who persisted with hopeless cases, while compensation awarded in successful cases has been paltry: in most cases the only compensation given is for injury to feelings and this is rarely more than £100. The only case in which substantial compensation has been given involved a radiographer awarded just under £2,000 when she failed to get a job at a leading London teaching hospital.[20,21] In March 1979, the first case under the new Act came before a county court: a West Indian woman was awarded £100 for injury to feelings after the judge found that she had been discriminated against on racial grounds when she went to view a flat.

Only one case of indirect discrimination had been among the early cases upheld by a tribunal, but a significant out-of-court settlement was reached in a dispute between seven Bangladeshi workers and the British Steel Corporation, in which workers who were refused re-employment on their return from Bangladesh alleged that the use of a language test had indirectly discriminated against them. The applicants received *ex gratia* sums ranging from £900 to £2,500; they were offered employment as labourers with in-plant English language training as a condition of their continued employment, and reaching the required standard according to a proper professionally devised test as the condition of opportunity to transfer to production line jobs.

Racial disadvantage

The 1975 White Paper contained a cautious recognition of the special needs of racial minorities. 'Some of the problems which coloured immigrants faced as immigrants, for example linguistic problems, have created handicaps for the second generation (West Indian as well as Asian) which will continue to require attention and resources for some time to come. Beyond the problems of cultural alien-ness, there are the problems of low status, of material and environmental deprivation which coloured immigrants and, increasingly, their children experience. To the extent that they share all or some of these problems with other groups in society, a general attack on deprivation will be relevant to their problems. But there may be a special dimension to their problems to the extent that the factor of racial discrimination multiplies and accentuates the disadvantages which are shared in part with others.' The White Paper therefore promised 'a more comprehensive strategy for dealing with the related and at least equally important problem of disadvantage'.

The fact that the White Paper contained such a declaration was largely the result of a fight waged by the Minister of State responsible for race relations and immigration, Alex Lyon, who had won a partial victory over the Home Office's reluctance to accept an analysis recognising special needs of racial minorities and the tendency of

Roy Jenkins' advisers to rely on anti-discrimination law alone. But the commitment came at an unpropitious time: such a strategy, the White Paper warned, had major public expenditure implications and could not be settled in advance of the outcome of the major review of public expenditure already underway. Roy Jenkins' own commitment to the reduction of public expenditure was stronger than his junior minister's conviction of the need for a new spending programme, and no progress had been made before James Callaghan's election as leader led to the ministerial reshuffle in which first Lyon and then Jenkins departed, the latter appointed to the EEC Presidency and the former sacked, as he himself put it, for 'trying to get justice for blacks'.

The two major ways in which funds had been available for local authority sponsored projects and programmes intended to meet special needs of racial minorities were grants under the urban programme and section 11 of the Local Government Act 1966. In both cases, grants were paid to local authorities at the rate of 75 per cent. Before the transfer of responsibility for the urban programme from the Home Office in 1977, under £30 million per year was granted in England and Wales; although the announcement of the urban programme had been Harold Wilson's response to Enoch Powell's 1968 'rivers of blood' speech, it is estimated that less than 10 per cent of the expenditure went on projects intended to counter racial disadvantage. Section 11 of the Local Government Act 1966 empowers the Home Secretary to make grants to local authorities 'required to make special provision in the exercise of any of their functions in consequence of the presence within their areas of substantial numbers of immigrants from the Commonwealth whose language or customs differ from those of the community'. In 1978/9, total section 11 expenditure was expected to reach nearly £38 million.

Under the plans set out in the 1977 White Paper on the Inner Cities, expenditure under the urban programme was to be more than quadrupled, to £125 million in 1979/80.[22] However, the relevance of this to many of the towns and cities where racial minorities shared in the most acute urban deprivation was limited by the concentration of resources on a small number of partnership authorities. Nine English cities figured both among the 12 areas of most acute deprivation as measured in the 1971 Census, and among the 12 areas with the most substantial racial minority populations: Inner London, Birmingham, Bradford, Manchester, Nottingham, Leicester, Leeds, Wolverhampton and Coventry. Of these, only Hackney, Islington

and Lambeth in Inner London, Birmingham and Manchester/
Salford were designated partnership areas, although all the remaining cities except Coventry were among 15 non-partnership authorities which would receive special attention, including up to £25 million
from 1979/80 onwards under the urban programme (see Chapter
15).

Section 11 expenditure, while it provided useful extra funding
largely for additional teachers in multi-racial areas (86 per cent of
the 1978/9 expenditure was estimated to be on education staff), made
no pretence of being a comprehensive strategy to tackle racial
disadvantage. It was available only to local authorities with 2 per
cent of 'New Commonwealth immigrant' children on their school
rolls: the number of authorities deemed eligible had grown from
46 to 88, but the statistics upon which eligibility was based had ceased
being collected in 1973, and related only to recent immigrants.
Funding was restricted to staff salaries, with no provision for capital
or associated revenue expenditure. Payment was by reimbursement
after the event. But the most serious deficiency was that no requirement was placed on local authorities to ensure that section 11
appointments were related to any general appraisal of need in their
area for special provision, or any strategy to meet this need. There was
no serious monitoring by the Home Office. The take-up by different
local authorities with similar proportions of racial minority children
was extremely uneven.

These defects were increasingly criticised by those in multi-racial
local authorities who sought improved provision.[23,24] Finally, in
November 1978 a Home Office consultative document itself acknowledged most of these deficiencies and proposed a new form of grant
extended to the health service as well as education, housing and social
services, with no statutory restriction on the purposes for which it
could be used or the form assistance should take. It was also to
be a specific aim of the new grant 'to encourage local authorities
to work out comprehensive strategies for dealing with problems of
racial disadvantage in their areas and to submit their claims for grants
for a particular year based on a strategy statement which mapped
out programmes for up to 3 years ahead'.[25] The new grant would
still be at the level of 75 per cent, but there was to have been a
greater commitment of resources: the increase was to be £10 million
in 1980/81 over expenditure previously planned for section 11 grants.
The proposals were going through Parliament as the Local Government (Ethnic Grants) Bill when the government fell.

The growing recognition of the need for action to combat racial disadvantage was reflected in a number of initiatives of questionable significance. The White Paper on Racial Discrimination announced the setting up of a Standing Advisory Council on Race Relations under the chairmanship of the Home Secretary, including other ministers, the TUC, CBI and members of minority communities. It is doubtful whether this to any significant degree compensates for Roy Jenkins' disastrous choice, in an excess of bipartisanship, of the former Conservative junior Home Office Minister, David Lane, as chairman of the Commission for Racial Equality. The Department of Employment established its own race relations advisory group, which by March 1979 could claim that 20 public sector bodies had or would soon have 'reinforced' their commitment to racial equality through a clear written statement of equal opportunity policy. The White Paper had stated in 1975 that it should be a standard condition of government contracts that the contractor would provide information about its employment policies and practices when requested by the Department of Employment; only in late 1978 did the government announce, to an angry reaction from the CBI, that such requests were to commence. When Shirley Williams left the Department of Education and Science, she had just appointed a committee of inquiry into the education of children from ethnic minority groups, which was to give priority to action to remedy the under-achievement of West Indian pupils. Even the Department of the Environment managed in September 1975 to respond after a mere four years to the Select Committee on Race Relations and Immigration's 1971 report on housing, and to make cautious noises in favour of local authorities collecting 'such information about the numbers and needs of coloured people as will enable them to make an informed judgement about the effect of their policies and programmes in relation to them'.[26]

Immigration and nationality

The new Labour Government began with intentions of cautious reform regarding nationality and immigration: immigration was not a major issue at either of the 1974 elections, and the manifesto promised a review of the law of nationality, 'so that our immigration policies are based on citizenship, and in particular to eliminate discrimination on grounds of colour'. The Labour opposition had voted against the Conservatives' 1971 Immigration Act, forthrightly denounced by James Callaghan, although in truth Labour's opposition was undermined by the extent to which the 1971 Act's concept of 'patriality' had been foreshadowed in Callaghan's own 1968 Commonwealth Immigrants Act. The Immigration Rules the new Government inherited had been described by Shirley Williams on behalf of the Opposition as 'offensive to natural justice, to decent human treatment, and to the long tradition of links between this country and the Commonwealth'.

Alex Lyon, the then Minister responsible, thus stated publicly that it was the government's intention to enact new legislation on nationality and then to repeal the 1971 Immigration Act within the lifetime of a full parliament. Nationality law was to be revised first, then immigration law; in the meantime, the harsher features of immigration control under the Conservatives' Act and Rules were to be mitigated by administrative action.

In April 1974, the government fulfilled its commitment not to use the retrospective provisions in the 1971 Act to remove Commonwealth citizens and citizens of Pakistan who had entered illegally before the Act came into effect on 1 January 1973. In August 1974, the Immigration Rules were amended to admit the husbands and fiancés of women settled here – reversing a piece of sex discrimination introduced when James Callaghan was Home Secretary in 1969 (see Chapter 9). In February 1975, the quota for the admission of UK citizens from East Africa whose statutory right of entry had been taken away by the 1968 Act was increased from 3,500 to 5,000 heads of household per year, an increase which soon led to the elimination of the queues in East Africa. The processing of entry certificate applications from wives and children in the Indian sub-continent was accelerated by posting additional staff, introducing priority categories and instructing officials not to defer cases unnecessarily.

Roy Jenkins' political caution stood in the way of any further formal relaxation of the Immigration Rules, and as the more rapid processing of entry certificate applications was reflected in the immigration statistics, Conservative pressure began to mount. The resistance of officials to Alex Lyon's policies became clear when, in July 1976, Enoch Powell released an internal Foreign Office report by a senior official, Donald Hawley. But by then Alex Lyon had been removed from office, immigration had returned to the headlines with the expulsion of a number of Asians from Malawi, and the National Front had gained sufficient electoral support in the local elections to cause the Labour Party serious alarm.

The arrival of James Callaghan at 10 Downing Street and Merlyn

Rees at the Home Office ended any likelihood of reform. The review of British nationality law was almost complete, but it was not to see the light of day until April 1977, in an abbreviated Green Paper.[27] The Green Paper proposals would have failed to restore an effective citizenship to British passport-holders outside the UK, who were to be redesignated 'British Overseas Citizens', would have allowed some children born to British Overseas Citizens to be born stateless and failed to specify the future rights of Commonwealth citizens settled in Britain to vote, work in the public service or register as UK citizens. Their most positive aspect was the intention to end aspects of sex discrimination in nationality law, which was partially anticipated when the Home Secretary announced that he would use his discretionary power to register as UK citizens the minor children of women born in Britain. But Merlyn Rees made clear that there was no longer any intention of legislating on nationality before a general election, and no review of immigration law ever commenced.

Indeed, in the second half of the Labour Government's period of office, the application of immigration control worsened in several respects. The proportion of entry certificate applications by wives and children overseas refused shot up as the officials responded to the mid-1976 climate of hostility to immigration. The immigration rules were changed so as to impose a 12-month probation period on the marriages of immigrant husbands, not only to frustrate alleged marriages of convenience but also to deny settlement to the husbands in genuine but short-lived marriages. The government refused, no doubt with an eye to the immigration figures in a pre-election period, to reallocate quota vouchers no longer being taken up in Africa to those East African Asians who had taken temporary refuge in India; thus in the government's last full year of office, 1978, only 1,752 voucher holders were admitted against a theoretical quota of 5,000, while the waiting period in India exceeded four years. A series of legal judgements extended the interpretation of illegal entrant to those who had employed some form of deception or concealed material facts, subjecting new categories of people to powers of arrest without warrant, detention without bail or time limit, and removal without prior right of appeal. The numbers of people in administrative detention under the Immigration Act increased in consequence.

The most that can be said for this period of Labour immigration control is that proposals for still greater restriction were firmly rejected. In February 1977, the Conservatives' proposal for a register of dependants was turned down – a politically easy task in view of the bipartisan report which showed that it would be a bureaucratic absurdity which could not meet its own objective of providing a certain estimate of future immigration.[28] The Select Committee on Race Relations and Immigration in its March 1978 report recommended a quota on immigration from the Indian sub-continent, the exclusion of children over 12, an end to the special voucher scheme, greater 'internal control', and an end to allowing all workers to become permanently settled after four years in approved employment.[29] Despite the support of the five Labour MPs on the Select Committee for these proposals, they were fortunately all rejected in the government's response.[30] The government left office, however, having administered for five years the Act and Rules denounced by Labour in opposition, and with no clear intention to undertake substantial reform if re-elected.

The political response

On a number of other issues, the government acted with scant sensitivity to the needs and treatment of racial minorities. The phasing out of child tax allowances in favour of child benefit would have meant the ending of support for the children overseas of people working in Britain; it took a major campaign before the government agreed for the time being to continue child tax allowances for children overseas. The call for the abolition of the offence under section four of the Vagrancy Act 1824 of being suspected of frequenting a public place with intent to commit an arrestable offence ('sus') became a symbol of opposition to police harassment of young West Indians in particular; despite evidence of the disproportionate use of the charge against blacks and the absence of any correlation with the prevalence of street crime or the involvement of blacks in crime, it took a major battle before the National Executive Committee overcame the outgoing Home Secretary's opposition to a manifesto commitment that a re-elected Labour Government would review section four of the Act with a view to its repeal.

For many members of Britain's racial minorities and others in the growing anti-racist movement, however, the Labour Government and the Labour Party will be judged on its response in a period in which racialism came to the centre of the political stage. A warning was already there in 1974, when the National Front in February gained its largest vote (3,662, representing 7.4 per cent) at Leicester East and in October gained its highest percentage poll (9.4 per cent) at Hackney South. Yet in early 1976 the Runnymede Trust could publish its annual report around the theme that Britain was 'emerging from a preoccupation with the numbers of coloured immigrants', and could see as the threat to future race relations the dangers of 'benign neglect'.[31]

There was no sign of an abandoned preoccupation in the press reaction when in May 1976 they discovered two Asian families from Malawi accommodated in a four star hotel by West Sussex Social Services Department ('We Want More Money, say the £600-a-week Asians' – *Daily Mail*) and learned that a number of Asian families were being expelled from Malawi ('Asian Flood Warning As More Fly In' – *Daily Express*). Nor was benign neglect the mood of parliament, which was not wildly exaggerated in the *Sun* headline 'MPs Rage Over Threat of New Asian Invaders'; Labour's former Chief Whip, Bob Mellish, providing a caption for leader writers in his declaration that 'Enough is Enough'. Only some 134 British Asians were ultimately expelled, but this fact was lost amid a second wave of press hysteria drawing its anecdotes of attempted evasion of immigration control in the Indian sub-continent from the Hawley Report. The press were meanwhile giving increasingly extensive and uncritical coverage to the National Front, which had won 18 per cent of the vote in local elections in Leicester, while in Blackburn two National Party councillors were elected. The climate had been created for a summer of racial violence in which four lives were to be lost.

This new crisis evoked two demands: that the law should be used more effectively to prevent incitement to racial hatred, and that the Labour movement should throw its full political weight into the opposition to racialism. The Race Relations Bill already before parliament proposed to strengthen the law against incitement to racial hatred by removing the requirement to prove intent on which prosecutions under the 1965 Act had foundered. There was widespread scepticism about the effectiveness of the law in this area when in January 1978 Kingsley-Read, leader of the National Party, was acquitted after an extraordinary summing-up by Judge Neil McKinnon on a charge of inciting racial hatred at a political meeting in Newham at the height of the racial tension of mid-1976; this despite his reference to the murder of an Asian in Southall in the phrase 'One down and a million to go'. This, however, was one of the last cases brought under the 1965 Act. The early cases under the 1976 Act have included both significant acquittals and convictions:

perhaps the best hope that the new law will be of greater effectiveness was given by the sentencing of Robert Relf to 15 months, reduced on appeal to nine months, for the distribution of racialist literature.

From mid-1976 onwards, the Labour Party belatedly lost some of its timidity on race and immigration. In conjunction with the TUC, the party committed itself to a national anti-racist campaign and for the first time made use of its party political broadcasts to attack the National Front. More significant, however, was the response of the local parties, many of which became involved in broad-based anti-racist campaigning; electoral inhibitions were discarded as it appeared that the racialist parties were checked by such campaigning and the Labour Party fared no worse where it was publicly identified with the anti-racist struggle.

The second period of major public debate on race and immigration was initiated by the television broadcast in which Mrs Thatcher identified herself with those who feared that Britain was being 'rather swamped' and promised a 'clear prospect of an end to immigration'. The immigration report of the Select Committee prolonged this phase of debate, and the complicity of five Labour MPs in its recommendations for further restriction might have compromised Labour condemnation of Mrs Thatcher's bid for racialist votes. But dissociation by both government and party was swift. It is little enough to claim, but for once a Labour Government refused to be panicked by the escalated demands of the Right into its own measures of restriction, although the subsequent White Paper on immigration set out clearly the limits to its own liberalism.

Two of the most important lessons of the experience of the 1974–79 Labour Government in the field of race relations lie, however, outside its record on combating racial discrimination and disadvantage or remedying the racialism of immigration policy. It is the failure or success recorded elsewhere in these essays, and in economic policy in particular, which is most fundamental to the racial climate: not only in the direct consequences for racial minorities as a section of the disadvantaged, but in meeting the aspirations of those whose absolute or relative poverty can be turned into a bitterness directed against racial minorities. Racial equality requires a society which is equal in all respects.

In the willingness of some of those who by tradition and by objective circumstances should be in its natural supporters to respond to the appeal of racialist politics, the Labour Party confronts its own most central failure: the inability to offer a convincing alternative to the failure of the economic and social policies of the 1960s and 1970s. The National Front is a spectre which compels the Labour Party to recognise its own decay; more than any other issue, the racialist threat has required local Labour parties to re-engage themselves in their local communities in support of a moral commitment which overrides immediate electoral expediency. It is not just progress towards racial equality which depends on their ability to take up that challenge.

9 Sex Equality

by Patricia Hewitt

When the 1974 Labour Party manifesto spoke of redistributing the balance of power and resources in favour of working people and their families, it did not refer specifically to the imbalance of power and resources which affects women in general and working class women in particular. But no discussion of equality would be complete which does not emphasise the economic, political, legal and social inequalities between men and women.

Since the early decades of this century, the life cycle of women has fundamentally changed. Well before the introduction of the pill, smaller families and increasing life expectancy meant that rearing children ceased to occupy the bulk of the average woman's adult years, and that most mothers could expect to spend at least as many years of adult working life without dependent children as with them.

In the last 15 years, the legal position of the sexes has been transformed. Serious injustices remain – notably, in British citizenship and immigration laws – but the momentum of legal reform, although it may be interrupted by the election of the Conservative Government in May 1979, is unlikely to be seriously diverted.

Nevertheless, the expectations and qualifications of girls leaving school have not caught up with women's need to maintain themselves (and, for many, their families) for most, if not all, of a 44 year working lifetime. Nor do boys leave school equipped to take an equal responsibility for the care of their children, or to face the demands (for an increasing number) of single parenthood. Women remain concentrated in as narrow a range of jobs as ever, forming the majority of the low paid as well and the majority of adults outside employment living in poverty. They remain grossly under-represented in decision making, whether in employment, in trade unions or in political institutions. (The 18 women MPs elected in May 1979 number one more than in 1951 and considerably fewer than in 1945 and 1950.)

In the early 1960s, women formed 35 per cent of the labour force, a proportion which had not altered much over the previous fifty years. What had changed was the participation of married women, often with children, in paid employment. Since then, women have remained the most rapidly-growing section of the work force, so that they now represent over 41 per cent. Women's earnings, far from being 'pin money', are crucial in keeping many families out of poverty. It has been estimated[1] that the number of families with incomes below the Supplementary Benefit level would have trebled if the wives had not been in paid employment.

When Labour came to power in 1964, women were second class citizens at home: fathers had sole guardianship of a legitimate child; women had only very qualified rights to matrimonial property; and most women were disbarred from jury service because of their non-householder status. In employment, women were paid considerably less than men, were segregated into a narrow range of semi-skilled and unskilled jobs and were rarely represented in the professions or management. The growth of the women's liberation movement, at around the same time as the much publicised equal pay strike of the women workers at Ford's Dagenham, focused attention not only on demands for equal pay and an end to discrimination in education and employment, but also on the need for women to organise themselves in trade unions and in women's groups. Statutory changes both reflected and encouraged these new demands.

The condition of women was not a high priority for the 1964 and 1966 Labour Governments, although time was given to Private Members' Bills – the Abortion Law Reform Act and the Divorce Reform Act – which significantly altered women's legal status. In 1968, when Labour movement protests concentrated on the Commonwealth Immigrants Act directed against the Kenyan Asians, the government also decided to ban foreign husbands of British women from entering this country except in the most exceptional compassionate circumstances, thus depriving British women and their families of a right which had existed for as long as immigration control. It was a mark of the absence of an organised women's movement, as well as of the Labour Government's desire to keep out Asian and black men at all costs, that the ban was introduced with little protest and was not lifted until 1974.

It was not until 1970 that the Labour Government introduced its Equal Pay Act (a century or so after the first TUC equal pay resolution). The Act provided equal pay, not for 'work of equal value', but for like work or for jobs which had been equally rated in a job evaluation scheme. A further five years was then allowed for employers to comply with – or find ways of avoiding – the Act before it became legally binding.

The manifesto for the October 1974 election promised 'a charter for women', to ensure that by the end of 1975 'Labour's Equal Pay Act will be fully effective throughout the land', to 'increase educational opportunities for girls, including further education, training and compulsory day release' and to provide maternity leave, free family planning, child benefits, family courts and so on. The Sex Discrimination Act came into force on the same day as the Equal Pay Act, 29 December 1975 – although whether either is 'fully effective throughout the land' even five years later is a different question. The Employment Protection Act 1975 included statutory provision for paid maternity leave and a right to return to work after the birth of a child. Two Private Members' Bills – the Sexual Offences (Amendment) Act 1976 and the Domestic Violence Act 1976 (both backed by the government) – removed some of the legal disabilities suffered by women who are victims of violence. The 1975 Social Security Pensions Act, with its home responsibilities provision, ensured that parents and those looking after elderly dependants would retain their pension rights despite breaks in employment and it provided for equal access by women and men to employers' pension schemes.

In 1978, some changes to the income tax system were announced by the government, although the fundamental reform which was promised was aborted by the 1979 election. A few months before, the Home Secretary announced that female UK citizens whose children were born abroad would usually be able to register those children as UK citizens even though the father was not himself a UK citizen. Although the Conservative Government has announced that it will continue with this policy, it is still pledged to restoring the ban on foreign husbands of British women.

Superficially, much has changed. The media are fond of telling women that they are 'equal now'. But a closer examination of the evidence and the impact of women's rights legislation shows that the fundamental fact of inequality has only just begun to be attacked.

Employment
In the early 1950s, only one-quarter of married women were in paid employment. By 1964, an increase of over one million in the female

labour force – most of them married – meant that about one-third of married women went out to work. In the last 15 years, the increase in women's share of the labour force has continued to reflect the rise in the economic activity rates of married women. Department of Employment estimates suggest that by 1986 women will constitute 49 per cent of the workforce.[2] Of those 11 million women, 68 per cent will be married.

At the same time, however, the economic activity rates of non-married women – the single, separated, widowed and divorced – have steadily decreased (from 45 per cent for all age-groups in 1971 to 41 per cent in 1977). In the older age groups, married women are nearly as likely as the non-married to be economically active: of those aged 45–54, 72 per cent of the non-married are economically active, compared with 68 per cent of married women.

The increasing demand by married women for jobs, at a time of growing unemployment, has meant higher unemployment rates amongst women. There were 401,000 women unemployed in January 1979, compared with 990,000 men.[3] Amongst school-leavers, unemployment fell almost impartially: 52,000 girls unemployed and 55,000 boys. But despite a growing tendency of married women to register as unemployed when out of a job, the DEP statistics continue to understate the size of female unemployment. The General Household Survey suggests that just under *half* of unemployed married women were actually registered as unemployed.[4]

Not surprisingly, the increase in women's participation in the labour market has been matched by the growing proportion of mothers taking full or part time work. In 1965, 15 per cent of mothers with the youngest child under 2 were in paid employment; 21 per cent of mothers whose youngest child was aged 3 or 4 were in employment, and 43 of mothers whose youngest child was aged between 5 and 15. By 1977, 27 per cent mothers with the youngest child under 5 were in employment (22 per cent part time, 5 per cent full-time); 45 per cent of mothers with a child aged 5 to 9 were working part time, and a further 15 per cent working full time; and 43 per cent of mothers with the youngest child aged 10 or over were working part time, with a further 28 per cent working full time.[4] In 1971, the General Household Survey showed that 39 per cent of mothers at home would return to work earlier than they intended if satisfactory child care facilities were available. Inadequate child care facilities are a major factor in preventing women from taking paid employment when they would like to. They are also a major cause of the growing proportion of part time workers amongst women: in 1976, 40 per cent of female employees were in part time jobs where they are particularly vulnerable to lack of legal protection, low pay rates and fewer fringe benefits, and inadequate union organisation.

Finally, along with the increasing employment of married women and the growth in part time employment must be noted the significant change in the nature of women's employment. Between 1961 and 1971, the number of full time women employees in manufacturing fell by 16 per cent while the number of part time women manufacturing workers rose by 21 per cent. The majority of new female jobs have been created in service employment (nearly 1.2 million between 1961 and 1971), and most of those new jobs are part time.

Earnings

Let us now consider the level of women's earnings, and their increase relative to men's, over the last 15 years and, in particular, over the $3\frac{1}{2}$ years following the Equal Pay Act coming fully into effect.

Looking at Table 9.1, it can be seen that there has been a real

Table 9.1   Relative earnings of men and women

	Women's weekly earnings as a % of men's	Women's hourly earnings as a % of men's
October 1973	50	60
April 1972		
Manual	53	61
Non manual	51	54
April 1975		
Manual	58	67
Non manual	58	61
April 1978		
Manual	61	72
Non manual	59	61

Source: *Department of Employment Gazette*, vol. 87 no. 3, March 1979 and Ministry of Labour figures, February 1964, quoted in *Women*, NCCL, 1965. Note: figures are for full time employees, excluding overtime pay. Hours from hourly earnings.

improvement in women's relative position, some of which is attributable to the Equal Pay Act. The exclusion of settlements and awards under the Act from statutory and voluntary pay norms, together with the use of flat rate increases, has allowed women to achieve higher percentage pay increases than men over the last decade. In 1970–71, 1971–72 and 1972–73, increases in manual women workers' basic hourly rates were 2 to 3 percentage points higher than men's; in 1973–74, 1974–75 and 1975–76, women's increases were 5 percentage points higher. But that higher percentage increase was, of course, a percentage of far lower rates, while a greater increase in basic rates will not compensate for the difference between men's and women's total earnings caused by the longer hours and greater overtime worked by men. (In 1978, men worked on average 43 hours, compared with women's $37\frac{1}{2}$ hours.)

Furthermore, the official figures used to measure the gap between men's and women's earnings exclude part time workers, whose *basic* rates are often lower than those for full time workers in the same or comparable jobs.

The impact of the Equal Pay Act has been limited by the fact that an individual woman can only bring a case to an industrial tribunal if she can show that she is doing the same or similar work to a man, or that her work has been equally rated under a job evaluation scheme.

Such cases have been few (1448 between January 1976 and May 1979 of which only 175 succeeded at a tribunal hearing). More significantly, the Act allows trade unions to refer discriminatory wage structures or collective agreements to the Central Arbitration Committee, which has made equal pay awards affecting larger numbers of women workers.

But the very limitations of the Act have served a useful purpose. By establishing that 'equal pay for equal work' (as defined by the Act) will still leave women earning less than three-quarters of men's rates, even after the differences in hours and overtime have been set aside, the Act has focused attention on the fundamental problems of job segregation and low pay.

In 1964, a study of women in the workforce showed that 50 per cent of female school-leavers went into three trades – clothing (14 per cent), textiles (7 per cent) and distributive trades (29 per cent). About 3 per cent of these girls obtained day release. By 1972, the picture had barely improved, with just under 77 per cent of all women employed working in four sectors: office and communications;

catering, domestic and related services; unskilled and semi-skilled production; and sales. Indeed, the concentration of women in certain sectors of employment has increased in the last decade. In 1966, 52 per cent of working women were to be found in three service industries: professional and scientific services (typists, secretaries, technicians, teachers and nurses); distributive trades; and miscellaneous services (including laundries, catering, dry cleaning and hairdressing). By 1978, 58 per cent women employees were concentrated in these three sectors. In the five sectors in which women employees outnumber men (clothing and footwear; professional and scientific services; miscellaneous services; distributive trades; insurance, banking and finance), the proportion of women in each industry considerably increased between 1966 and 1978.

Not only are women segregated into a narrower range of jobs than men, in a narrower range of industries but they are also largely concentrated in low paid employment. For instance, the professional and scientific services (whose average full time *male* earnings are 90 per cent of the average earnings for all industries and services) employed 24.5 per cent of all female manual employees. The miscellaneous services sector (average full time male earnings 81 per cent of the average) employs 16.3 per cent of all female manual workers. Clothing and footwear, with average male earnings of 88 per cent the average, employs 7 per cent of all female manual workers. In all three sectors, women are the majority of manual workers.

Earnings figures for 1978, as set out in Table 9.2, show the distribution of average male and female earnings.

Table 9.2   Gross weekly earnings of full time adult workers, April 1978

	Lowest decile	Lower quartile	Median	Upper quartile	Highest decile
Non-manual workers					
Male	57.7	72.0	91.8	117.4	150.4
Female	37.1	44.2	53.9	68.7	88.8
Manual workers					
Male	53.4	63.2	76.8	93.1	112.2
Female	33.7	39.6	47.6	57.0	67.1

In 1978, nearly half the female work force was earning less than £50, compared with about 10 per cent of the male work force. Policies for tackling the problem of women's pay must, therefore, be inextricable from policies for low pay generally.

The Sex Discrimination Act

The Sex Discrimination Act was designed to affect this segregation of women into the low paid, less skilled jobs. To what extent has it succeeded?

The task of equipping girls with the skills and confidence to move into new and better paid areas of work starts with the schools. Discrimination is no longer as crude as in 1961, when local education authorities (LEAs) provided lower sums for science facilities for girls than for boys (69p for a boy in a grammar school, compared with 57p for a girl). The Sex Discrimination Act outlawed both direct and indirect discrimination by LEAs, boards of governors and head-teachers (although single sex schools can continue to exist). A 1975 survey by the DES showed widespread sex segregation in timetabling and, despite complaints to the Equal Opportunities Commission (EOC), the Act does not appear to have abolished segregated time-tabling. More importantly, allowing an individual girl to opt into woodwork or technical drawing where the rest of the class are boys, or allowing a boy to opt into an otherwise female needlework lesson, does not encourage equality of opportunity or enable either sex to acquire the range of skills which both will need, as workers and as parents. In 1975, O level results (A to C grades) reflected the sex stereotyping of subjects: 61 per cent of maths passes were from boys; 58 per cent of physics passes were from boys; 60 per cent of biology passes from girls; 58 per cent of French passes from girls; 98 per cent of cookery passes from girls; and 98 per cent technical drawing passes from boys. Since technical drawing is often a prerequisite for an apprenticeship leading to skilled work, the vast majority of girls are effectively excluded from a wide range of higher paid jobs even before they leave school.

Resources directed towards unemployed school-leavers have not been used as they could have been to compensate girls for the inadequacies of their schooling and to equip them for a full range of jobs. While, in 1970, only 35 per cent of unemployed young people aged 16–17 were girls, by 1977 49 per cent of this age group of unemployed people were female. In that year, only 21 per cent of places on Job Creation Schemes were taken by girls, with 41 per cent of the Youth Employment Subsidy payments being made in respect of girls and 46 per cent Community Industry placements going to girls. Of 25,000 people qualifying from skill centres in 1978, less than 1,000 were women. Nor has the re-training of older women done much to affect the traditional segregation of the workforce. Of the 41,000 women who completed training in 1977 under the Training Opportunities Scheme (TOPS), 76 per cent trained for traditionally female occupations on courses such as typing and office skills.

The Sex Discrimination Act has so far had little effect on the under-representation of women on day release, in industrial apprenticeships and in training for non-traditional work. The Act requires employers and training organisations not to discriminate, directly or indirectly, against someone applying for a job, for training or for promotion. But in order to establish that she has been discriminated against, the woman also has to show that she and the man with whom she is comparing herself were in the same 'relevant circumstances'. A woman cannot successfully complain of unlawful discrimination if she was not qualified for a particular job, or if she did not even have the prerequisite school results for a particular training programme. Nor can the Act's enforcement procedures through individual complaints tackle the problem that low expectations, fear of discrimination and an entirely justified fear of the treatment that a lone woman will receive from a primarily male workforce, prevent the majority of women from considering training for a job in, say, engineering, the construction industry or vehicle maintenance.

Potentially the most far reaching of the Act's provisions is the outlawing of unjustifiable 'indirect discrimination'. In the case of Belinda Price – a 35-year-old mother who was refused employment in the civil service executive officer grade – it was decided that the age limit of 28, although applied equally to men and women, discriminated against women who were particularly likely to be out of employment in their 20s and 30s caring for small children. Since the age limit could not be justified as necessary for workforce planning or promotion and training, the civil service were ordered to redraw their age limit requirements before 1980. The indirect discrimination provision therefore makes it possible to challenge other requirements – such as mobility conditions, lengthy residential training or a condition that a foreman must have worked on night shifts – which disqualify many women from certain jobs.

But not even the ban on unjustified indirect discrimination can alter the fact that many women do not have the basic qualifications to train for skilled work, nor the confidence or expectations of themselves to move into non-traditional areas. In recognition of the fact that more is needed to undo years of inequality, the Act permits positive discrimination by employers and training organisations, who can run special courses for women in fields where they have previously been under-represented. These sections of the Act have barely been used, and there is no compulsion on an employer or on the Manpower Services Commission to use them. By contrast, in the United States of America, affirmative action programmes require institutions and companies receiving federal funds to analyse their hiring and personnel policies and the composition of their workforce, and to draw up programmes to increase the representation of women and minority group workers in jobs where they have been under-represented. By establishing goals and timetables, but not fixed quotas, institutions and companies are encouraged to undertake special recruitment and training programmes, to redesign jobs in ways that provide opportunities for people lacking accepted work skills and to make efforts to provide in-service training for people locked into dead-end jobs. The problems encountered in the United States in implementing equal opportunities laws should not be underestimated (women's earnings as a proportion of men's have actually dropped), but affirmative action programmes have assisted many women in overcoming the barrier of segregation, both in skilled manual work and in middle management grades.

A measure such as the Sex Discrimination Act can never be expected to have instant effects. Nonetheless the early years' experience of the Act has been disappointing. During 1976 and 1977, 472 complaints of unlawful discrimination were made to tribunals (126 by men). Of these, 98 were settled through ACAS; 175 were withdrawn, some with a private settlement; 155 were dismissed by the tribunal; and 41 were successful after a hearing. Of 111 compensation payments (after settlement or by tribunal order), 59 were under £100 and only 6 were over £500. A major problem for those alleging sex discrimination is that the burden of proof is on the applicant (by contrast with unfair dismissal cases where, once the fact of dismissal is established, it is up to the employer to justify the dismissal). In addition, however, the Act has affected the practice of many credit firms and building societies although an EOC survey of the latter reveals the persistence of discrimination against women earning more than their husbands.

But individual complaints of discrimination are only one of the enforcement methods provided by the Act. The other, and arguably more important, is the establishment of the Equal Opportunities Commission with wide powers to investigate, make recommendations and issue non-discrimination notices. The Commission's record, in its first three and a half years, has hardly been impressive. Its first formal investigation concerned Tameside's allocation of girls and boys to selective schools and came to the conclusion that there was no sex discrimination involved. Its second, so far uncompleted, involves Electrolux where women workers have complained for years of unequal pay. The Commission has preferred a 'conciliatory' approach which, despite useful documents on child care and tax discrimination, has borne little fruit. Studies by the Equal Pay and Opportunity project at the LSE, and a survey of major employers by the EOC itself (a survey which omitted the unions represented at those workplaces), show that there is widespread ignorance of the detailed provisions of the Act, which has had little effect on the policies of most managements. The EOC's failure to develop an aggressive and effective strategy reflects in part the absence of an organised cohesive women's movement. Much of the energy involved in publishing and campaigning for a Sex Discrimination Act seems now to be used in practical forms of help to women, for instance in women's aid centres, rather than in ensuring that the Act is properly implemented.

It is difficult to assess the impact of the maternity pay and leave provisions introduced in 1976 under the Employment Protection Act. The pay levels set (6 weeks' pay for a woman employed for 16 hours or more per week for 2 years) are considerably below those in most other western European countries. Because they have not been accompanied by a major publicity drive, many women and their employers remain ignorant of the statutory provisions. The right to return to work for up to 29 weeks after the baby's birth is meaningless for a mother who cannot arrange for someone else to care for the child. Both the pay and the leave provisions exclude women who have not been in the job for the minimum 2 years, as well as part timers (those employed for less than 16 hours per week or between 8 and 16 if they have been employed for 5 years).

The EOC stresses that a major expansion in child care facilities will be essential if the restrictions on women's working hours are to be lifted. Indeed, it is the unmet demand for child care facilities which makes the legal right to return to work after the birth of a child useless in practice for many women, and which accounts in part for the dramatic rise in part time work amongst women.

As long ago as 1965,[5] it was estimated that one million mothers required day care places for their under fives and that over one million needed out-of-school places for their over fives. In 1974, 64 per cent of mothers wanted some form of day-care for their under-fives[6], while a survey of three inner city areas in London found that 90 per cent of mothers wanted day care for their three and four year olds. But local authority targets for day care places remain 8 per 1,000 under-fives; priority waiting lists were 12,601 in 1976; and the total estimated number of under-fives in any form of care in 1973, including those placed with childminders, was one million or 29 per cent of the total under-five group. Full time care in a local authority day nursery was available for only 0.7 per cent. Without a massive expansion of resources to meet the needs of children and their parents, and without a change of attitudes on the part of employers, fathers and the community generally, enabling and encouraging fathers to share the task of looking after children, anti-discrimination laws are unlikely to make more than a dent in the problems of women in employment.

Taxation and social security

The notion of man as breadwinner and woman as dependant used to be offered as the main justification for unequal pay. This myth corresponds less and less with the reality, which is that one in six of non-pensioner households relies on a woman for financial support (the majority of these households containing dependants). In around 5 per cent of households where both husband and wife earn, the woman earns more than the husband. The number of families below the poverty line would be trebled if it were not for the wife's earnings. Nonetheless, the income tax system and, to some extent, the social security system continue to perpetuate the assumption of the wife as dependant on the husband breadwinner.

Under income tax law, a married man living with his wife owns her income for tax purposes. He is responsible for declaring it to the Inland Revenue and for paying tax on it; he is entitled to any rebate on the tax (although most married women will in future receive rebates on their own income). On marriage, a man becomes entitled to a higher personal allowance; a woman loses the single person's allowance, although her husband can claim a wife's earned income allowance at the same level, but which can only be offset against her earnings. The wife's earned income election (under which her earnings, but not her unearned income are taxed separately) is advantageous only for higher rate taxpayers, while separate assessment (under which a couple's tax bill is divided in proportion to their income and outgoings) is very little publicised and does not give either partner financial privacy.

In 1978, the government announced administrative changes which would allow women to receive their own rebates, and which would extend certain additional allowances (such as for a housekeeper) on non-discriminatory terms. But more fundamental changes are needed to deal with the problem of the ownership of income for tax purposes, and the question of the married man's allowance. At least as far as earned income is concerned, disaggregation and the taxation of a married person as an individual in his or her own right is likely to be the only satisfactory solution. And if the tax system is not to continue subsidising married men for no other reason than that they are married and male, a way will have to be found of equalising personal allowances and concentrating assistance through cash benefits on those households who need it because they include children or other dependants. Separate taxation of unearned income might, of course, encourage tax avoidance through the transfer of capital from husband to wife; the danger of reduced revenue could, however, be met by continuing to aggregate unearned income, by levying capital gains tax on inter-spouse transfers or by withdrawing personal allowances from unearned income (except possibly, as the Meade Report suggests, for certain categories of taxpayers).

The Social Security Pensions Act 1975 ended some of the most glaring forms of sex discrimination within the social security system, particularly by providing that a married woman would in future receive the same level of personal sickness or unemployment benefit. The phasing out of the married woman's option to pay reduced stamps will not only ensure that an increasing proportion of women qualify for both short and long term benefit in their own right, but will also provide additional income for the National Insurance fund. It is therefore particularly disappointing that the Labour Government has refused to equalise dependency benefits and abolish the rule whereby a married woman receiving sickness or unemployment benefit can only qualify for additions for her husband and children if the husband is incapable of self-support. An EEC Directive on equal treatment in social security systems, adopted in November 1978, directs member states to eliminate sex discrimination in a wide range of benefits, including dependancy additions, but it is possible that in order to comply with the Directive (which has a six year implementation period), the government may reduce men's entitlement to dependancy additions.

Citizenship and immigration

Mention has already been made of the immigration controls imposed in 1968 on foreign husbands of British women. Although the ban was lifted in 1974 under the new Labour Government, a man seeking to enter or remain in this country as a fiancé or husband will only be granted an initial 12 months' stay and may be refused even that, or any extension of that period, if the immigration officers believed the marriage was one of convenience. Inevitably, where the husband or both partners are black or Asian, couples have found themselves particularly liable to inquisitions by the police and immigration officials, many of whom seem to have accepted the prevailing myth that an arranged marriage is one of convenience. No such problems worry British men who have married Commonwealth or alien women: a woman is entitled, on marriage, to register as a UK citizen. The Labour Government's Green Paper on nationality and citizenship, published in April 1977, promised to end sex discrimination in the transmission of citizenship to a spouse, not by giving husbands the same rights which wives now enjoy, but by establishing a more restrictive right for a spouse to apply for registration as a UK citizen. Meanwhile, female United Kingdom passport holders in East Africa, if married to a non-UK citizen, have been denied the right to apply for entry vouchers under the quota system on the grounds that only a man (or a woman married to a disabled man) can be a 'head of household'. However, no Bill on citizenship was published before the 1979 election and the reform of citizenship laws is now in the hands of the Conservative Government.

Violence against women

The Domestic Violence and Matrimonial Proceedings Act 1976 followed the recommendations of the House of Commons Select Committee on violence in marriage. It enabled a married woman to seek an injunction against a violent husband without commencing divorce proceedings, enabled married or single women to obtain injunctions under an emergency procedure, if necessary, and gave the courts the power to attach a power of arrest to the injunction. The law has undoubtedly improved the legal remedies available to a battered woman although, as its sponsor Jo Richardson MP said, it cannot provide the resources needed to maintain refuges and women's aid centres for women who have been forced to leave home. Clear as the intentions of the new law were, it took an appeal to the House of Lords in the case of Davis and Johnson to establish that an unmarried woman could evict her cohabitee from a council home which was in their joint names for a temporary period while she found other accommodation.

Following the recommendations of the Heilbron Committee, the Sexual Offences (Amendment) Act 1976 provided a right to anonymity for both the victim and the defendant (until and unless convicted) in a rape case. It also placed some limitations on the evidence which can be brought about a woman's previous sexual history, although the judge still has a discretionary power to admit such evidence.

Political and trade union activity

The Equal Opportunities Commission has calculated[7] that trade union membership amongst women has risen from 27.2 per cent of potential membership in 1967 to 37.1 per cent in 1976 (compared with an increase from 52.9 per cent to 61 per cent of potential male membership over the same period). Although union organisation still affects less than half women workers, it is significant that membership is increasing extremely fast amongst women, having gone up by over 55 per cent since 1967 compared with a rise of only 12 per cent amongst men. Representation at the upper levels of the movement remains depressingly inadequate: in no union are women represented in the same proportion as amongst the membership amongst full time officials, on their executives or as TUC delegates. COHSE, 70 per cent of whose members are women, had 5 full time women officials out of 40, 1 woman NEC member and no female TUC delegates in 1976. In the same year, the National Union of Tailors and Garment Workers, with an 88 per cent female membership had 6 full time women officials out of 40, 5 women NEC members and 5 TUC women delegates. The number of women active as shop stewards and conveners appears to be increasing and some unions – despite a lack of female representation at their higher levels – are organising positive campaigns to negotiate higher pay and better conditions particularly for their women members. However, many unions remain complacent about discriminatory attitudes and structures and they ignore the need for positive action to ensure that women members play an active part in their unions as well as to improve women's position in the workplace. It is significant that a number of unions are reluctant to recruit or negotiate for part time workers – the vast majority of whom are women – who, while admittedly difficult to organise, are seen as a threat to the conditions of full time workers, instead of as an integral part of the workforce.

Conclusion

The economic, legal and social status of women is a crucial measure by which to judge the impact of Labour Governments' policies in 11 out of the last 15 years. Despite important legal advances and the recognition given to the need to tackle inequalities between the sexes, the principle that law and social policy must be based on equal rights, equal responsibilities and equal opportunities is not yet fully accepted. In matters as basic as the definition of who is a citizen of this country and of who is a taxpayer, the Labour Government retained fundamentally discriminatory laws. In the area of employment, the principle – although not the practice – of equal pay and equal access to jobs is widely accepted. But equal opportunities cannot be achieved without policies and resources which tackle the basic fact of a workforce segregated by sex, where the women are largely under-trained and low paid. Positive action against discrimination will have to involve compensatory training on a massive scale to meet the particular needs of school-leavers, of those already employed and of those returning to work after bringing up a family, together with a breaking down of the attitudes and practices which bar large areas of employment to women.

Finally, it is not equality to improve women's position in law and at the workplace while leaving the burden of caring for children and other dependants, and performing domestic duties, largely to women. Better maternity leave provisions and the massive expansion of child care facilities – although urgently needed – will alleviate, but not deal with the issue. Equality between the sexes demands a radical alteration in the organisation of work, in employment and in the home, so that men, as well as women, take a full part of the responsibility for caring for children and other dependants, and women, as well as men, are enabled to gain access to the full range of employment and to play a full part in trade union and political activity.

PART V

Redistribution Through Income Support

10 Social Security

by David Piachaud

A fair test of the extent to which a society is civilised is its treatment of the weak – those who must, more than most, depend on others because of age or disability or illness or the lack of the opportunity to work. In modern industrial societies, social security is central to the just treatment of these groups; it is the most potent instrument for allocating income in accordance with needs rather than on the basis of economic power.

This chapter will review the commitments of the last Labour Government and its record, considering in turn the aggregate changes, the level of benefits, provision for the elderly, the disabled and the unemployed, supplementary benefits and poverty. Social security in relation to children in one and two parent families is discussed in Chapter 11 and other aspects of policy of direct relevance to income maintenance in Chapter 5.

The Labour Government was elected in 1974 on a manifesto that stated the intention to: 'Eliminate poverty wherever it exists in Britain.... Achieve far greater economic equality – in income, wealth and living standards. ... Increase social equality by giving far greater importance to full employment, housing, education and social benefits.' In the section of the manifesto headed 'Social Justice', the approach was outlined: 'Clearly a fresh approach to the British crisis is required, and Labour insist that it must begin with an entirely new recognition of the claims of social justice.' More specifically, there were three commitments. First to: 'Bring immediate help to existing pensioners, widows, the sick and the unemployed by increasing pensions and other benefits to £10 for the single person and £16 for the married couple, within the first Parliamentary session of our government. Thereafter these figures will be increased annually in proportion to increases in average national earnings. We shall also follow this by replacing the Conservative Government's inadequate and unjust long term pensions scheme by a comprehensive scheme designed to take future pensioners off the means test and give full equality of treatment to women.' Second there was a commitment to 'introduce a new scheme of help for the disabled'. The third and final commitment on social security was for a new system of child cash allowances.

Aggregate changes

Between 1973/4 and 1978/9, total expenditure on social security nearly tripled, an increase of £10 billion per annum. The great majority of this increase was due to inflation. In real terms, spending on social security (excluding child benefits and family income supplement) grew by 30 per cent. The change in expenditure by groups of recipients is shown in Table 10.1.

Table 10.1   *Change in expenditure 1973/74 to 1978/79 at constant prices[a]*

	£m	Proportion
Elderly	+1760	+27%
Disabled and long term sick	+560	+47%
Short-term sick	−30	−4%
Unemployed	+630	+91%
Widows and orphans	−10	−1%
One parent and other benefits[b]	+220	+52%
Total Expenditure[c]	+3220	+30%

[a] 1978 Survey prices.
[b] Supplementary allowances to one parent families and those looking after elderly parents and maternity benefit.
[c] Excludes Family Allowance/Child Benefit and Family Income Supplement but includes administration.
Source: *The Government's Expenditure Plans, 1979/80 to 1982/83*, Cmnd 7439, 1979.

Over half of the increase in expenditure went to the elderly; one-fifth went on increased expenditure on the unemployed and rather less on the disabled. The biggest percentage increase in expenditure was on the unemployed, on whom spending nearly doubled during the five years of the Labour Government; the next most rapid growth was on one parent families and the disabled.

Overall social security rose as a proportion of total public expenditure from 18.4 per cent in 1973/74 to 21.5 per cent in 1978/ 1979; in the latter year, expenditure on social security, £15,361 million, was far and away the largest public expenditure programme, the next largest being education with £8,722 million. In relation to gross domestic product, the growth of social security was even more marked from 7.9 per cent in 1973/74 to 9.8 per cent in 1978/79. Thus in the course of the Labour Government, the share of income devoted to social security increased by almost 2 per cent of GDP.

Social security expenditure therefore increased during Labour's period in office in real terms, as a proportion of public expenditure and as a proportion of GDP. Ironically, the biggest increases in social security spending were in the early years of the Labour Government when the economy as a whole was static or declining. In the government's last year, when the economy was growing fast, there was little advance in social security. Whether, given this performance, it is true that redistribution can only take place when there is economic growth must be in some doubt.

Social security was, with one exception, largely exempt from the cuts that afflicted many areas of social policy. The exception was the change from the 'historic' to the 'forecasting' method of uprating which, while not a formal 'cut', deprived pensioners of some £500 million per annum which they would otherwise have received. Overall, however, social security was given very favourable treatment and exempted from the most substantial cuts.

In aggregate, to have achieved a shift to social security at a time when real incomes were static or declining was a major achievement.

The level of benefits
There were six main upratings of social security benefits during Labour's period in office. The first was in July 1974, an accelerated uprating which would not normally have taken place until October; the single and married couple's standard retirement pensions were increased to £10 and £16 respectively. This increase in pensions was well above the increase in prices or earnings and represented a 14 per cent increase in the real value of the pension. The government decided, however, that it could only afford to introduce the £10 and £16 benefit rates for pensioners and widows, not for the sick and the unemployed. The manifesto commitment of 1974 was thus fulfilled only in part. The changes in benefits in each of the upratings are shown in Table 10.2.

Over the whole five year period, both short and long term benefits

Table 10.2   *Percentage change in social security benefits, prices and earnings since previous updating*

	Unemployment and sickness benefit[a]	Retirement pension[b]	Prices[c]	Average earnings[d]
Uprating:				
July 1974	17.0	29.0	13.5	12.9
April 1975	14.0	16.0	17.7	17.4
November 1975	13.3	14.7	11.7	10.7
November 1976	16.2	15.0	15.0	12.8
November 1977	14.0	14.4	13.0	9.6
November 1978	7.1	11.4	8.1	14.6
Total increase October 1973 – November 1978	114.3	151.6	109.6	107.9

[a]Single person.
[b]Single pensioner under age 80.
[c]General index of retail prices.
[d]Average gross weekly earnings of full time adult male manual workers. For November 1978, October 1977 to October 1978 increase used.
Source: *Social Security Statistics 1977* and author's calculations.

increased at least as fast as prices or average earnings. In April 1975, benefits were not fully restored to their July 1974 level but this deficit was made good in subsequent upratings. Comparing November 1978 with October 1973, unemployment and sickness benefit had increased in real terms by only 2.2 per cent whereas retirement pensions had increased in real terms by 20 per cent.

Supplementary benefit scale rates were uprated broadly in line with national insurance benefit rates, with a similar distinction between short term (ordinary) and long term rates. Table 10.3 shows these rates in relation to gross and net incomes of the average earner.

Both ordinary and long term supplementary benefit (SB) rates increased in relation to gross and net earnings in the years up to 1977 but declined in 1978. This pattern is more marked in relation to *net* earnings since, broadly speaking, in the early years the burden of tax was increased whereas in the later years of the Labour Government it was decreased. Over the whole period, the ordinary rate increased by 3.7 percentage points and the long term rate by 9.6

Table 10.3   Supplementary benefit rates as proportion of gross and net income at average earnings, married couple

End of year[a]	As % of gross average earnings		As % of net income[b] at average earnings	
	Ordinary rate	Long term rate	Ordinary rate	Long term rate
1973	28.5	31.4	37.9	41.8
1974	28.1	33.6	38.8	46.5
1975	29.8	36.2	42.4	51.5
1976	30.8	37.1	43.9	52.9
1977	32.3	38.9	44.1	53.1
1978	30.6	37.8	41.6	51.4

[a]October for Gross and Net Income at Average Earnings, December for Supplementary Benefit Rates.
[b]Gross earnings less income tax and national insurance contributions.
Source: *Social Security Statistics, 1977* and author's calculations.

percentage points relative to the net income of the average earner.

As has been seen, in the course of the Labour Government, the real value of the retirement pension increased significantly while the value of unemployment and sickness benefits remained virtually constant. The uprating of 1974 in effect drove a wedge between short and long term benefit rates. The wedge was driven deeper by the upratings policy which increased pensions in line with the higher of earnings or prices but increased short term benefits only in line with prices. The resulting difference between short and long term benefit rates is set out in Table 10.4.

Table 10.4   Supplementary benefit: long term scale rate as proportion of ordinary rate (%)

Date of introduction	Single	Married couple
1973	14.0	10.3
1974	23.8	19.8
1975 (April)	25.0	20.4
1975 (November)	25.7	21.4
1976	23.6	20.3
1977	23.4	20.4
1978	28.0	23.5

The long term addition to supplementary benefit which was only 60p per week in 1972 had increased to £6 per week for a married couple by the end of 1978. The size of this differential is out of all proportion to the original justification – that short term recipients can delay purchasing capital goods until their circumstances improve. For the unemployed, this differential is particularly serious since they are never allowed to receive the long term rate however long they have been unemployed, an unjustifiable form of discrimination which was not, unfortunately, rectified by the Labour Government.

Provision for the elderly
The increase in the real value of the retirement pension and in the long term supplementary benefit level has been set out above. Social security is not, however, the sole determinant of the incomes of the elderly: they also depend on incomes from work, occupational pensions, income from savings and on deductions from their income. The change in real disposable income between 1972 and 1977 (the latest for which data are available) is shown for retired and non-retired households in Table 10.5. There has been a relative improvement in the position of the retired, who gained 8 to 10 per cent whereas the non-retired had on average gained virtually nothing.

Table 10.5   Change in real disposable incomes (%)

	Change in real disposable income 1972 to 1977	Disposable income as proportion of average disposable income for all households, 1977
One adult, retired	+8.2	35.7
Two adults, retired	+10.2	60.2
One adult, non-retired	+1.7	64.1
Two adults, non-retired	+0.2	107.8
Two adults, 1–4 children (almost all non-retired)	−1.0	111.9

Source: 'The effects of taxes and benefits on household income 1977', *Economic Trends*, January 1979 and author's calculations.

These results must, to a limited extent, be qualified. The change in real disposable income was calculated using the General Index of Retail Prices (RP) which from 1974 to 1979 rose 111 per cent. By contrast, the one person pensioner price index rose 115 per cent and the two person pensioner index rose 113 per cent. Thus the prices facing pensioners have tended to rise slightly faster than for households in general. Nonetheless, the conclusion still holds good that the elderly made real gains during Labour's period in office. The fulfilment of Labour's commitment to pensioners was a major achievement – possibly the most substantial single achievement of the Labour Government.

Thus far we have been concerned primarily with the impact of social security policy on existing pensioners. Of less immediate effect, but of more importance for the future, was the introduction of the government's new pension scheme.

Heralded by the White paper, *Better Pensions*,[1] and enacted in the Social Security Act 1975, contributions for the new pension scheme started to be paid in April 1978. The scheme is designed to provide in the future increased pensions, related to the individual's earnings and fully protected against inflation. Full pensions for those retiring will be paid in 20 years' time (1999); those retiring between now and then will receive lower levels of pension. When the scheme is fully mature, an individual's pension will be calculated on the basis of his earnings in his 20 'best years' and will be based on a redistributive formula: a single pensioner on average earnings will receive a pension of 44 per cent of earnings; on three-quarters of average earnings the pension will be 50 per cent of the individual's earnings; and on $1\frac{1}{2}$ times average earnings the pension will be 38 per cent of earnings. The new scheme allows for members of occupational pension schemes which meet certain standards to be contracted-out and receive reduced state benefits in return for a reduced level of contributions. For those contracted-out, the government undertakes, within certain limits, to supplement occupational pensions to protect them against inflation above 3 per cent per annum. When the scheme was introduced in April 1978, 11 million people were contracted-out.

The new pensions scheme was essentially a compromise. The Crossman scheme of 1968 just failed to reach the statute book and was scrapped by the Conservative Government. The Joseph pension plan was enacted in the Social Security Act of 1973 but in terms of making adequate provision for old age it fell far short of the Crossman plan. Pension plans which are scrapped before they ever come into operation serve little purpose so that the Labour Government not unreasonably sought to produce a plan which would have the acquiescence, if not support, of the Conservative Party. To gain this support, and to avoid offending certain powerful interests, the government had to reach an accommodation with the occupational pension schemes. Crossman had conceded generous terms for contracting-out. Barbara Castle offered the added inducement of government inflation proofing for occupational pensions. This open ended commitment to bolster up pension funds appears to have been adequate to gain Conservative Party support and there is not, at the moment at least, any indication that the scheme will be altered.

While the new pension scheme may have been the best available compromise, it is not about to cause a sudden transformation in the circumstances of those retiring. It will be well into the next century before most pensioner couples have a pension of half average earnings. The White Paper estimated that the new scheme would raise the pensioner's share of total personal consumption from 10 per cent to 13 per cent over the next 40 years; this may be compared with the shift of $1\frac{1}{2}$ per cent of gross domestic product to social security over Labour's five years. The pension prospects of women are certainly better under the new scheme than under previous proposals and the prospects for widows who will be able to inherit their husbands' pension rights are markedly improved. But those already retired gain nothing from the new scheme. (Although the White Paper stated, 'With the introduction of the new scheme, the position of existing pensioners will be further reviewed in the light of the development of the economy', nothing was done.)

The new pension scheme is far from an ideal socialist solution. The massive dependence of pensioners on supplementary benefit remains, and will remain for a long time to come. There continues to be a very high incidence of poverty amongst the elderly and pensions remain much lower in Britain than in many other countries. Thus, while there has been progress, much more remains to be done.

Disability benefits
Three new benefits for disabled people were introduced by the Labour Government. In 1975 the Non-Contributory Invalidity Pension (NCIP) was introduced for people of working age who have been unable to work for at least six months and who lack sufficient national insurance contributions to get invalidity benefit. In 1976, the Mobility Allowance was introduced; it now provides for people between age 5 and age 65 (and those over 65 who are already in

receipt of the allowance) who are unable, or almost unable to walk and who could benefit from increased facilities for mobility. Also in 1976 the Invalid Care Allowance (ICA) was introduced for men and single women of working age who are unable to work because they have to stay at home to look after a severely disabled relative.

The Beveridge plan, based on the insurance principle, largely excluded those disabled people who had never been able to work and thus satisfy contribution conditions. The introduction of the Attendance Allowance in 1971 and the three new benefits in 1975 and 1976 has in part rectified this deficiency but only subject to major qualifications.

The Mobility Allowance, now paid at the rate of £10 per week, has brought real gains for those people who previously lacked any assistance with mobility. The gain for those who chose it instead of the hazardous invalid three-wheeler has been much less but the principle of extending assistance to a wider group is surely right.

The NCIP and ICA represent advances but they are still unsatisfactory in two principal respects. First, the level of each of these benefits is only 60 per cent of the normal long term rate of benefit and as such is way below supplementary benefit level. In 1979, 130,000 people were receiving NCIP but only 10,000 of these were thereby taken off supplementary benefit. Most recipients of NCIP and ICA are, at the end of the day, no better off since they simply receive less supplementary benefits, and they are probably more confused and irritated because they now apply for two benefits instead of one. Second, the treatment of married women is deficient if not downright discriminatory. For NCIP, married women must satisfy a contentious condition that they be unable to do normal household duties; this condition is not applied to men or single women. In the case of the ICA, married women are not eligible; since most invalid care is undertaken by married women this is a fundamental defect.

Once again, as with the elderly, there has been some real progress in providing adequately for disabled people but much more remains to be done. There is still not a comprehensive and coherent policy for meeting the income needs and meeting the extra expenses resulting from disability. It is nevertheless to its credit that the Labour Government paid more attention to the disabled than any preceding government.

The Unemployed

The record on unemployment of the Labour Government is bad. While there was a massive increase in social security expenditure on the unemployed (91 per cent in real terms), this was almost entirely attributable to the increase in the numbers of people out of work – from 600,000 in 1974 to nearly 1.4 million in 1978. Contrary to much ignorant opinion, unemployment benefits scarcely altered in real terms over the course of the Labour Government; nor did they vary substantially relative to net incomes at work, as is shown in Table 10.6.

Table 10.6   Unemployment or sickness benefit as percentage of net income[a] at average earnings[b]

	Single person		Married couple		Married couple with two children	
	Exc. ERS	Inc. ERS[c]	Exc. ERS	Inc. ERS[c]	Exc. ERS	Inc. ERS[c]
1965	27.0	27.0	41.2	41.2	49.3	49.3
1970	25.0	53.3	38.4	65.2	48.3	72.7
1973	24.8	48.4	38.7	61.5	49.5	70.6
1974	25.6	48.6	39.5	61.6	50.2	70.3
1975	24.5	45.9	38.0	58.4	48.3	67.0
1976	24.9	46.7	38.3	59.1	48.4	67.3
1977	25.8	47.9	39.1	59.9	49.7	68.8
1978	25.4	45.1	38.8	57.4	49.6	66.9

[a]After allowing for income tax and national insurance contributions.
[b]Average earnings of adult male manual workers.
[c]Earnings Related Supplement calculated using average earnings in October of the relevant tax year.
Source: *Royal Commission on the Distribution of Income and Wealth, Report No. 6* and author's calculations.

It will be seen that, excluding earnings related supplement, benefits in all years were at most one-half of the net income of an average earner. The inclusion of the earnings related supplement raised this proportion to around 70 per cent for a married couple with two children (a higher proportion than if they were receiving supplementary benefit with normal housing costs). As the table shows, there is no evidence whatsoever to support the notion that benefits in relation to incomes at work were suddenly and substantially increased, as many people seem to have imagined. Indeed a quite different conclusion would seem appropriate: for most people, short term benefits were providing very low levels of benefit compared to incomes at work.

One other aspect of social security in relation to the unemployed must regrettably be mentioned since it received more public attention than any other aspect of social security, namely the emotive subject of scroungers, the 'workshy' and social security fraud. The role of parts of the press and of certain Conservative politicians in what became at times an hysterical witch-hunt was utterly beneath contempt. The Labour Government did increase the number of investigators and prosecutions for fraud but it took account of the fact that tightening up controls aggravated the hardship of those genuinely unemployed. All the facts suggest that the extent of social security fraud is very small indeed and it remains the case that the government is deprived of resources to a far greater extent from tax evasion than from social security fraud. Cynically, some of those who most condemn the latter take pride in the former: by reducing legitimate revenue, tax evasion is no different in effect from snatching the book from the schoolchild or kicking away the crutches of a cripple, and remoteness does nothing to lend respectability. It is all the more deplorable that the shameful hounding of the unemployed took place when more and more were losing their jobs through no fault of their own.

Supplementary benefits

One of the primary goals of Labour's social security policy has been to reduce dependence on means tested supplementary benefit. For example, the new 'Better Pensions' scheme is primarily designed to achieve this in the future. Over Labour's term of office, the number of supplementary benefit recipients increased, as shown in Table 10.7. The number of pensioners and of the sick and disabled on SB declined but the number of unemployed recipients more than doubled and of one parent families increased by 43 per cent. In all, by 1979, 5 million individuals had their level of income determined by the supplementary benefit levels.

In 1976, a comprehensive review of the supplementary benefits scheme was initiated by the Department of Health and Social Security. While this review was a model of open government, in terms of content, it unfortunately concentrated on details of claiming, assessment and appeals. The review team was shackled by the Treasury's 'zero cost' condition and therefore could not examine the relationship between national insurance and SB levels; yet this

Table 10.7   *Supplementary benefit recipients (thousands)*[a]

	Pensioners	Unemployed	Sick and disabled	One parent families[b]	All supplementary benefits
1973	1840	249	280	228	2680
1974	1810	301	260	245	2680
1975	1680	441	242	276	2790
1976	1690	654	243	303	2940
1977	1740	671	229	309	2990
1978	1730	602	220	327	2930

[a]Recipients of regular weekly payments in November.
[b]Excluding one parent families included in other groups.
Source: *Social Security Statistics, 1977.*

relationship is what determines the number of people who are eligible for supplementary benefit. The *Review*[2] has been examined in detail by the Supplementary Benefits Commission itself[3] and by the Child Poverty Action Group.[4] Both have concluded that any reform of the system must involve additional expenditure if there are not to be unacceptable losses.

There still remains a major task of coordinating and integrating national insurance benefits with the SB safety net. This can only be achieved by closer integration of social security and income taxation, yet virtually no progress was made in this area, apart from the introduction of child benefits; indeed one step, the introduction of the income tax age allowance (for which there was no mandate or justification in terms of social policy) was a move in the opposite direction. The choice remains as to whether means testing is to be concentrated on the poorest as now happens or whether everyone is to receive adequate benefits which are then rendered selective by taxing those better off – in effect, sharing the burden of means testing.

Poverty
The ultimate test of social security must be its effectiveness in tackling poverty. The most recent official estimates of the extent of poverty are shown in Table 10.8.

In terms of individuals, there were estimated to be over 1 million living below 90 per cent of supplementary benefit level and 10 million

Table 10.8   *The incidence of poverty 1976*

	SB level or below	Above SB but within 20% of it
Proportion of families (as % of total) with incomes:		
Elderly single people	46	20
Elderly couple	21	24
Single adult	11	3
Couple without children	3	2
Couple with children	5	7
One parent family	48	4
Total	15	8

Source: *Social Trends, 1979*, Table 6.26, data for December 1976.

living below 120 per cent of SB level in 1976. The number below current SB levels rose between 1974 and 1976, particularly among the unemployed, as discussed in Chapter 2. Using a constant poverty level (that is, adjusted only for inflation), the number at or below the real SB level when Labour took office declined by over one-third.

Nevertheless the numbers at or very close to the SB level – a harsh enough poverty level by any standards – remains very high. Some on the Right have concluded that this fact points to the ineffectiveness of social security. Certainly it indicates that there are deficiencies and that further improvements are necessary. It does not however mean that social security is ineffective. Beckerman has estimated how many would have been in poverty in 1975 without social benefits and how many were poor even after receiving benefits as shown in Table 10.9.

Benefits raised about 85 per cent of families below SB level up to or above this level. So, despite all the defects and room for improvement, it is important not to forget what our present social security programmes successfully do to relieve hardship and to increase security and freedom from want.

Conclusion

This chapter has described the main changes in social security that

Table 10.9   Number of families below SB level

	Before benefits '000s	After benefits '000s	Average poverty gap per family per week
Pensioners	5,429	603	£1.8
Single adults	1,054	260	£5.5
Couples without children	293	61	£7.4
Couples with children	482	132	£9.4
One parent families	389	46	£11.6
Total	7,648	1,102	£5.0

Source: Royal Commission on the Distribution of Income and Wealth, *Lower Incomes*, Cmnd 7175, Table 4.9.

occurred between 1974 and 1979. Many other changes took place, some of great importance for those affected – the abolition of the 'wage stop', the neglect continued of Maternity and Death Grants, the relaxation of the Earnings Rule, steps towards equal treatment of men and women, for examples. For reasons of space, the discussion has had to be concentrated on those changes that were of most general significance.

The Labour Government's record on social security is generally good in relation to its commitments and to the economic circumstances. Very much more might have been done but the government's sights were set on compassion and social justice.

Now, when the Conservative Government is renouncing the search for social justice – as though it were merely a minor and undesirable aim rather than a prerequisite for a united, civilised and dynamic society – social security is under attack and must be defended. Looking further ahead, the understanding and support of the public must be won so that the next Labour Government can make further progress with social security, for very much more needs to be done. Social security has never been the most evocative feature of socialism and many on the far Left have neglected it totally. Yet the task of relating income to needs in an equitable manner is central to socialism and social security is central to that task.

While poverty in Britain remains to the extent that it does, the Labour Government's record on social security cannot be a source of complacency or of pride. But it need not be a source of shame.

11 Family Policy
by Ruth Lister

What is 'family policy'?

'Family policy' is an all embracing concept which, according to
Margaret Wynn, who pioneered its use in this country, covers 'all
social arrangements as they affect the family'[1]. The key element
which concerns us here is the distribution of resources as between
families and other groups in the population and, to quote Margaret
Wynn once more, 'family policy proposes the redistribution of
national wealth and income in favour of children or, in other words,
the transfer of resources to investment in future generations.'
Although family policy must also concern itself with those with the
care of disabled or elderly relatives, there is general agreement that
its first priority should be families with children. Family policy aims
to redress inequalities in living standards which arise not just from
the unequal 'vertical' distribution of rewards in our society but also
from the very different needs of households of different sizes and composition. A family with children requires more money to achieve
the same material standard of living as a single person or childless
couple. Policies to achieve greater equality must therefore aim at
the 'horizontal' redistribution of resources to those with family
responsibilities as well as the more familiar 'vertical' redistribution.

The justification for greater 'horizontal equity', which involves
the childless two-thirds of the adult population subsidising the other
third responsible for raising children is twofold. First, children can
be regarded as 'a nation's most crucial resource'[2] or, in the more
stirring words of the UN Charter for the Declaration of the Rights
of the Child: 'Mankind owes the child the best it has to give.' Second,
the majority of people are responsible for children at some stage
in their life; a horizontal redistribution of resources also means a
redistribution over the lifecycle of the individual, concentrating
financial support on the child-rearing years when it is needed most.

The political, social and economic climate

When Margaret Wynn wrote *Family Policy* in 1970, she observed that 'no political party in the UK has yet identified itself with the social and economic interests of the family'. Eight years later, the political parties were falling over each other to be seen as the party of 'the family'. This remarkable shift in the political climate is particularly marked in the change in attitude towards cash benefits for children which is the main subject of this chapter.

The 1964–70 Labour Government faced demands for an increase in family allowances in the wake of the 'rediscovery' of family poverty. These demands were made against a background of years of political neglect of family allowances which reflected general public indifference and even antipathy towards them. Their unpopularity has been ascribed to a number of causes, the most important probably being the (unfounded) association in many people's minds with overpopulation and the encouragement of large families and the fact that about two fifths of parents (those with only one child) did not receive family allowances. Furthermore the benefit to better off families with more than one child was reduced through taxation. This was aggravated by the introduction of 'clawback' which left the majority of families confused, resentful and no better off after the October 1967–April 1968 family allowance increases.

The turning of the political tide for family allowances can partly be traced to two events. The first was the suggestion in the Tory Government's Green Paper on Tax Credits that the child credit (which would amalgamate family allowances and child tax allowances) should be paid to the father. This provoked a storm of protest and a petition with 300,000 signatures showing that family allowances were far from unpopular with mothers. The second was the controversy surrounding the Labour Government's decision to postpone the introduction of its promised child benefit scheme and the subsequent leaking of Cabinet minutes by Frank Field in *New Society*, which drew child benefit to the centre of the political arena. Since then the tax free child benefit scheme has created its own momentum and ex-Cabinet ministers are now able to report favourable reactions from their constituents. Moreover, the child benefit scheme is seen as a means of helping all families, not just the poorest, so that, as Frank Field has noted, a 'family lobby' is emerging around the scheme which can make use of the 'sharp elbows of the middle class in getting the needs of families to the top of the political agenda'.[3]

The political revival of family allowances also reflected growing awareness about how the living standards of families have been falling in relative terms. The Child Poverty Action Group (CPAG) and the Low Pay Unit have produced a succession of reports demonstrating the extent of the shift in the burden of taxation towards families, the 'poverty trap' created by this trend in interaction with the extension of means tested benefits and the above average inflation rates experienced by low income families. However, the politicians' new found enthusiasm for a family policy also appears to reflect their deeper sense of unease that 'the central role of the family' in society is being undermined. Rising divorce rates, family violence, juvenile crime and other 'social problems' are being linked with the need to strengthen the family as an institution. One effect of the increase in the divorce rate has been a growing number of one parent families. It is estimated that between 1971 and 1976 there was a 32 per cent increase in the number of one parent families, from 570,000 to 750,000. By 1976, one parent families constituted 11 per cent of all families with children, compared with 8 per cent in 1971, and 1¼ million children were being raised in these families.[4]

James Callaghan specifically related his concern about 'the family' to the fact that 'as there is now a larger number of women going out to work than ever before, a number of changes are needed if we are to preserve and enhance the family's dimension and the family circle, which I believe to be a very precious asset in our national life'.[5] Similarly, Patrick Jenkin, now Secretary of State for Social Services, has complained that 'the pressure on young wives to go out to work devalues motherhood itself'.[6]

The growing participation of married women in the labour market has been one of the most striking economic trends during the period under review. It reflects a number of social changes including the compression of child rearing into a shorter time span and the changing attitudes about the position of women. In 1961, the economic activity rate for married women was 29.7 per cent; by 1974 it was estimated to be 47.7 per cent and the Department of Employment projection for 1979 is 51.3 per cent.[7] As Patricia Hewitt points out in Chapter 9, the earnings of these women have made an important contribution to the family income, even though the majority of them work part time. Layard *et al.*'s analysis of the 1975 General Household Survey found that if no wives worked, 37 per cent of couples where the husband worked would be living at below 140 per cent of the supplementary benefit level compared with the 13 per cent who were.[8] Those families in which the wife did work would otherwise on average have been poorer than other families. Although a growing proportion of mothers of young children are in paid employment, they are still much less likely to be going out to work than other married women. Thus the growing participation of married women in the labour market has the least impact on the incomes of their families at the time when two incomes are needed most. This helps to explain why the presence of young children marks one of the troughs in the 'life cycle of poverty'.

Married women have also suffered disproportionately in recent years from the increase in unemployment. Between 1974 and 1978, there was a five fold increase in the number of married women registered as unemployed. (We do not know how many actually were unemployed because of the tendency of many married women not to register.) Although unemployment has not hit men with families harder than those without, there has nevertheless been a big increase in the number of families with children dependent on unemployment or supplementary benefit because of the father's unemployment: from 222,000 in November 1964 to 462,000 in 1974 and 959,000 in 1977.

While this chapter traces how the new concern for 'the family' has contributed to a welcome redistribution of resources to those raising children, there are dangers that this concern could be translated into measures which attempt to reverse many of the gains made by women in recent years in order to bolster up 'the family'. As is argued below, the future development of family policy should be contributing to further improvements in the position of women, who are regarded as being, in James Callaghan's words, 'usually the centre of the family', and not be a vehicle for attempts to push them back into the home as a means of reducing unemployment.

The Record 1964–74

The record for the decade 1964–74 cannot be judged on the basis of any intended 'family policy', as there was none. It is only with hindsight that politicians have been made aware of the overall negative impact of income maintenance and taxation policies on families with children during this period (and in earlier ones). The 1964–70 Labour Government can take credit for the first increase in the family allowance since 1956. The increases of 35p in April

1968 (October 1967 for fourth and subsequent children) and a further 15p in October did restore the value of the family allowance relative to average earnings to that in the early 1950s. However, the gains to individual families were offset by increases in the price of school meals and welfare milk, NHS charges and national insurance contributions and, for tax paying families, the 'clawback' of the whole of the 35p increase through the tax system. The Tory Party took office in 1970 committed to a further increase in family allowances, but failed to increase them once during its term of office. Instead, it quickly introduced the means tested family income supplement scheme together with a further package of increases in school meal prices, NHS charges and the abolition of free school milk for 7–11 year olds and of cheap welfare milk. By 1974, the family allowance had fallen back to its low 1964 level in relation to average earnings.

The failure to maintain the value of the family allowance during this period was paralleled by the growing burden of taxation on families with children. Child tax allowances (CTAs) were not increased at all between 1964 and 1970. The Conservatives increased them in 1971 and 1973 but even after these increases CTAs in 1973–74 were only a fraction of their value relative to the single person's allowance ten years earlier. Between 1964 and 1974, the tax threshold for families with two and four children fell by 33 and 40 per cent respectively; that for a childless couple fell by 27 per cent and for a single person by only 8 per cent. Table 11.1 illustrates the drop in the real combined value of family allowances and CTAs between 1964 and 1974.

Policies since 1974: the emergence of child benefits

The key issue for family policy has been the chequered history of the child benefits scheme. In addition, this section covers the development of policies for one parent families and the Labour Government's record on education benefits.

From family allowances/child tax allowances to child benefits
Labour's October 1974 manifesto promised an 'attack on family poverty by increasing family allowances and extending them to the first child through a new scheme of child credits payable to the mother'. Families had to wait until April 1975 for an increase in family allowances although there had been some gains from the increase in CTAs and the food subsidies programme announced in

the April 1974 Budget. In the wake of press speculation that family allowances would be doubled in 1975, the actual increase to £1.50 was disappointingly low and failed to restore their 1968 value. The 1975 Budget proved to be even more disappointing. CTAs were not increased, the increase in personal allowances was insufficient to compensate for inflation and it was announced that the introduction of the child benefit scheme was to be delayed until April 1977 because of administrative difficulties. The Child Benefit Bill went through Parliament with all-party support but the government resisted attempts to write in a commencement date and a benefit rate. The essence of the new scheme was that CTAs and taxable family allowances would be replaced by a tax-free benefit paid to the mother. It was envisaged that CTAs would be phased out over a two year period.

1976 represented the nadir of the Labour Government policy for families. An increase in CTAs in the budget proved to be a mixed blessing as it meant more money would have to be transferred from the 'father's wallet into the mother's purse' under the proposed child benefit scheme. Worried about the implications of this transfer for its pay policy, the government lost its nerve and announced the indefinite postponement of child benefits. In compensation, a family allowance of £1 would be paid to the first child from April 1977. The family allowance would continue to be taxable and subject to 'clawback' and CTAs would remain. The net cost would be £95 million. The reaction, both inside and outside parliament, was overwhelmingly hostile and was further fuelled by the leaking of Cabinet minutes which revealed the political manoeuvring that had led to the reversal of the government's child benefit policy. In order to diffuse the mounting campaign to save the child benefit scheme, the government set up a working party from the TUC/Labour Party Liaison Committee. From this emerged a compromise scheme which gave no extra money to families but did at least ensure that the framework of a tax free child benefit was established and that the full scheme would be phased in by 1980.

The first consequence of the compromise scheme, which committed the Government to the phasing out of CTAs, was, ironically, a budget involving £2¼ billion in tax cuts in April 1977 which did nothing to help families with children. Instead of announcing an interim November increase in child benefits as he had been pressed to do, Denis Healey, the Chancellor, declared: 'I am proposing a substantially larger increase in the married allowance so as to provide the family man with special help during the transition to the child benefit scheme'.[9] However, the announcement in July of a child benefit rate of £2.30 in April 1978 hinted at a dawning realisation by the government of the need to transfer resources to those with children. The Minister for Social Security explained that 'the Government is putting over £300 million extra into family support next year because we recognise that the budgets of families with children have been particularly squeezed in this difficult economic period'.[10]

The final stage of the government's conversion to the cause of child benefits came in the 1978 Budget, subsequently dubbed by Denis Healey a 'family budget'. But the 'family budget' was only squeezed out of a very reluctant Chancellor after intensive pressure from MPs, trade union leaders, the Churches and the 'poverty lobby'. The Chancellor announced a further increase in child benefit of 70p for November 1978 to be followed by a £1 increase in April 1979. The latter increase was to be partially offset by the abolition of the under-11 CTA and, in a subsequent statement, it was announced that the residual CTAs for older children would also be abolished in April. The April and November 1978 and April 1979 increases together represent a net transfer of £830 million to the support of children.

One parent families

It is no longer possible to view one parent families as some kind of 'aberration', when they comprise over one in ten of all families and this proportion could well increase still further. The big increase in the number of one parent families is reflected in the growing numbers dependent on supplementary benefit. (The proportion on supplementary benefit has, however, in recent years remained fairly constant, at 44 per cent.) In 1964, 110,000 lone mothers were claiming national assistance; by 1974, the number had more than doubled to 261,000 (plus 8,000 lone fathers) and between 1974 and 1977 there was a further substantial increase to 326,000 (plus 14,000 lone fathers). Three out of five families raising children on supplementary benefit are headed by one parent; they include nearly 600,000 children. In addition, a disproportionate number of one parent families are living below the supplementary benefit level: just under one in six families below SB level are headed by a lone parent on a rough official estimate of 40,000 lone parents caring for 60,000 children in 1976.[11]

In July 1974, the Finer Committee, which had been appointed by the previous Labour Government, reported on the position of one parent families. It concluded that 'in terms of families with children ... there can be no other group of this size who are as poor as fatherless families, of whom so many lack any state benefit other than supplementary benefit or family allowance, whose financial position is so uncertain and whose hope for improvement in their situation is so remote'.[12]

Five years later, no progress has been made on any of the report's key recommendations. The guaranteed maintenance allowance proposed by Finer, as a means of lifting one parent families off supplementary benefit, was rejected on the legitimate grounds that it was means tested but the Labour Government refused to commit itself to a non-means-tested benefit for lone parents. The recommendation that the maternity grant should be made non-contributory, which would cost only £1.5 million, was ignored on the grounds that 'it could only be considered at some future time when more resources became available and even then there would be difficult questions of priorities'.[13] However, the abolition of the contribution conditions and an increase in the £25 grant (which has not been raised since 1969 and is now worth less than £9) is part of Labour Party policy and was promised in the 1979 manifesto. The idea of a special addition to the supplementary benefit rates for lone parents in recognition of their special needs was rejected and no action was taken on the proposal that the long-term rate should be paid after one, rather than two, years to all families with children. Only a number of minor cheap reforms of supplementary benefit which favour lone parents were implemented.

On the credit side, the Labour Government accepted in 1975 the recommendation that the additional personal tax allowance available to lone parents should be raised to give lone parents an equivalent tax allowance to married men. Lone parents also received special treatment under the child benefit scheme. A child interim benefit of £1.50 was paid to the first children of lone parents in 1976. Lone parents continued to receive the extra 50p for the first child when the £1 child benefit was introduced and this 50p was doubled to £1 in April 1978 and again to £2 in November 1978. The government did, however, come under attack from the National Council for One Parent Families for the fact that lone parents on supplementary benefit have not benefitted from this extra £2 because it is offset against their supplementary benefit. The most recent concession to one parent families was the agreement to implement, in April 1979, the Finer proposal that the qualifying hours for family income supplement should be reduced for lone parents. When asked to make a statement in parliament on its record on help to one parent families, the Labour Government pointed to these measures and to the fact that expenditure on benefits received by lone parents had trebled between 1974 and 1979. But by the end of its term in office there was some uncertainty as to whether the Labour Government did regard one parent families as a group requiring special help. According to *Labour's Programme 1976*, 'Labour has always favoured the principle of special help to Britain's (750,000) one parent families' yet David Ennals, the then Secretary of State for Social Services, questioned whether they should expect special help since, he said, they do not comprise a majority of poor families.

Education benefits
The Labour Government's policy on school meals prices was set out in its 1976 Public Expenditure White Paper. The intention was to reduce the subsidy of 62 per cent by about half by 1980 through a series of price increases starting with a 5p increase that year. The 5p increase was cancelled following pressure from the trade unions but, despite continued opposition, a 10p increase went through the following autumn. This was accompanied by a big rise in the income limits for free school meals. A further increase of 5p for 1978 was averted in the Chancellor's 'family budget' but only to be delayed until autumn 1979. According to the 1979 Expenditure White Paper, it was now the intention 'to maintain the subsidy at about 50 per cent of the average cost of providing a meal'. The government also announced in 1978 that local authorities could, if they wished, reintroduce free school milk for 7 to 11 year olds under an EEC subsidy scheme; two thirds of local authorities declined the invitation. Local authority policies had a harmful impact on families' living standards in the field of provision for school uniform and essential clothing. The evidence collected by CPAG and the Supplementary Benefits Commission shows that discretionary school uniform and clothing grants were a prime target for public expenditure cuts at a time when the price of clothing had soared. The government refused pleas to place these grants on a mandatory basis.

The impact of policies
The impact of the above policies can be assessed in a number of

ways. The child benefit is now worth more than the family allowance ever was but, for the great majority of families, the most important comparison is with the combined value of family allowances and CTAs. In 1976, David Ennals told the Cabinet that the overall level of child support was then worth less than in 1970–72 and the late 1960s. By 1978, the Child Poverty Action Group was pointing out that 'family support is lower than that provided by the 1945 Attlee Government'.[14] Stan Orme was able to announce that the 1978/9 child benefit increases 'will take the real value of child support for most families to a higher level than the peak reached in 1971'[15]. Laudable as this is, as Table 11.1 shows, the level of child support

Table 11.1   Combined value to standard rate taxpayer of child tax allowances, after clawback, and family allowances/child benefit for each child expressed at November 1978 prices for selective years (£)

	1 child under 11[a]	Married couple with: 2 children under 11[a]	3 children under 11[a]	4 children under 11[a]
August 1946	2.99	3.54	3.70	3.80
April 1950	3.20	3.69	3.85	3.93
April 1955	3.91	4.53	4.75	4.85
April 1960	3.10	3.66	3.94	4.10
April 1964	3.15	3.64	3.90	4.04
April 1970	2.54	2.93	3.13	3.23
April 1971	2.96	3.36	3.55	3.64
April 1972	2.78	3.16	3.34	3.43
April 1973	2.53	2.85	3.00	3.08
April 1974	2.90	3.17	3.30	3.36
April 1975	2.54	3.03	3.19	3.27
April 1976	2.66	3.07	3.21	3.28
April 1977	2.56	2.75	2.81	2.84
April 1978	3.05	3.05	3.05	3.05
April 1979[b]	3.84	3.84	3.84	3.84

[a] Information on the value of child support for children aged over 11 is not available for the years 1958–71. In 1971 and 1972 support for children aged over 11 was higher than in 1979 for some families and in 1973–76 it was higher for families with three or four children aged over 16.
[b] The April 1979 child benefit rates have been deflated to November 1978 prices to reflect an annual inflation rate of 8.5 per cent for April 1979.
Source: House of Commons, *Hansard*, 1 February 1979, cols 525–6.

in April 1979 was still less than that achieved in the mid-1950s and few would try to argue that the mid-1950s level was itself adequate. And, for families with dependent children aged over 16 or with more than two children aged 11–15, the April 1979 child benefit was still worth less than the combined value of CTAs and family allowances in 1971. Moreover, Table 11.2 shows that, as a percentage of average earnings, the value of support for the majority of children was lower in 1978/79 than it had been throughout most of the post-war period.

Table 11.2   Value of the child tax allowance and family allowance/ child benefit as a percentage of gross earnings of male manual workers[a]

| | Children under 11 years | | | Children between 11 and 16 years | | |
	One child	Two children	Four children	One child	Two children	Four children
1946/7	4.5	9.3	14.7	4.5	9.3	14.7
1950/1	3.9	9.3	16.5	3.9	9.3	16.5
1955/6	4.1	10.2	17.8	4.1	10.2	17.8
1960/1	4.1	9.6	19.8	5.2	11.0	19.8
1963/4	4.3	10.1	19.1	5.1	11.5	19.1
1964/5	4.5	9.8	19.9	5.3	11.4	19.9
1968/9	4.0	9.1	20.0	4.8	10.9	23.0
1969/70	3.7	8.5	18.6	4.5	10.1	21.8
1970/1	3.2	7.5	16.5	4.0	8.9	19.3
1971/2	3.7	8.5	18.4	4.3	9.6	20.7
1972/3	3.2	7.4	16.1	3.8	8.5	18.2
1973/4	2.8	6.3	13.7	3.3	7.3	15.7
1974/5	3.1	6.7	14.2	3.5	7.6	16.0
1975/6	2.7	6.4	13.8	3.1	7.2	15.4
1976/7	3.0	6.8	14.6	3.3	7.5	15.9
1977/8	3.0	6.4	13.3	3.3	7.0	14.5
1978/9[b]	3.7	7.5	14.9	4.0	8.0	16.0

[a]The figures take account where appropriate of the family allowance deduction (clawback) and earned income relief.
[b]Estimated.
Source: House of Commons, *Hansard*, 6 March 1979.

One of the main arguments originally put forward in favour of a child benefit scheme was that it would help those working families too poor to pay tax and thus benefit from CTAs. But, between the original conception of the scheme and its eventual implementation, the fall in the tax threshold had reduced substantially the number of families in this 'happy' position. For the small minority still below the tax threshold, the phasing in of child benefits meant a straight gain of £4 for the first child and £2.50 for each further child. Similarly, in two parent families the child benefit scheme has effected an important redistribution of resources within the family from father to mother. However, it must be remembered that the gains for families in receipt of rent and rate rebates were substantially less because of the drop in their rebates (some families actually lost money) and for families on social security benefits there was no gain at all (see below). Also, during the same period, parents of school age children had to pay an extra £1 a week for school meals during term time (taking into account the November 1979 price increase announced while Labour was still in office). Although the eligibility limits for free school meals are now much more generous, the 1977 price increase led to a drop of over half a million in the number of children eating school dinners and an increase of about 170,000 in the numbers of children eligible for free school meals but not receiving them. There is also evidence that cutbacks in school uniform and clothing grants had a damaging impact on low income families' budgets.

How far the £4 child benefit goes towards meeting the actual cost of maintaining a child is difficult to say, as there is no accurate information about what it does cost. However, Mimi Parker has attempted an estimate which, updated to allow for inflation, sets the minimum cost of maintaining a child aged under five at £7.58, and children aged 5–12, 13–15 and 16–18 at £11.80, £15.42 and £18.09 respectively.[16]

Another way of assessing the extent to which the policies of the Labour Government redistributed resources to families with children is to look at changes in the tax free income and net weekly income of different family groups. Table 11.3 shows that, while the amount of tax free income enjoyed by all groups was lower in 1978/9 than in 1973/4, childless married couples have done relatively well compared with single people and those with children. Even after taking account of the October 1978 child benefit increase, the tax threshold (which includes the value of the tax free child benefit) for a couple with four children was 17 per cent less in 1978/9 than in 1973/4; the fall for a childless married couple was only 5 per cent. If we compare the 1978/9 tax thresholds with those in the peak year of 1963/4, the picture is even less impressive. Childless married couples and single people have 6 to 7 per cent less tax free income; families with children have between 19 and 38 per cent less than in 1963/4. One of the consequences of this trend has been the increasing numbers of families caught in the 'poverty trap' (see Chapter 5).

Table 11.3   Changes in tax free income in real terms
(a) 1973/74 = 100, (b) 1963/64 = 100

Year	Single	Married	Married, one child under 11	Married, two children under 11	Married, two children under 11, one aged 11–16	Married, three children under 11, two aged 11–16
(a)						
1973/4	100	100	100	100	100	100
1974/5	89	95	96	98	100	101
1975/6	77	84	83	84	85	85
1976/7	73	83	84	86	88	89
1977/8	82	97	90	91	89	89
1978/9	79	95	87	86	84	83
(b)						
1963/4	100	100	100	100	100	100
1974/5	104	94	90	84	79	76
1975/6	91	83	78	72	67	64
1976/7	86	82	78	74	69	67
1977/8	97	96	84	77	71	67
1978/9	93	94	81	73	67	62

Source: Calculated from House of Commons *Hansard*, vol 961, 25 January 1979, cols 212–4.

Similarly, by the end of the Labour Government's term of office, the child benefit scheme had not yet made a significant impact on the net weekly income (defined as take-home pay plus family allowance/child benefit) of those with children relative to those without. Table 11.4 shows that the ratio between the net weekly incomes of couples with children and of those without was nearly the same in 1978/9 as it was when the Labour Government came to power. There is no consistent pattern during the intervening years; for most families the ratio between those with and without children remained pretty stable but for those with four children, particularly those on half average earnings, there was a short lived improvement just before the child benefit scheme was introduced.

Table 11.4   Real weekly net incomes of couples with children relative to childless couples 1973/4 to 1978/9. (100 = net income of a childless couple)

Half average earnings			2/3 average earnings			Average earnings		
One child under	Two children under	Four children, two under 11, two	One child under	Two children under	Four children, two under 11, two	One child under	Two children under	Four children, two under 11, two
11	11	11–16	11	11	11–16	11	11	11–16
1973/4	106	114	128	105	111	125	103	108	118
1974/5	107	115	129	105	112	127	104	109	119
1975/6	106	115	134	105	112	127	104	108	119
1976/7	106	116	135	105	112	128	104	109	120
1977/8	107	114	129	105	111	125	104	108	118
1978/9	107	115	130	106	112	125	105	109	119

Source: calculated from House of Commons, *Hansard*, 26 January 1979 and 5 March 1979 (as corrected in a letter from Robert Sheldon to Jo Richardson MP).

Table 11.5, which expresses the difference between the net weekly incomes of the different family groups in cash terms, provides some measure of the very limited horizontal redistribution of resources

Table 11.5   Cash differences between the net income of couples with children and childless couples in 1978/9 (£)

Half average earnings			2/3 average earnings			Average earnings		
One child under	Two children under	Four children, two under 11, two	One child under	Two children under	Four children, two under 11, two	One child under	Two children under	Four children, two under 11, two
11	11	11–16	11	11	11–16	11	11	11–16
3.00	5.90	11.90	3.00	6.00	12.40	3.20	6.50	13.50

Source: as for Table 11.3.

that has been achieved so far particularly for those with below average earnings. For example, in 1978/9 a couple with two children on below average wages had only about £6 more a week than a childless couple earning the same wage.

An earlier chapter of this book has shown how poverty increased particularly amongst people of working age. It is too early to assess the extent to which the introduction of the child benefit scheme has reversed this recent dramatic increase in the numbers of poor families. The estimates for families suggest that the number living below the supplementary benefit level more than doubled from 110,000 to 230,000 between 1974 and 1976 (some of the figures being subject to considerable sampling error). The number of children affected rose from 260,000 to half a million. As a proportion of all people living below the poverty line, those living in families with children rose from a third to two-fifths. The number of people living in families with children at incomes less than 40 per cent above supplementary benefit level increased by 84 per cent to 6,920,000 and in 1976 represented 46.5 per cent of all people living in or on the margins of poverty compared with 36 per cent two years earlier. The biggest increase was among working families which partly reflected the growing tax burden on low income families and the failure to raise family allowances in line with increases in social security benefits. The growing number of lone parents and of families affected by unemployment has also contributed to the increase in family poverty. The child benefit scheme was a promising start but it did not make up for this general increase in economic insecurity.

Plans for the future
The central plank for future policy for families must continue to be the child benefit scheme. It is the aim of the Labour Party to raise child benefits at least to the level of child support provided for the unemployed and short term sick. 'Once this rate has been established, the government must be required by law to increase it regularly in line with other benefits.'[17] This is crucial if child benefits are not to repeat the history of family allowances. But even then the level of family support would be lower than that provided in many other EEC countries. The eventual goal should be to raise child benefits to the level provided for those on long term social security benefits. The possibility of relating the benefits to age should also be examined together with consideration of the Meade Committee's

proposal for a home responsibility benefit for all (including those in paid employment) with the care of children or other dependants.

Although an adequate child benefit scheme is of crucial importance, it does not of itself comprise a 'family policy'. For instance, it does nothing to help the growing number of families forced to depend on supplementary benefit. The DHSS's own evidence suggests that 'the supplementary benefits scheme provides, *particularly for families with children*, incomes that are barely adequate to meet their needs at a level that is consistent with normal participation in the life of the relatively wealthy society in which they live' (emphasis added).[18] The children's scale rates have fallen in value relative to the adult's and need to be increased substantially. Similarly, lone parents on supplementary benefit gained nothing from the extra tax allowance and child benefit that helped employed lone parents. The most constructive means of help would be a non-means tested benefit which would lift most lone parents off supplementary benefit. Single parents would also be helped by the abolition of the contribution conditions for the maternity grant and the restoration of its real value. As a growing number of people are likely to be spending some part of their lives in a one parent family, any 'family policy' worthy of the name must take account of the special needs of these families.

James Callaghan admitted that the Labour Government's family policy had 'not been totally co-ordinated'.[19] What is needed now is not simply better co-ordination but a coherent positive strategy. We could learn much from the example of Sweden where family policy has aimed to provide a framework in which both parents can combine paid employment with their family responsibilities. Such an approach in Britain would require a fundamental shift in attitude towards the role of married women for, as David Ennals has pointed out, 'we have been slow in coming to terms with the greatest social change of the past 40 years – the increase in the proportion of married women at work'.[20] A Labour Government's future plans for developing a family policy should include a massive expansion of good child care facilities (including those for school age children), improved maternity and paternity provisions and more flexible employment policies as well as further improvements in financial support for those raising children.

PART VI

Equality and the Social Services

12   Health

by Nick Bosanquet

The 1974–79 Labour Governments made an attempt at reducing inequalities in the NHS which was without precedent in its scope and ambition. There was the RAWP (Resource Allocation Working Party) scheme which was aimed at reducing inequalities in spending between regions.[1] There was also a statement on priorities which set out an intention of increased relative spending on the services for the elderly, the mentally ill, mentally handicapped and children as well as more spending on community and primary care.[2] Other new initiatives were directed towards areas with high rates of perinatal and infant mortality – an important aspect of class inequality – and towards increased prevention. This aspired to reduce the inequality inherent in being ill at all.

All these policies, especially RAWP, attracted a volume of criticism. There was much protest both from those who felt a particular policy went much too far and those who felt that it did not go far enough. We need to look both at whether the aims were the right ones in the first place and at how far they were achieved. On its own terms the RAWP programme achieved some success. The programme really did show a beginning of some equalisation with a promise of much more to come. The attempt to shift priorities towards neglected groups met with more mixed success. The record in primary care was rather more satisfactory.

There was some continued development of services for the elderly, the mentally handicapped and children. The main failure was with services for the mentally ill. However, the successes such as they were have to be seen against a slow growth of expenditure. The growth of spending in real terms, even on most of these services, was slower than it had been over the previous five or ten years. This was the central and over-riding development of the government's period in office before which the attempts at redistribution faded into insignificance. The government's special policies did give a measure of protection to the neglected services but gave no new impetus. The attempts to deal with class inequalities were tentative and unfinished. In the case of prevention, the results were generally disappointing, the greatest disappointment falling in the sphere of the Ministry of Transport rather than the DHSS. This was the failure to reduce casualties on the road by legislating on the compulsory wearing of seat belts and by tightening up the laws on drink and driving.

The effects of these policies have to be assessed at a time when the health service was being shaken by a great number of other changes, including reorganisation, conflict in industrial relations and the slow overall growth in spending. Apart from these developments there were also changes in mood which can affect judgement. Thus, for much of the period, the health service was thought to be in a 'bad way'. There were also swings of mood about the personalities of health ministers.

At the end there were some unresolved tensions between these various policies. The first tension was between RAWP and any policy for dealing with inequalities between client groups and between classes. The main effect of RAWP seemed to have been on the acute services in the traditionally deprived regions. It made for difficulty in improving neglected services in other regions. But the most important tension was between the government's statement of priorities, between client groups and yet another important commitment which was to the expansion of medical education. Thus while RAWP was trying to take money away from central London the University Grants Committee was being asked to expand the number of medical students in London teaching hospitals. The longer term dilemma was even greater. Could a health service on the new lines be built with doctors trained in the traditional way? There were several official points made for the defence. The first was that medical education was changing anyway, though for many the changes seemed cosmetic. The other argument was that the extra doctors were needed to replace immigrant doctors. But similar effects could have been achieved by taking further steps to increase the partici- pation rate of women doctors or by changing hospital career structures, even assuming the most unlikely forecasts about the disappearance of immigrant doctors were accurate. The debate on priorities still remained a dialogue of the deaf between government and doctors.

Over the years of the NHS and before, there have been swings in intensity of interest in the issue of equality. Thus early interest was great. One of the main reasons for setting up a National Health Service was so that the state could ensure that 'an equally good service is available everywhere'. With a locally controlled system 'there will tend to be a better service in the richer areas, a worse service in the poorer'.[3] 'The inequalities which existed under the old system were gross. In the early years simple forms of rationing in GP and in consultant posts did achieve a steady equalization'.[4] For a long period in the 1950s and 1960s interest in the subject of equality was low and centred instead on the costs of the service and then on the hospital building programme. The first revival of interest in equality arose from worry about the care of the mentally ill in the early 1960s – a concern which was later extended to the elderly and to the mentally handicapped. It was only in the Crossman era that the question of regional inequality again came to life.

As well as changes in intensity of interest, there have been changes in the scope and kind of inequalities which have attracted most attention. Thus in the later 1930s and early 1940s it was the inequalities between classes on which interest focused. In the late 1970s, official anxiety seemed to be about inequalities between regions.

The main aspects of inequality with which we could potentially be concerned are: inequalities between regions; inequalities between areas within regions; inequalities between class groups; inequalities between client groups; inequalities in treatment between private care and care within the NHS; inequalities in the enjoyment of good health. Any consideration of these inequalities suggests a need for evidence that more spending on health care can in fact contribute to better health.

The RAWP programme supplied the main working definition of equality in this time. The aim is 'equal opportunity for access to health care for people at equal risk'.[1] This definition summons up issues ranging from measurement of risk or need on to policies for improving access, as well as the older question of the volume of spending on services. Earlier definitions were in terms of expenditure per head and concentrated on the supply side.

Changes in philosophy

The period 1974–79 was one in which attitudes to the health service were changing rapidly. At the broadest level, public expectations of the NHS were still great with the usual publicity for dramatic technological advances in medicine but a substantial minority were beginning to look at the health service in rather a different light. There was some greater realisation that 'health' and the NHS were not synonomous and that the demand for health care was without practical limit. Doubts which had been the prerogative of the few in departments of social medicine came to be more widely shared.

The government's policies developed from some of the older issues such as the division of funds between regions and between client groups, but they also touched on some newer (or revived) ones such as the right balance between preventive and curative medicine. The government's policies were also worked out against a background of waning faith in general market solutions in the field of health care. The bold calls for a larger private sector or for payment through insurance which had been such a feature of documents such as the Porritt Report in 1962[5] or the BMA Report in 1970[6] were now rarely heard. However, while there were fewer advocates of a private sector as a general replacement for the NHS, there were increasingly strong voices urging that the private sector could in specific ways supplement the NHS. This carried the possibility that in certain forms of treatment, two standards of services might become even more strongly established.

The Record 1964–74

In general this was a period of high activity for the NHS with rapid increases in revenue spending, a capital programme on an entirely new scale and new commitments in care. Revenue spending grew on average by 4 per cent a year in real terms and many new hospitals were opened. New commitments were made towards community care for the mentally ill and the mentally handicapped and towards better services for the elderly. It was a period of optimism about the performance of the service and of relative certainty in its role. The 1970 Green Paper wrote of how there had been 'striking improvements in standards of health during the 21 years since the National Health Service was established. ... Not all this progress is due to the establishment of the NHS but much of it must be due to the virtual removal of financial and geographical barriers to the use of health services and to the increase in resources which have been devoted to the health service'.[7] Also in this period the NHS waited for re-organisation, with three successive plans put before it. Finally, it was a period of growing anger in pay bargaining and growing strength in union membership within the NHS.

The incoming Labour Government in 1974 had a very mixed legacy. There was a major immediate crisis about pay which was resolved in the short term although not in the long. There were commitments to client groups and on regional equality which had been sonorously made but only partly followed through. There was the possibility of cuts in public spending following on the cuts in the capital programme which had already been made in December 1973. Finally, it inherited the results of the hospital building programme. A large capital programme had been undertaken but it was far from clear that adequate revenue allowance had been made to support this level of capital spending.

Policies and their impact

The incoming government was then faced with crises. In most cases these were soon resolved but extreme difficulties over the new consultant contract continued for two years. Barbara Castle and David Owen turned with impressive speed both to a restatement of the aim of equality and to devising new instruments for bringing it about. The two central pillars were RAWP and the restatement of priorities. The new planning system was to be used and was to be aided by the important innovation of joint funding. But a number of other measures were indirectly related to the aim of equality. Thus *Democracy in the Health Service* announced an increase in the proportion of Community Health Council (CHC) and local authority representatives on Area Health Authorities (AHAs).[8] It was hoped that such a change would be to the advantage of neglected groups. A paper on community hospitals set out to provide an alternative in hospital development which could direct resources and interest towards long stay patients. New policies on pay beds aimed at ending inequalities between NHS and private patients within the service. The assessment here concentrates mainly on RAWP, on the drive to change priorities between client groups and on the attempt to reduce the burden of sickness through prevention.

The impact of these policies has to be seen against other changes which were unconnected but which undercut them. The proportion of GDP accounted for by NHS spending rose over the period as a whole from 1973 to 1979, but this change reflected first the large size of public sector pay settlements in 1974 and then the slow growth of GDP after that. It did not reflect any planned decision to raise the share of national resources going to the NHS. In fact the planned decision when it came was to reduce the NHS share in GDP. The service was immediately affected by a slowing down of the growth rate of spending which came about abruptly in 1976. From 1975/76 to 1978/79 revenue spending rose in comparison with the previous ten years. Capital spending was reduced by one-third from about £636 million at 1978 prices in 1973/74 to £450 million in 1978/79. In its 1979 white paper on public spending, the government's plan for the future was to raise spending on the NHS by less than 2 per cent per annum – below the best estimate for the expected growth rate of GDP.[9] This was even below the planned rate of growth in defence spending.

The cuts in capital spending were partly made to protect the growth rate of revenue spending. This was thought to be the line of least resistance in view of the strength of political pressures towards more revenue spending, although strangely enough when AHAs were given the choice of greater *virement* between capital and revenue spending, they chose mainly to vire money towards capital spending.[10] Some efforts were made to soften the blow on the capital side by distributing spending on a fairer basis between regions and by using it more effectively through building hospitals in phases starting with a nucleus of a more common design. However the fall in capital spending combined with the slow growth in revenue was an unpromising context in which to raise the issue of equality – although one in which it become even more urgent.

Lower capital spending meant that more money would have to be spent in patching up old buildings. As the Regional Plan for one of the deprived regions, the West Midlands, made clear, even with their relatively favourable allocation the proportion of buildings over 60 years old would be higher in the year 2000 than today.[11] The Labour Party's evidence to the Royal Commission spelt out how changes in acute hospitals together with 'a complete rethinking of the functions of primary care and the development of new patterns of service for the mentally ill, handicapped and elderly (would) require wholesale replacement and resiting of buildings'.[12] There would now be little chance of any such developments. It was also pointed out in the evidence that 'while half the nation's schools and nearly half the housing has been renewed since the war, only about a quarter of the acute hospital plant has been modernised or renewed in the same period'. While the instinct of 'putting people before buildings' may have been the right one in a crisis, in the long run it would make little sense to employ more and more staff working in poor conditions, in out-of-date buildings.

The impact of RAWP

From Bevan onwards, ministers had aspired to equalise spending between regions. The RAWP scheme had important differences from the main actual attempt to do this under Richard Crossman and Sir Keith Joseph. It related allocations to measures of need. The proposals were argued out at length in a published document. They were worked out by a group made up of staff from within the NHS as well as of civil servants. The formula and methods used could be applied to budgets at other levels of the NHS and not just to the initial division of money between regions. The RAWP scheme applied to teaching hospitals and to capital works. Finally, it was accompanied by a timetable.

The RAWP report sets certain 'target' allocations related to each region's 'need'. Need is measured mainly in terms of demographic data and of mortality experience. A 'fair' allocation is then measured in terms mainly of the amount of spending which would follow from the regions mortality experience if each region were spending the UK average for in patient treatments. Adjustments are made for the extra costs of medical teaching, for the cost of London weighting and for patients crossing over regional boundaries. The target allocations show that the London regions are much above their targets while most other regions are below.

This exercise can be judged on two levels. First it can be seen whether the RAWP plan achieved its intentions. Certainly the redistribution *was* much more significant than that under the Crossman formula. The formula used under that scheme had a number of weaknesses. It excluded the teaching hospitals and it included in its weighting the number of beds in the area thus favouring those which were better off to start with. However the evidence suggested that there was some redistribution before 1973 in spite of these defects. RAWP has since sharpened this redistribution both in capital and in revenue terms (Tables 12.1 and 12.2). The general restriction in spending, however, meant that in absolute terms the growth rate of real spending even in the main regions to gain such as Trent and East Anglia were *below* what they had been over the previous five years.

Thus real revenue spending on the hospital services grew by 6–7 per cent a year in East Anglia and Sheffield from 1969/70 to 1973/74.

Table 12.1   Revenue spending at constant 1978 survey prices by region
(£ million)

	Hospital services provided by regional hospital boards			Hospital, community and family practitioner services			
	1969/70[a]	1973/74[a]	Growth rate p.a.		1975/76	1978/79	Growth rate p.a.
Newcastle	159	208	6.9	Northern	351	372	1.9
Leeds	177	214	4.9	Yorkshire	394	420	2.1
Sheffield	199	254	6.3	Trent	452	496	3.1
East Anglia	76	99	6.8	East Anglia	190	207	2.9
NW Met	212	257	4.9	NW Thames	491	494	0.2
NE Met	195	229	4.1	NE Thames	496	503	0.4
SE Met	191	232	5.0	SE Thames	484	502	1.2
SW Met	207	238	3.5	SW Thames	383	391	0.6
Wessex	107	133	5.6	Wessex	282	305	2.6
Oxford	91	114	5.8	Oxford	236	245	1.2
South Western	174	212	5.1	South Western	350	372	2.0
Birmingham	241	301	5.7	West Midlands	544	581	2.2
Liverpool	130	142	2.2	Mersey	300	312	1.3
Manchester	233	295	6.1	North Western	463	505	2.9
Total	2392	2928	5.2	Total	5416	5705	1.7

[a] 1969/70 and 1973/74 figures relate only to services provided by RHBs. They therefore understate total spending particularly in Met regions which includes spending by boards of governors. 1974/75 figures are not available.
Source: *Hansard*, Written Answer, 24 May 1979.

Table 12.2 Capital expenditure at constant 1978 survey prices
(£ million)

| | 1969/70 | | 1973/74 | | 1977/78 | | 1978/79 | |
	£m	% of total	£m	% of total	£m	% of total	£m	% of total
Northern	16.7	4.8	30.8	6.7	23.7	7.3	23.1	6.9
Yorkshire	17.0	4.9	28.9	6.3	22.0	6.8	26.3	7.9
Trent	28.8	8.4	51.1	11.1	51.1	15.8	40.8	12.3
East Anglia	20.1	5.8	22.6	4.9	13.6	4.2	17.9	5.4
NW Thames	40.9	11.9	44.0	9.5	17.6	5.4	20.4	6.1
NE Thames	27.1	7.9	40.6	8.8	19.8	6.1	25.7	7.7
SE Thames	34.4	10.0	38.8	8.4	17.9	5.5	19.6	5.9
SW Thames	19.8	5.7	24.4	5.3	22.7	7.0	16.7	5.0
Wessex	13.5	3.9	22.3	4.8	19.7	6.1	18.7	5.6
Oxford	18.4	5.3	29.2	6.3	15.3	4.7	13.2	4.0
South Western	28.1	8.2	32.8	7.1	18.4	5.7	20.6	6.2
West Midlands	26.0	7.6	39.2	8.5	23.2	7.2	28.1	8.4
Mersey	20.5	6.0	23.5	5.1	24.8	7.7	26.4	7.9
North Western	32.6	9.5	32.6	7.1	33.4	10.3	34.9	10.9
Total	343.9	100	460.8	100	323.2	100	332.4	100

[a] estimated
Source: DHSS, letter to author.

From 1975/76 to 1978/79 the growth was only 3 per cent.

RAWP gave some measure of protection from what would have been a disaster. The shift in capital spending has been rather more impressive. Thus Trent has a higher capital programme now than in 1969/70 in real terms (see Table 12.2). In the North West, East Anglia and the West Midlands spending levels have been maintained.

RAWP was implemented through permitting a much higher growth of spending in some regions than in others, varying from about ½ per cent per annum in real terms to 3 per cent. If all regions had increased spending at the same rate, Trent would have had £20 million less than it had in 1978/79 and the North West £18 million less. RAWP has meant a great deal for some deprived areas within these regions. Thus in Wigan, the most deprived area within one of the most deprived regions, RAWP has made it possible to renovate a building for a nurse training school and to upgrade an accident and emergency department.[13] On the staffing side more district nurses and health visitors could be recruited and employed and the psychiatric community nursing service expanded. RAWP also held out the possibility of an earlier start on a new maternity unit and on a new district general hospital.

RAWP was more commonly judged however from quite another point of view by those who argued that the exercise was misconceived. There were some fundamentalists who argued that the exercise was a completely false one. Some argued for an organic view of a health service as a kind of body with 'centres of excellence' as the heart. Other implied that the extra health spending in central London was just a bare minimum of compensation for its great social problems.

The second and larger band of critics were those who might in principle have been willing to accept some equalisation but argued that the data were much too bad for it to be feasible now. The most common contention was that RAWP did not use data on morbidity. This would have been highly desirable even if difficult. The use of such figures would certainly have made some difference, even though there is a clear correlation between mortality and morbidity. Thus Yorkshire and Humberside would have had a greater 'need' using morbidity figures as they had a good deal of chronic illness.[14] But it is highly unlikely that full use of morbidity figures would have resulted in an outcome very different from the RAWP exercise. More accurate data would have altered the degree of redistribution but not its general direction. In any case, the redistribution was to take place over ten years and there was surely scope for refinement in the method well before the last pound had been transferred.

The argument about morbidity raged but had little effect on policy. It was anxieties of a different kind which led to some slowing down of the pace of RAWP in 1979/80. It had always been well known that some of the greatest inequalities in spending were within regions and not between them. The original RAWP plan had nothing to offer to low spending areas within high spending regions apart from the exhortations to regions to use the principles of RAWP in distributing money between areas. By 1979 it was clear that the two metropolitan regions most concerned were planning only a very slow redistribution between Inner London and areas such as Essex and Kent. In reality the metropolitan regions were hardly applying RAWP at all. These regions were then given extra revenue spending of 1 per cent partly to make it easier for them to increase spending in districts such as Medway which was still using Oliver Twist's workhouse as one of its hospitals. Anxieties too about class inequalities also led to some weakening on the aim of saving money on maternity services in face of a lower birth rate. Thus areas were to be allowed to maintain spending in order to reduce perinatal and infant mortality. Finally the problems of adjustment in some central London districts with 'inner city' characteristics led to extra funds being allocated for their community services. In the shadow of the teaching hospitals, community services were often very weak, as was argued both in relation to King's College Hospital and the London Hospital. One effect of RAWP for London was to raise the share of the district's spending going to the teaching hospital while other hospitals of a community hospital character were closed.[15] There was a strong case for a much more sympathetic initiative to deal with the low standards of GP service, high infant mortality among immigrants and single parents and the special problems of elderly people living alone – which marked some inner city districts. Progress here however could have been made without discarding RAWP as a whole and by steps other than raising block allocations to teaching hospital districts.

On balance, RAWP seems the 'least worst' of the options which were open to the government. Its most serious weakness was that it put the righting of inequalities in the acute services well in front of action against inequalities between client groups and between classes. The drive towards equality was unbalanced. There was very little explicit attempt to deal with inequalities in access arising from class. The use of SMRs (reflecting class differences in mortality) did in theory take some account of class in allocating expenditure, but serious problems of standards in care and access remained in all regions – both those which lost and those which gained. Nor did RAWP reconcile tensions between the drive to improve the average level of service in some regions and the aspiration of improving neglected services in all regions. For example, the aim of redistributing money from the Thames regions to the Trent Region may cut across the aim of improving the geriatric services in the Thames Regions (which may be as bad as those in Trent). Spending per head on services for the elderly in the Trent region in 1975/76 was actually higher than spending per head on these services in three out of the four Thames Regions.[16] AHAs in all regions were not able or willing to cut down spending on acute services, and some neglected services suffered in the regions which 'lost'. One of the research teams working for the Royal Commission on the NHS noted how the first effect of RAWP had mainly been to improve acute services.[17]

Table 12.3   *Current expenditure by programme on health and personal social services, England (£ million at 1978 prices)*

	1975–76		1977–78		Growth rate % 1975/76 to 1977/78	Growth rates p.a.[a] 1970/71 to 1973/74
	£m	% of total	£m	% of total		
Primary care	1202.9	20.1	1258.9	20.3	2.3	1.7
General and acute hospital and maternity services	2319.5	38.7	2399.1	38.6	1.7	3.7
Services for the elderly and physically handicapped	789.3	13.2	820.6	13.2	2.0	9.0
Services for the mentally handicapped	250.6	4.2	263.0	4.2	2.4	8.0
Services for the mentally ill	455.7	7.6	464.7	7.5	1.0	3.6
Services mainly for children	329.7	5.5	351.8	5.7	3.3	0.5
Other services	641.5	10.7	655.2	10.5	1.0	—
Total	5989.2	100	6213.1	100	1.8	4.3

[a] These are not directly comparable because of changes in accounting practices. Figures cover capital and current spending. Figures for 1974/75 are not available on a comparable basis.
Source: DHSS.

The government's statements on priorities backed by 'joint funding' were the main links between the regional aims and those for client groups. The aim was to redistribute funds towards the care of the mentally ill, the mentally handicapped, children's services and the elderly and also away from hospitals towards community care. The record here was mixed, with redistribution to primary care showing the most success. In the first major priorities document, the government set out its aspirations both in terms of aggregate shares in spending and in terms of detailed policies. The picture in terms of relative shares in health and social service spending is given in Table 12.3. The shares of spending on the mentally handicapped and the elderly were maintained, while that for the mentally ill declined, from 7.6 to 7.5 per cent. Real spending on the elderly and the mentally handicapped rose faster than spending overall. But spending on services for the elderly has to be seen against a background of growth in need. In terms of spending per potential client, there was probably a *fall* in real spending. For the mentally ill spending in real terms hardly rose at all. By 1977/78, £10.1 million was being spent in the whole of England on community care of the mentally ill. Such rates of growth of spending have to be set against a background of improvement in staff conditions and commitments on the maintenance of buildings which often represent first claims on real spending, and which were not adequately adjusted for in arriving at 'real' spending.

In general the directions of change were those intended, with the share of the hospital service declining for the first time for many years. However the slow overall growth in spending meant that there was a net loss on the past record.

The detailed policies set out in the document also met with mixed success. The long running struggles to increase the number of geriatricians, to get them assessment beds in District General Hospitals and to improve the quality of long stay care for the elderly continued but there was no change in tempo in the years after the statement on priorities. In fact the DHSS's main planning circular for 1979 spoke ominously of the pressures being exerted by the increasing numbers of very elderly patients on all acute hospital services.[18] There was some success in directing more medical research towards the health problems of the elderly from the position in which virtually nothing was being done on such major problems as dementia or incontinence. The old problems of medical attitudes to geriatrics continued. The community hospital failed to catch on as a more successful local form of long stay care for the elderly. Perhaps the most glaring failure was in community care and long stay places outside psychiatric hospitals for the elderly mentally infirm. Here the decline in number of places in psychiatric hospitals continued – but without an alternative. The main role of joint funding was to turn what would have been a disaster into a serious set-back.

The government issued a long and complex plan for *Better Services for the Mentally Ill*.[19] This showed yet again just how behind we are in terms both of day places and residential places in the community. Some progress was made even within the grim record of low spending. The biggest success was in the increasing number of community psychiatric nurses – from a handful in 1974 to 1,500 in 1978. But, in general, community care for the mentally ill remained an illusion in most parts of the country.

The issues involved in the care of the mentally handicapped showed a definite change in scope over the period. There was some progress in providing places in the community in line with targets set in *Better Services for the Mentally Handicapped*.[20] The numbers of residential places rose from 6,473 in 1974 to 9,751 in 1977. The numbers of day care places rose from 31,604 to 38,682 over the same period. Some success was registered in improving community care especially for mentally handicapped children. Ironically, however, there was growing scepticism about the direction of change even at a time when aims as defined in the usual 'numbers game' were being met. Some wanted to see much more emphasis on family support in the community, involving a network of services such as day places and respite care. Others felt that the aim of reducing hospital places was unrealistic. Certainly there was an odd slowness of reduction in hospital beds at a time when residential places in the community were increasing. Towards the end of the period there were signs of breakdown in any sense of direction – the endless exhortation put out by the National Development Group; a vicious argument about the Wessex experiments in community care; and finally a great controversy about the future of training for staff and the recommendations of the Jay Report. In spite of some good progress locally, there were worrying signs that the whole movement to community care might falter. There were certainly few signs that the barriers in the way of care of the severely handicapped had been overcome. Most of the residents in the new hostels were quite lightly handicapped and had come from the community. The government's policies were adequate in terms of the standards set in the past but they had little to offer in face of these new difficulties.

There was greater success with the family doctor service reflecting the consistent progress since the Family Doctor Charter in the mid 1960s and helped by the expansion in medical education since then.

Average list size fell from 2,478 in 1970 to 2,384 in 1974; it fell again to 2.331 in 1977. There were above average reductions of list sizes in all the eleven authorities with the largest lists in 1974. The share of spending going to primary care rose and the numbers of doctors practising in health centres rose considerably. General practice became more popular with medical graduates. By 1976, 30 per cent of graduates were putting it as their first choice. For GPs, vocational training was compulsory at long last. There was also progress with the community services. Spending on district nursing rose by 9.4 per cent and for health visiting by 6 per cent from 1975/76 to 1977/78, a period over which spending grew by 3.7 per cent. There was a worry, however, about a fall in the numbers of nurses starting community training in 1977/78.

Prevention

There is a basic inequality between the state of illness or injury and the state of health. Prevention aims to reduce this inequality. The government's aim was that 'in future much greater emphasis should be given to prevention'.[21] This aim had to be translated into specific policies for four main hazards: smoking, alcoholism, road accidents and handicap among children.

The government certainly made some brave statements as well as giving more money to the Health Education Council. However once prevention ceased to be a generality and had to be translated into policies the scope for initiative seem to have been drastically reduced. Commercial vested interests, considerations of fiscal equity, anxieties about public opinion, all helped to produce a generally disappointing return to effort.

Death and disease caused by smoking are now a major cause of death and one with a growing class bias. Smoking probably accounts for 50,000 deaths a year as well as a great deal of suffering from bronchitis, heart disease and emphysema. As a result of reductions in smoking among social classes I and II, these effects are increasingly concentrated among the less well off. The government had to accept inevitably that reductions in smoking would be a gradual process, because of existing addiction. The aim was one of persuasion in co-operation with the industry, with some possible use of the tax effect held in reserve. The main success was in securing that higher tar brands were not advertised and the highest taken off the market. Other steps taken included (a) encouraging general reduction in the tar and nicotine content of cigarettes; (b) restricting advertising in medium and content; (c) doubling the tax on cigarettes in money terms between 1974 and 1977 although the increase in real terms was substantially less; (d) the health warning on packets; (e) encouraging extension of non-smoking areas in public places; and (f) attempting to get more compliance with the law banning sales to minors. Other more drastic measures such as a major increase in the relative price of cigarettes had to be ruled out because of their impact on low incomes and because of the low price elasticity of demand for cigarettes.

There is little hard evidence on the effectiveness of these policies. The trend towards reduced smoking by some social groups was well established and big general declines (though mainly temporary) seemed to be related to the Royal College of Physicians Reports in 1962 and 1975. It was argued that the government should have somewhat strengthened its policies, even though at the cost of losing co-operation with the tobacco industry. Thus it could have banned all advertising (as has been done in Norway), introduced a much stronger message on packets and paid for a big publicity campaign against smoking. A minority government might not have had options – but they would have to be faced by any majority Labour Government.

Public opinion on alcoholism is even less well formed than about smoking, and the social difficulties in the way of using tax rates as a disincentive are almost as great. The government's main approach was to encourage the treatment of alcoholism by the NHS. It seemed doubtful whether this was very effective in view of known relationships by which excessive drinking grows with statistical inevitability as average consumption rises with income.[22] The government never really got alcoholism into focus as a problem in social prevention. This led to a serious neglect of the problem of drinking and driving.

Every year 7,000 people are killed on the roads and 85,000 injured. The casualty rate is particularly high among children and young people and among pedestrians. On present probabilities one out of every 50 school-leavers will be killed or maimed for life on the roads within ten years. There were 51,000 children injured on the roads in 1976. At least in the case of smoking there were serious problems about individual freedom and social equity in the way of further action. In the case of road safety, it is not only the rights of drivers that need respect but those of their passengers, of pedestrians and of other road users. Evidence showed that a sharply rising proportion of drivers killed in accidents (which must often have involved others) had excessive amounts of alcohol in their blood. Yet the government did nothing to tighten up the very lax laws on drinking and driving, even to the extent recommended by the Blennerhassett Report in 1976.[23] There was a similar failure to legislate successfully on the wearing of seat belts, in face of reliable evidence from Australia and elsewhere that such a move might reduce fatalities and serious injuries on the roads by 10–15 per cent. Work by the Transport and Road Research Laboratory suggested that if every driver and front seat passenger wore belts 12,000 fewer people would be disfigured, injured or killed each year.[24] A Bill to make seat belt wearing compulsory fell when parliament was dissolved. Many of the costs of these failures were borne by pedestrians and by 'innocent' drivers. Official responsibility must fall to the government as a whole rather than just to the DHSS.

Lastly there was the sad tale of immunisation. It is well known that serious illness in early childhood can cause handicap and delay development. Nothing has done more for child health than immunisation from poliomyelitis, diphtheria, whooping cough and measles. Take-up dropped because of a sudden surge of worry about vaccine damage. The effect was to increase the number of children who contracted diseases such as polio and whooping cough. Undoubtedly there were far more cases of long term disablement arising from the diseases than had ever been caused by vaccine damage but these did not get the same degree of attention from the media. The DHSS decided not to try to stem the initial tide of panic by showing that the costs arising from vaccinating fewer would be much greater than the costs of carrying on with the vaccination programme. It was felt that such a campaign would have been counter-productive. When it did try to reverse the tide through publicity, it was very late. It is likely to prove very difficult to restore coverage. This episode also blighted the attempt to reduce handicaps through immunising girls of school age against German measles.

The pattern of class inequality in standards of health varies between age groups. People in social class V have much higher levels of mortality and morbidity from infancy throughout life. Men in social classes III and IV have above average life chances until they are 45 and have a much worse experience between 45 and 65. It would appear that some social class differences in health standards have been worsening over time, although the halving of numbers in social class V makes such comparisons difficult over long periods. Thus the 'problem' of class inequality in health can be summed up in terms of very high rates of infant and child mortality and on through life among a minority of social class V households, plus poor life chances after 45 for a very much larger number of manual workers drawn from social classes III and IV as well as from class V. There is a social bias in sickness; there is also one in use of the health service. The better off have less sickness and also tend to make more use of the NHS.

The government published some eloquent statistics about early mortality among middle aged men. They showed that for every 100 men in England and Wales who reached the age of 45, only 73 would draw their pension compared with 81 out of 100 who would survive in Sweden.[25] However, the difficult question of how to improve access to health care for this group was never really raised even assuming that such care could help. There could have been, for example, experiments in late opening of GP surgeries. The problem was an important one not only for its direct effect but for its indirect results in terms of widowhood. High local rates of perinatal and infant mortality were the one issue in class inequality which did receive attention. Thus in December 1978 the government called for reports from the 16 AHAs with the highest such rates. This was in a context of continued reduction in the general rate. Infant mortality was particularly high among immigrant families. Various steps might have helped, ranging from better antenatal care to larger numbers of special care baby units and closure of GP maternity beds. It remained to be seen whether the government's initiative would have any great impact without specific backing in money or special assistance with medical staffing.

Private medicine

The government also tried to reduce the inequalities involved in private care. The main strategy was to phase out private beds from the NHS but with little change in the ability of NHS consultants to undertake private practice. In fact the new contractual arrangements made it if anything easier for them to do so. The 1976 Health Services Act represented a compromise between the views of the unions and those of the consultants. It provided for a gradual phasing out of pay beds from the NHS and for the licensing of large new private hospitals. By the government's fall, only about 1,000 of the least used pay beds had been phased out and the powers of control over private developments were proving to be ineffective. There were also worrying signs of a growth in the income and membership of the major provident associations. Given the difficulty of controlling private medicine outside the NHS which would face even a very determined Labour Government, it may well turn out to have been a mistake to have disturbed an established compromise which had bipartisan support. The revulsion against pay beds within the NHS may have been understandable, but the old compromise did set limits to the growth of private practice both directly inside the NHS and indirectly through lack of incentive outside the NHS.

Health service workers

The government was also committed to action on another type of inequality: pay between workers in the NHS and elsewhere. It inherited a situation in which pay had fallen well behind. It was able to repair some of the damage through large increases in pay in 1974 but it did not put in hand the changes in methods and institutions which would have made sure that the problem did not recur. By the end of 1978, the government was faced with exactly the same situation of worsening relative pay, particularly for ancillary workers and for nurses, as it faced in 1974. It had not managed to reform the process of pay bargaining so that it produced sensible results either in terms of differentials within the NHS (as was clear from the works supervisors dispute of 1978) or in terms of relativities between pay in the NHS and that outside. The setting up at the twelfth hour of the Standing Commission on Pay Comparability only confirmed the depth of the failure. No act of omission did more to damage the reputation of the NHS in its day to day affairs. This failure in means did make it that much more difficult for the NHS to make progress towards its ends.

A quiet decision on medical education might in the long run prove to be the most important single measure taken by the Labour Government. This was the decision to make the expansion of the intake of medical students to 4,000 in the early 1980s the 'highest priority'. In fact the target was pushed back from 1980 during the government's life but it still represented a major undertaking. The ghost of the Willink report still stalked the Health Service. There were some compelling reasons for this. Thus it made sense to open new medical schools in Nottingham and in Leicester. These were under-doctored areas and doctors tend to practice where they train. It also made sense to worry about the high dependence on immigrant staff. Above and beyond such arguments of substance, there was a good deal of wishful thinking. Thus David Owen wrote about how 'a long overdue re-appraisal of the medical school curriculum was taking place'.[26] In many places this amounted to tackling on short courses in geriatrics and general practice without changing the core of the course. The social class bias in recruitment to medical schools remained as strong as it had ever been.

The government could have followed a different policy by pressing reform in the staffing structures for hospital doctors which were universally recognised as being out of date and on a more minor key by going even further in using the talents of women doctors. These measures could have complemented a steadying of intakes to medical training. The long term resource consequences of the government's decision will be very important. On the most probable assumption about future numbers of medical graduates there would be a rise in hospital expenditures of 47 per cent by the year 2000.[27] This would represent a reduction compared with the 100 per cent growth of such spending from 1948 to 1978, but spending on the service as a whole was likely to be growing much more slowly. Training more doctors would create an irresistible momentum towards the kind of medicine which they wanted to practice.

The government had set out in the statement on 'Priorities' a view of the kind of health service best suited to the needs of society. This view met with wide approval outside acute teaching hospitals. It was difficult though to see how such a service could be created given the pattern of interest within the medical profession. There was little pressure through new developments and increased numbers of trainees towards more spending on neglected kinds of care. Nobody wished to set aside professional competence as the main source of initiative in the service – but were we training the right professionals to look after the right patients? There are many other ways that well trained professionals could have been nurtured – for example in starting the new caring profession for the mentally handicapped. But most of the investment was still in one particular type of professional – doctors as trained in British medical schools.

Within the NHS there was still a great tension between its role in looking after acute illness and its role of central responsibility for the life chances of 200,000 'long stay' patients. RAWP was a useful step but one whose main results would be within the acute services. The deeper dilemmas remained and were even increased by the government's decisions. The problems of choice in care first posed in the 1960s would be there in an even more serious form in the 1980s.

Proposals for the future

The main priorities for a future Labour Government are simple. They are, first of all, to give a better chance of life for the 200,000 long stay patients who are among the most deprived people in the whole of society. It is in the long stay wards of hospitals for the mentally ill, the mentally handicapped and the elderly that life too often is without hope and without dignity. We may have to take new and bolder initiatives. Our view of community care has been based on a theory of incremental optimism, that if we just let things continue on their present course, we will one day have different forms of care. After 20 years, in the case of the mentally ill, and 10 in the case of the mentally handicapped, such an approach may in fact now be so much wishful thinking. After nearly 20 years of attempting to give priority to the care of the mentally ill in the community we were spending in 1977/78 just £10.1 million in the whole of England on such provision. We must examine the case again for giving these services a much more independent standing with their own sources of funds. Their interests have been badly damaged both by competition for resources from acute medicine and by the division between the NHS and local government. We perhaps need to think in terms of a separate national service for the mentally handicapped and more special funding for services in the community for the mentally ill.

The second main priority must be to seize opportunities for prevention both in terms of reducing road accidents and reducing smoking and alcoholism. It is here that we could make the most immediate gains in terms of lives saved. Finally there is the difficult task of running the acute services. The needs of neglected groups point to restrictions on spending but unless there is a good service to people generally we will probably see the growth of a larger sphere of private medicine offering service on demand and leaving the NHS with emergency care and the care of the elderly. A higher rate of growth in spending overall will certainly help but there will still be difficult problems of choice and of finding a different style in running these services.

13 Education

by Tessa Blackstone

Education has been seen as an important method of redistribution by socialists for many years. A person's life chances can be substantially affected by the nature and extent of his educational opportunities. Education is a route to greater material wealth, more power and higher status in the community. Educational qualifications have become a frequent requirement for entry to social positions with prestige, power and high material rewards. A society with a great deal of opportunity for those who begin life with little access to wealth, power or status to rise through the system and obtain them does not, however, necessarily mean a more equal society. It simply means a more mobile society. Yet, to turn the argument round, it is likely that in a society where inequalities of wealth, power and status are relatively small the opportunities for mobility through education will be good. For many years it was argued that equality of opportunity should be a central goal in education. It is now increasingly recognised that this is unrealisable without first achieving a greater measure of equality in society itself. How can a child living in a slum without a book in his house, perhaps with little encouragement to learn and few aspirations for the future, be expected to grasp equality of opportunity, however accessible the educational system is in theory? The long term aim must, therefore, be greater equality not simply equality of opportunity, which in practice is enormously difficult to fulfil.

A great deal of energy has gone into trying to get improvements in the opportunities offered to working class children at school and in the educational system after compulsory schooling. So far, however, it would be complacent to claim a great deal of success. Recent figures on entry to higher education demonstrate that the top of the educational system is being reached by a much smaller proportion of children from some backgrounds than others. Instead of the expected improvement in the proportions of young people from working class homes going into higher education, there has been a slight decline. There are, of course, other measures of improving educational opportunities than entry to university or polytechnic but the amount of progress made in many other areas also remains small. For example, the number of young people getting day release from work for further education has hardly grown, nor has the number of adults being provided with recurrent or continuing education. This still remains a pipe-dream. In spite of the existence of the Open University (OU), those who 'miss the boat' early in life find it extremely difficult to catch up later. Moreover, the requirements of OU courses are too demanding, and their content often inappropriate for those who left school aged 15 without qualifications 20 years earlier.

It has now been recognised that a redistribution of educational resources towards girls, women and minority groups as well as towards the working class is required. Whilst it is true that more girls now obtain A levels and go to universities and polytechnics than in the past, many more girls than boys who leave school at 16 fail to get any further education or training on a part time basis. Young blacks, particularly West Indians, are leaving school with few qualifications and are more likely than their white peers to become unemployed. Any failure to meet the educational needs of minority group children could have serious consequences for harmonious race relations in the long term. In that sense their poor representation in certain parts of the educational system is even more serious than that of women and girls. There is now talk of multi-cultural education but relatively little action.

Looking back over the last 15 years to 1964 when Labour was returned to power, progress towards educational equality has not been as great as some hoped at that time. There has, in fact, been a gradual disenchantment with the power of the educational system both to promote economic growth and (more important for the purposes of this discussion) to reduce inequality. There has been a dramatic change of climate in which the optimism of many social democrats in the early sixties has been undermined. It is important to be realistic when considering the potential scope of education to alter life chances. Nevertheless the amount of pessimism about this has been unduly great. Research undertaken in the United States by Coleman, Jencks[1] and others suggesting that schools make little difference to equality has contributed substantially to this. The impact of this research (which incidentally has been widely misinterpreted) is now beginning to be muted by new findings. Michael Rutter and his co-authors' study of secondary schools in London provides a rather different view of the differential impact schools can have on children of similar social backgrounds and levels of ability, and suggests that they need not be quite so impotent.[2]

But there is undoubtedly still a malaise about the potential contribution of education to a more socially just and equal society. Education is now on an unsure philosophical and policy basis. There is, perhaps, a need during the next five years in opposition for Labour to undertake a fundamental reappraisal of the role of education in relation to other social institutions. This may lead to the need to re-examine the future of certain educational institutions, for example, is the 'school' still a suitable form for older adolescents? Amongst other things, this will have to take into account the attitudes of the consumers. But any such reappraisal must also take account of the fact that education is a massive allocator of revenue: public expenditure of over £8 billion can have large distributional effects.

Labour's record in the 1960s

The following section describes the 1964–70 government's attempts at educational reform in the interests of greater equality. It is possible to identify 5 main areas of growth or change during this period.

1. The expansion of the colleges of education in order to meet the demand for teachers of a growing school population and in order to bring down pupil/teacher ratios.
2. The expansion of higher education to meet the Robbins' principle of providing sufficient places for the able and willing.
3. The introduction of the binary policy which entailed development and expansion of higher education in polytechnics run by the local authorities.
4. The decision to abolish selection at 11 and to create comprehensive secondary schools.
5. Following the Plowden Report, the introduction of educational priority areas and the attempt to implement positive discrimination by spending more in deprived areas than elsewhere.

Much of the expansion that took place during 1964–70 was in higher education, as a consequence of the first three policies listed above. This expansion and the growth in the numbers of children coming into the school system as a result of the increasing birth rate in the late 1950s and early 1960s accounted for most of the growth in expenditure during the period. There was a 69 per cent growth in spending on education between 1963 and 1968 but it would be wrong to see this as exceptional. It was, in fact, part of a much longer period of growth from the early 1950s through to the mid 1970s. Between 1953 and 1973, expenditure on education grew by 274.5 per cent. It grew much faster than total public expenditure whose growth through the same period was 99.9 per cent.[3] Table 13.1 illustrates this growth in expenditure on education between the early 1960s and the late 1970s.

Table 13.1   UK education expenditure[a] as % of GNP, 1960 to 1978 (£ million)

	Educational expenditure[b]	GNP[c]	Educational expenditure as % GNP
1960/1	947	26,188	3.6
1965/6	1,644	36,578	4.5
1966/7	1,842	38,955	4.7
1967/8	2,077	41,057	5.1
1968/9	2,218	44,310	5.0
1969/70	2,398	47,630	5.0
1970/1	2,740	52,699	5.2
1971/2	3,140	59,059	5.3
1972/3	3,708	66,284	5.6
1973/4	4,237	74,384	5.7
1974/5	5,528	88,336	6.3
1975/6	7,020	109,901	6.4
1976/7	7,849	126,745	6.2
1977/8	8,342	146,082	5.7

[a] Excluding meals and milk.
[b] Expenditure figures at out-turn prices.
[c] GNP at market prices.

In the context of this growth in educational expenditure, can it be said that the 1964–70 Labour Government was successful in re-distributing resources towards the less privileged members of the community? The answer is 'no'. There are two main reasons. First, there was the failure at every level of education to give high priority to redistribution in favour of the deprived whether via positive discrimination of the kind Plowden favoured or via reorientation of programmes to meet the educational needs of such groups. Second, there was the concentration of growth in the higher education sector. This is the stage of the educational system most used by the middle classes and the well off and the least used by the working classes and the poor. It is also the stage of education where unit costs are particularly high (and higher in the UK than in many other countries – see Table 13.2). Consequently, the share of resources going to the privileged is higher in education than in other social services. The most useful analysis of who benefited most from education during the 1960s was provided by Howard Glennerster in the earlier Fabian volume:

> The highest social class, professionals and senior managers, constituted 5 per cent of all married couples in 1966 but 8 per cent of the extra expenditure benefited them. The other non-manual groups received more than their share of the extra resources devoted to education. Skilled manual workers families benefited in direct proportion to their numbers, but semi-skilled and unskilled families received a significantly smaller share than their numbers would lead one to expect. They constituted 28 per cent of the married population in 1966 but received only 19 per cent of the additional expenditure on education. Put another way all the non-manual groups enjoyed a greater improvement in their educational standards than the average improvement for the whole population. In brief then the expenditure on higher and sixth form education which largely benefited middle class children effectively outweighed the other attempts that were made to spend more on those types of education that primarily benefited the less fortunate. In this sense society did not 'positively discriminate' in the sixties, it did the reverse.[4]

Developments since 1974

What might Labour have done since 1974 to rectify this? What lessons might it have learnt from this experience? Labour's 1974 manifesto listed the following aims: (a) end the 11 plus and other forms of selection for secondary education. Continue to give priority to nursery school and day care provision, full time and part time; (b) stop the present system of direct grant schools and withdraw tax relief and charitable status from public schools, as a first step towards our long term aim of phasing out fee paying in schools; (c) continue to move towards a fairer system of student grants; (d) provide increased opportunities for further education and training, including compulsory paid day release, especially for young people who leave school early; and (e) legislate for an annual review and an annual report to parliament on youth services.

Whilst all these aims are acceptable and some are even highly desirable as methods of increasing equality in education (see for example, the two Public Schools Commission Reports for the case on tax relief and charitable status and direct grant schools), not much progress has been made in implementing a number of them. Thus, in spite of falling rolls in primary schools, there has been much less expansion of nursery education and day care than the 1972 White Paper on Educational Expansion anticipated. Although the direct grant schools have been abolished, withdrawal of tax relief and charitable status of public schools is not much further ahead than in 1974. Student grants are still unfair in that many courses only carry an award at the discretion of the local authority, although the government did increase the number of further education courses carrying mandatory awards in 1976. Although opportunities for further education and training have improved in some respects (for example, courses sponsored by the Manpower Services Commission), others may have got worse, partly because it is an area that local authorities find easy to cut in times of public expenditure constraint. Perhaps the manifesto aim which is closest to being realised is the abolition of selection at 11. However there were still seven recalcitrant authorities that had refused to submit acceptable plans for achieving this at the end of Labour's period of office.

Not only did the government fail to deliver a number of these manifesto commitments it also failed to take sufficient action on the findings of Glennerster's review of what happened last time around. It failed to make sure that cuts in the growth of expenditure did not hit some areas of education where working class children or adults were most likely to be affected; nor did it make much impact on redistributing existing resources. Perhaps the manifesto itself should have provided a better guide but there is a suspicion that the problem has not been a shortage of ideas but a lack of political will at both central and local levels.

No attempt is made here to provide a chronological account of the Labour Government's education programme between 1974–79. Instead certain areas of policy which are important from the point of view of equality will be considered. Before examining these, it is necessary to mention one important background factor. This is the decline in the birth rate every year except one between 1965 and 1978.

This has dramatic consequences for the number of children at school. The school population in England and Wales is likely to fall from nearly 9.1 million in 1977 to about 7.3 million in 1986. The decline in the primary school population began during the Labour Government. It is expected to fall from 4.9 million in 1973 to about 3.3 million by 1986. In contrast, the secondary school population was growing throughout the period, reaching a peak of 4.1 million in 1979. However, during this period it became clear that it would probably fall to as low a figure as 2.8 million by the early 1990s. The impact of this change was considerable in that all planning and future expenditure plans were affected by it. In the competition for extra resources within Whitehall, education began to be treated as a relatively low priority, particularly because of these demographic changes.

In the first two years of the Labour Government one of its main preoccupations was trying to complete secondary reorganisation. From 1976 on it became more preoccupied with the question of education standards and with how to adapt the content of education to meet the requirements of industrial growth. Relatively little emphasis was placed on the potential of education as a mechanism of redistribution. This was partly the result of the general malaise about the effectiveness of education which has already been described. But it was partly the result of the major constraint on expansion imposed by reductions in the growth of public expenditure from 1976 on. The fact that little extra money is around does not of course mean that redistribution is impossible but it is often claimed that it is easier to achieve when services can be expanded.

Table 13.2 shows that the overall cut in real expenditure was only about £50 million between 1974/5 and 1978/9. This has to be seen in the context of a budget of nearly £8½ billion. The biggest cuts were on the capital programme; overall revenue expenditure went up by about £320 million over this period. The cuts appear to have affected higher education, further education and teacher training more than nursery, primary and secondary education, all of which show small increases in recurrent spending. Table 13.3, showing unit costs and how they have been changing, tells a similar story.

Table 13.3 shows the great differences in unit costs at the different stages of education. Thus, a child in a primary school cost only £297 per annum in 1976/7, whereas a university student cost on average £2,400 per annum. Within the secondary sector, considerably more was spent per head on the minority who stay on after the age of 16

Table 13.2 Expenditure on education including libraries
(£ million at 1978 survey prices)

	1974/5	1976/7	1978/9
Schools			
Under fives			
Capital	26	9	15
Current	148	165	208
Primary, secondary and other			
Capital	606	510	321
Primary			
Current	1,612	1,675	1,620
Secondary			
Current	2,044	2,160	2,260
Other			
Current	418	487	478
Meals	450	455	415
Milk	19	18	16
Higher and further education			
Universities			
Capital	115	117	85
Current	698	708	607
Further education and teacher training			
Capital	112	94	68
Current	1,037	1,004	980
Student support	412	438	593
Libraries			
Purchase grants	4	5	6
Other	227	226	221
Miscellaneous educational services,			
research and administration			
Youth services, etc.			
Capital	20	17	16
Current	78	84	85
Research and other services	13	15	20
Administration	331	302	301
Total education and libraries			
Capital	878	747	505
Current	7,492	7,742	7,811
Total	8,370	8,489	8,316

Source: *Public Expenditure White Paper, 1979*, Cmnd 7439, HMSO, 1979.

Table 13.3   Net recurrent institutional expenditure and % changes in it per full time pupil/student from public funds at constant 1977 survey prices

	Expenditure per head (£)		% Changes in expenditure per head			
	1974/5	1976/7	1973/4 to 1974/5	1974/5 to 1975/6	1975/6 to 1976/7	1973/4 to 1976/7
Nursery schools	603	714	27.5	12.6	5.2	51.0
Primary schools	279	297	24.6	3.2	3.1	32.3
Secondary schools						
pupils under 16	421	422	17.9	−0.5	0.7	18.2
pupils over 16	813	773	27.0	−5.8	0.9	20.8
Special schools	1,317	1,461	21.6	5.2	5.4	34.9
Evening Institutes	185	195	19.4	10.8	4.9	25.8
Major FE establishments (excluding poly-technics)						
non-advanced work	920	890	15.0	−2.2	−1.1	11.25
advanced work	1,430	1,370	16.3	2.1	−2.1	11.4
Polytechnics						
non-advanced work	1,410	1,240	14.6	3.5	−15.0	0.8
advanced work	2,190	1,930	15.3	3.2	−14.6	1.6
Colleges of Education	1,290	—	15.2	20.2	—	—
Universities	2,400	2,400	−1.0	1.0	−1.0	−1.0

Source: DES, *Finance and Awards 1976*, Vol. 5, HMSO, 1978.

than on those under 16. Similarly, non-advanced work in further education (FE) and polytechnics had lower unit costs than advanced work. The table also shows that between 1973/4 and 1976/7 the amount spent per head went up in the schools sector quite considerably. This is especially true of nursery, primary and special schools. In the more selective post-school stage, they went up by much smaller amounts; in the universities they actually declined slightly. The year by year changes indicate the impact of public expenditure cuts towards the end of the period. They show that increases, per pupil, in expenditure in schools have become much smaller. Nevertheless, cuts have not, as some people have feared, reduced the amount spent per pupil. However, at the post-school stage, particularly in polytechnics, there have been reductions in expenditure per head. There has, therefore, been a small improvement in the distribution of resources towards the universal part of the system from which all benefit relative to the selective parts from which only a minority benefit.

'The Great Debate'

Perhaps the Labour Government's most highly publicised initiative in education was the launching of a 'Great Debate'. Late in 1976, the Prime Minister made a speech at Ruskin College, Oxford in which he exhorted the educational system to provide more relevant education and training to meet the needs of industry. In particular he lamented the low status attached to such fields as engineering and, implicitly at least, blamed the educational system for it. He also made some remarks about the importance of maintaining high standards in basic skills. The Department of Education and Science (DES) responded to this by producing a document on school education which suggested the need for a core curriculum and more links between schools and industry. It also set up a number of regional conferences to debate some of the issues raised by the Prime Minister and its own paper. Lastly it asked local education authorities to undertake a survey of the curriculum, the outcome of which is not yet clear.

Whilst rightly focusing on the contribution education might make to our industrial regeneration, the result of these activities has been disappointing. One reason for this is that there was insufficient emphasis on some of the key areas concerning the education of industrial workers. Little attention, for example, was given to such matters as how to introduce positive discrimination towards the less advantaged in the provision of careers advice. Similarly, there was little mention of ways of expanding trade union education by, for example, courses preparing adult members of the industrial workforce and their leaders for industrial democracy. Developments of this kind could both redistribute educational resources and increase the relevance of education to industrial needs.

During the last part of Labour's five years of office in 1978 and 1979 it became increasingly preoccupied with the introduction of a Bill. This Bill had little to offer those hoping to reduce educational inequality. Much of it was concerned with questions of administration and resource management. Perhaps it is too much to ask for an Education Bill being put through a parliament where the government does not have an overall majority to demonstrate any socialist idealism. Moreover, there were useful items in it. It covered: school government; admission limits to schools; school attendance orders; the employment of teachers in day nurseries; awards and grants; advanced FE and various miscellaneous items. The school government proposals were desirable in that they involved increased parent and teacher participation in governing bodies. However, the impact of the Bill's clauses on the educational opportunities of most working class children seems unlikely to have been great. The section on awards and grants would have made possible educational maintenance allowances for 16 to 19 year olds in full time education, although even if the Bill had been passed before the government fell there was no guarantee that they would be introduced (see below). How far all the work that went into this Bill was wasted remains to be seen.

The establishment of comprehensive education

The government would probably have claimed that its greatest success was its progress towards the abolition of selection for secondary schools. Nearly one thousand new comprehensive schools were established between 1974 and 1979 so that by the end of that period over 80 per cent of children were attending such schools. This compares with just under 10 per cent at the time that Circular 10/65 was sent out inviting local authorities to submit proposals for the abolition of selection. The 1976 Education Act gave the Secretary of State new powers to require those local education authorities which had not yet done so to submit proposals for comprehensive reorganisation. As already mentioned, all but seven had done so by 1979, though only 44 authorities had *completed* reorganisation by this date. It also went ahead with the abolition of direct grant schools. In 1975, of 174 of these, 54 were Roman Catholic, most of the others being owned by foundations or trusts. A disconcertingly high proportion of them (121) are becoming independent; 46 of them will become maintained schools and the remainder are closing down.

The reorganisation of secondary education, although not quite complete, is clearly an important achievement. The previous selective system was grossly unfair to the 75 per cent of children who were sent to secondary modern schools, with their lower status and fewer resources than the grammar schools. Opportunities for these children have been greatly improved. Some of the concern about standards in recent years may be a consequence of the greater social and academic mix of comprehensive schools. When the average and below average child was 'out of sight' in the secondary modern schools, few people cared about their standards of education. An indirect consequence of 'going comprehensive' has been to focus attention on this – attention which was perhaps overdue and could further improve opportunities for working class children.

The fact that a considerable number of Conservative local education authorities have been strongly opposed to reorganisation has made what has been achieved all the more praiseworthy. Yet, there do remain a number of doubts about it. It might have been more effective to have introduced legislation in the mid-1960s and set up a national pattern of secondary education at that time. Had this happened, it seems likely that there would, by now, be fewer selective schools left. Moreover, there would have been a more uniform system throughout the country which would have made geographical mobility for parents within this age group easier. The repeal of the 1976 Act, by the new Conservative Government, will mean that many of the remaining selective schools will survive, creaming the most able children from the comprehensive schools until Labour is re-elected.

Nursery education and day care
Turning to the second of the items listed in the October 1974 manifesto, priority to nursery and day care provision, less success can be claimed. Although the number of children attending nursery schools or classes in England and Wales had risen from about 140,000 in 1974 to about 210,000 in 1977, the Labour Government was far from achieving the target figures proposed by the Plowden Report in 1967. Twelve years have passed since then, for nearly nine of which Labour was in power. Moreover, in recent years demography has been on the side of policy makers attempting to expand provision in this area.

In spite of this the CPRS was able to claim late in 1978 that:

There are four main aspects of the services for children where existing policies are inadequate:
(a) There is a lack of direction and no clear priorities as to the ways in which services should progress.
(b) There is confusion in the administration of services for children under five. The provision of services is fragmented and responsibility is divided.
(c) The consequences of the present situation for the children and

their parents are both unjust and inequitable. There is a serious lost opportunity for preventative work at an early stage.

(d) It is widely recognised that children benefit from some education and care outside their homes between the ages of three and five. A substantial number of children are denied this benefit because adequate provision is not available.[5]

Few people disagree with the view that nursery education and day care are of high priority. There is, however, some disagreement on how education and care for this age group should be provided. If the service is to provide for those in greatest need and, hence, have some redistributive impact, it is essential that priority should be given to the expansion of full time provision, particularly in inner cities and other deprived areas. One of the poorest groups in our society are single parent families. In order to give these parents, approximately five out of six of whom are women, the chance to earn a reasonable living, it is vitally important to make available places for their children under five. As well as this group there are now many working class women who both want and need to work to secure an adequate standard of living for their families. The priority that has been given to the growth of part time places in nursery classes attached to primary schools must be changed. Resources should be switched to some sort of provision, preferably in primary schools rather than separate day nurseries, which provides education and care for a full working day. Falling rolls in primary schools make them the obvious location for such provision; this opportunity should not have been wasted. This location will require improvements in the co-ordination between education and social services departments at both central and local levels. Although the central government authorised building programmes for nursery education, local authorities were reluctant in many cases to take up the opportunities available. Public expenditure cuts left them unwilling to finance any additional recurrent expenditure. This meant that in some areas places which might easily have been filled with children under five were left empty. The solution to this would have been legislation which gave parents the minimum right to a part time place when their child reached the age of three, with a right to a full time place for certain categories of need. Local authorities would then have to be given a period of, say, five years to reach a position where they could meet this right. The government failed to make substantial progress in nursery education and day care.

Independent schools

The inclusion of reductions of indirect government support for independent schools crops up like a hardy annual in every Labour manifesto. In some ways it is wrong to attach too much importance to these schools. Only 5 per cent of the school age population (though more 17 to 18 year olds) attends them. However, they have a symbolic importance far beyond their actual importance. No Labour Government can claim success in eliminating educational inequality whilst it continues to subsidise schools which are confined to a social and intellectual élite and which convey to their pupils advantages in later life which are not equally available to the great majority. The removal of charitable status for certain public schools is the first priority. The Labour Government failed to achieve this because it allowed itself to be paralysed by the complexities of the law of charity and to do nothing until a more general review of this was completed. It would, however, have been a relatively simple exercise to have withdrawn rate relief and relief from the national insurance surcharge. The first of these would have generated additional revenue of around £6 million a year had it been introduced at the end of the government's period in office. The abolition of all indirect subsidies to these schools would save over £100 million.[6]

It would, of course, be wrong to suppose that measures of this kind would have led to the demise of the independent system. What else might have been done other than outright abolition, which is not a politically realistic option? First, the substantial numbers of children of public servants abroad who attend these schools at public expense should be accommodated in the state sector. In 1977 the cost to the government of paying the school fees of these children was £36 million. Falling rolls in secondary schools would make possible their inclusion in comprehensive schools at relatively low cost. Boarding houses attached to such schools in London and in other areas where military personnel work whilst in the UK should be built. When public servants working abroad are posted home many of their children could, as a consequence, live at home without changing schools, returning to a boarding house when their parents are sent abroad again. There are adequate English-speaking schools for children up to the age of eleven in most places abroad where British military or diplomatic personnel work. A second policy which should be considered is the withdrawal of access to free higher education for those who have not spent, say, a minimum of three years in the state secondary system. This would be little different from the system that applied to direct grant schools in the past. Another analogy is that of private patients in the health service. Those who pay for private consultancies, and thereby jump the queue for a hospital bed, now have to pay the complete cost of their treatment in private hospitals.

Further and higher education

The manifesto also promised fairer student grants. The student élite in universities and polytechnics doing full time degrees or their equivalent are more generously treated than those on lower level courses. In this sense the system is regressive. The issue to which the last Labour Government devoted much attention was, however, how to improve participation in full time education between 16 and 19, whether in school or in further education colleges. For many years a system of providing cash benefits on a means tested basis for this group has been in operation. However, it was discretionary and varied from authority to authority in the amount paid. As such it was unsatisfactory in that in some cases a young person had a much better chance than others of receiving an award. It was also unsatisfactory in that the amounts paid by most authorities were so small as to be almost derisory.

The case for extending these awards is twofold. Firstly, many people who might stay on at school or go to college after the age of 16 still do not do so. International comparisons in this area are difficult. However, league tables suggest that the UK has a lower proportion of this age group in full time education than in some other comparable countries. Secondly, poor families must make a considerable sacrifice in terms of loss of earnings to keep their children in full time education. How far a much more generous system of mandatory awards would encourage more young people in this age group to seek full time education is not entirely clear. However, some unpublished evidence suggests that some would certainly stay on who might not otherwise do so.[7] Moreover, a system of mandatory awards on a means tested basis would certainly help those families improve their standard of living who are at the moment making considerable sacrifices to keep their children at school. The Secretary of State for Education was unable to persuade her Cabinet colleagues at the time that the extra £100 million that such a scheme would cost could be spared. She was, however, able to get agreement to a system of pilot schemes to try out a new system of educational maintenance allowances. This would have been a useful beginning towards achieving a scheme which would undoubtedly have had some redistributional benefits.

The last of the manifesto promises which might have contributed to the more equal sharing of educational resources was the expansion of opportunities for further education and training including compulsory day release. This applied especially to those who leave school as soon as they are allowed. At present some 47 per cent of 16 to 19 year olds are in employment and not receiving any further education and training. Whilst nothing at all is being spent on their education their more privileged peers attending university are benefiting from expenditure of approximately £2,400 per annum (average unit costs) on each of them. Concentrated in the former group are some of the least able and most disadvantaged young people. The decline in the number of unskilled jobs makes it all the more important to provide some training and skills for this group so that their prospects of long term unemployment are reduced. For years the TUC and others have identified this group as one which has been particularly neglected. The last Labour Government undoubtedly shared this view, yet failed to deliver the kind of comprehensive scheme that is required.

There has been a courageous attempt to provide some education and training, however limited, for all school leavers who have been unemployed for six months or longer. The Youth Opportunities Programme, which set out to do this, has been developed by the Manpower Services Commission rather than by the DES and local education authorities. However, the DES has provided some extra money for the further education sector to help the young unemployed. But the largest numbers in this age group are to be found amongst those with jobs who are following no course of any kind. When the government fell it was working towards a White Paper which was to put forward plans for the development of education and training for 16 to 19 year olds including vocational preparation for all young people in the group described above. Although policy changes of this kind are complex and require substantial amounts of extra public expenditure (the cost of vocational preparation for all young people, including compensation to employers for releasing them from work, could not be much less than £100 million a year) it is hard to excuse the failure to get this White Paper out earlier. Had the government tackled it with the urgency it deserved as soon as they came into office it seems unlikely that they would have failed.

Conclusion

This chapter has tried to highlight some of the areas where educational reform is desperately needed in the interest of greater equality. Some issues, like the expansion of educational opportunities for adults including those in their early twenties, have not been discussed. The fact that the number of LEA discretionary grants fell during the latter period of the Labour Government is a depressing indication of failure. However, the adult literacy scheme is one of the success stories for which the government should be given credit. In general, the system of post-school education provides lavishly for the élite minority and does too little for the great majority.

Even if the Labour Government had been successful in expanding opportunities in all the areas that have been identified, this would not be enough. Labour's future programme needs to stress that within every sector of education a programme of positive discrimination is necessary which involves teachers and local authorities as much if not more than central government. It entails not only more resources in deprived areas but changes which do not require much extra money. For example, there need to be better opportunities for the participation of minority group parents in their children's schools. The educational system must recognise that we have a multi-cultural society. The Labour Government was all too slow in honouring its promise to set up a Committee of Enquiry to look into the education of minority groups. Basic and in-service training of teachers must place more emphasis on the dangers of sex role stereotyping which limits the aspirations of girls in our society. If the necessary changes in the content of education and in teaching methods to meet the needs of disadvantaged children of ethnic minorities and of girls are to be introduced, better guidance from the centre is needed. This means politicians must make administrators more aware of these needs and the Inspectorate must become more effective at implementing policies to meet them.

This raises the more general question of the relationship between central government and local education authorities which are responsible for providing the service. This chapter has concentrated on the role of central government but the role of the LEAs is, of course, crucial. Blame for some of the failure to make progress rests with them. Nursery education, discussed above, is one example of a central government initiative in providing funds, but some LEAs declined to take advantage of them. In-service training for teachers is another. If a Labour Government wishes to be certain of getting changes implemented in a reasonably short time scale it must either make more use of specific grants or fall back on legislation with supporting regulations. A move in this direction need not prevent local innovation, which, in any case, has recently been somewhat lacking with respect to reducing inequality in both Labour and Conservative local authorities.

In a climate of public expenditure constraints and falling numbers it will not be easy to achieve greater equality. But, in such a climate it will be all the more essential to put forward positive policies to use some of the spare capacity properly. The last Labour Government's greatest problem in education was to devise and implement such policies for 16 to 19 year olds, at present outside the system altogether; it was also its greatest failure. Unless such policies are devised we could find that a higher proportion of privileged middle class young people, neither particularly well motivated nor particularly well qualified, will enter higher education leaving many working class young people and adults no better off than before. If this is allowed to happen, expenditure in education will become more, rather than less, regressive.

14   Housing

by David Webster

In reviewing Labour's housing policies in 1974–79, the main developments of the preceding decade need to be borne in mind. Here they are briefly summarised.[1] There was a continuing expansion in the number of households, despite a cessation of population growth by the end of the period. Thus there was a continuing shortage of housing in general, and a need for new construction. The main features of the three main housing tenures were unaltered, and their relative size was changing in the same way as it had done over the previous half century. Owner occupation was continuing to expand, helped by tax concessions. Council housing was also expanding its share. The private rented sector was continuing to shrink, though less fast absolutely than relatively.

This changing pattern of housing tenure was leading to problems of access to housing for the poor and mobile, which gradually became more acute and were seen in their most dramatic form in the officially recognised problem of homelessness. Housing obsolescence was a major problem. The oldest unrehabilitated housing was to be found in the private rented sector, and the impact of bad conditions there fell disproportionately on the elderly and on poor families. Largely unrecognised by central government, obsolescence was also becoming a major problem in the council sector, due both to age and, in the case of more recently constructed housing, functional inadequacy.

The spatial pattern of urban settlement was also changing quite rapidly. Following trends taking place in the United States ten or more years earlier, people and jobs were leaving the old urban cores for smaller settlements on the fringes of or outside the conurbations, leaving behind a complex of problems including relatively high unemployment, a disproportionate number of elderly and dependent households, physical obsolescence and declining public and private services, compounded by the special problems of the ethnic minorities.

Finally, there were important changes in financial conditions. After many years of low inflation and moderate interest rates, with a low but positive 'real' rate of interest, there were rapid changes in the burden of housing payments in both public and private sectors in the early seventies as a result of increased inflation.

The 1964–70 Labour Government had by and large a good record, but in some ways stored up trouble for the future. It embarked on a massive housebuilding and slum clearance programme which continued at a high level even after the cuts following the devaluation crisis of 1967. In 1967 it put into effect most of the higher standards for council house building recommended in the 1961 Parker Morris report which had lain unimplemented by the previous Conservative Government. However, it has since become accepted that much of the building has failed to provide an acceptable living environment, because of deficiencies in design, layout and constructional soundness. The reasons for this failure are complex, but they include the search for high densities by urban authorities facing a shortage of land within their areas; the dominance of certain architectural fashions based on an inadequate understanding of the way people live, and the power of architects who succumbed to these fashions; the influence over public construction of lobbyists from the construction industry (which took forms ranging from the presence of advisers within the Ministry of Housing and Local Government to overt corruption as in the Poulson case); and the failure of the institutions and procedures for regulating constructional innovation. What is perhaps the most important political lesson for the Labour Party is that it was the absence of effective consumer sovereignty within the council sector which allowed these mistakes to occur on so massive a scale.

For the owner occupied sector, the 1964–70 government did little except introduce the option mortgage scheme, a valuable and egalitarian measure. Towards the end of the period, however, and still more after 1974, its importance was being reduced by the downward drift of the income tax threshold – a drift which had been helped on its way by Roy Jenkins' abolition of the lower rate tax bands. For the private rented sector, the government introduced security of tenure for unfurnished lettings, and the system of fair rents and its accompanying rent officer service which has since proved politically so robust. Generally, given the denial of state subsidy to the sector, this system has been reasonably favourable to tenants, but it is essentially a form of rough justice made necessary by the absence of more fundamental reform.

Perhaps the most serious political failure of the government was its 1969 Housing Act. In spite of lengthy internal discussions of proposals similar to the Housing Action Areas introduced in 1974, it drew back from any attempt to devise measures which would seriously tackle poor working class rented housing by rehabilitation. The ineffectiveness of this Act in reaching the worst off was well documented by the House of Commons Expenditure Committee in 1973[2]; it left tenants vulnerable to the effects of the property boom of 1971–73 and continued the bias in public policy towards large scale clearance, with all the disruption involved.

The period of the Heath Government from 1970 to 1974 was marked by two main features. The first was the 1972 Housing Finance Act, one of the most savagely inegalitarian measures of this century. It was inegalitarian not *ipso facto* because it involved large rent increases – although this was what permitted the widespread political mobilisation which finally destroyed the Act – but because it proposed the reduction and eventual elimination of subsidies to council tenants while retaining unaltered the system of mortgage interest tax relief for home owners. In practice, this intention was temporarily thwarted by the rise in inflation and interest rates; this has led many commentators to claim that the Act would never really have done what it intended. But there can be no doubt that, had it remained in force, it would eventually have achieved exactly what it set out to do. Even if the figure of 50p per year for the progression to 'fair rents' had been retained, by 1978 the average council rent would have risen by £4.50 a week compared with an actual average increase of well under £3. One feature of the Housing Finance Act proved durable: its introduction of a national system of rent rebates and allowances. The Labour Party had failed to tackle the problems of low income tenants, partly because of ambivalence about means testing and partly (in the local authority case) because of the traditional view that council housing should itself be used to redistribute income to a broadly defined working class.

The second principal feature of the Heath period was the property boom of 1971–73, and the Tory Government's majestic impassivity in the face of it. Motivated by the general philosophy of non-intervention and by specific *laissez-faire* policies, in particular 'Competition and Credit Control', the Conservatives refused either to stabilise the credit market for house purchase or to intervene to mitigate the effects of property speculation on tenants. Only the near collapse of the credit system in 1973 led to a change of policy. As a result, on taking office in March 1974, the Labour Party inherited from the Conservatives two policies. These were the approach to private sector improvement of the Housing Bill, passed in modified form as the Housing Act 1974, and the establishment of a non-statutory Joint Advisory Committee (set up in 1973), to bring together the Building Societies Association and the government for regular consultations on the management of house purchase credit.

One development of a bipartisan nature during the Heath period was the spread of housing aid and advice centres, following the recommendation of the Seebohm Committee in 1968. Although costing relatively little, it helped to alter the balance of power in the housing market in favour of the consumer, and in particular the poorer and less educated consumer. Its benefits, however, were rarely extended to council tenants.

On taking office in 1974, the Labour Government had the advantage of a very radical political climate, which for over two years more than made up for the small size of its parliamentary majority. This radicalism was in large part due to housing issues, in particular over the Housing Finance Act, and the discrediting of market processes even among homeowners by the anarchy of the property boom. It was a time of opportunity for fundamental reform. It is clear that this opportunity had to be seized quickly or forfeited altogether.

A brief narrative, 1974–79
In contrast to 1964, the Labour Party came into office with fairly comprehensive housing policies already formulated in its 1973 programme. While these were on the right lines, they were not fully adequate and anyway many did not find their way into the manifestos of February and October 1974. Of those that did, two of the most important were never implemented – security of tenure for council tenants and the setting up of a National Housing Finance Agency. All the other manifesto policies were carried out. During the first six months when the party had no majority in parliament, two major housing measures were passed. One was the Rent Act, giving security of tenure to furnished tenants (followed in 1976 by an Act giving security to farmworkers in tied accommodation), and the other was the Housing Act based on the Conservative Bill. Little about the latter was distinctively Labour rather than Tory; the main

difference was a more sceptical attitude towards housing associations. However, the commitment to housing associations (already contained in the 1973 programme) was a major new departure for the Labour Party. A rent freeze was also introduced for both council and private tenants; this lasted until 1975. On obtaining a parliamentary majority, the government moved swiftly to fulfil its pledge to repeal the Housing Finance Act and to pass the Housing and Rents Subsidies Act 1975 as an interim measure setting up a temporary subsidy system for local authority housing – which has in fact not yet been replaced by a permanent system. To consider permanent reform of the system of housing finance, the government set up an internal Housing Finance Review. Many consider this a major strategic error. The Review took well over a year to complete its work, and by the time its conclusions were available a change of Secretary of State had already meant a loss of impetus. By the time the Review was published as the *Housing Policy Review* in June 1977, the government had lost its parliamentary majority, and there was no sign of a radical policy in the document. A parallel Review of the Rent Acts, likely to be equally tame, was completed but shelved pending the 1979 general election and never published.

From 1976 onwards, government strategy was dictated by economic events, with much attention focused on cutting or controlling housing expenditure and on the new machinery of control – cash limits and Housing Investment Programmes. Other housing initiatives were few: the revival of interest in the inner cities in late 1976 and 1977 under Peter Shore,[3] and an associated White Paper and Act; the Housing (Homeless Persons) Act, an 'adopted' Liberal private member's bill on a topic on which the government did not originally wish to legislate; and the Savings Bonus and Loan Scheme to help first time owner occupiers. This latter measure was one of those suggested in the Housing Policy Review and put into the legislative programme ahead of the others because it was expected to be electorally popular. The remaining proposals requiring legislation were contained in the Housing Bill published at the end of March 1979 and lost as a result of the 1979 election.

An appraisal of policy, 1974–79
A preoccupation with equity on a fundamental level in the housing finance system was a notable characteristic of the Labour Government; 'a more equitable and balanced distribution of assistance' was a main objective of the Housing Finance Review.[4] In the end, how-

ever, the government did little and the Review recommended no major change. Why was this? The Housing Finance Review did demonstrate, via a more comprehensive examination of the problems than ever previously made, how difficult it is to design financial arrangements across all three tenures, even across the two main tenures, which will both effectively secure equity of treatment and be administratively feasible. The Review section on 'Fairness Between Tenants and Homeowners' presents the results of comparisons based on very limited definitions of fairness and concludes that to make an objective and comprehensive comparison taking into account all payments, costs and benefits is impossible on account of the sheer number of assumptions involved.[5] To design acceptable arrangements to ensure a balance of advantage between tenures automatically over a long period is impossible both for this reason and because changing economic circumstances affect each tenure in different ways. The Review also effectively demonstrated the difficulty of designing an adequate universal housing allowance system in the absence of a consistent 'current value' basis for pricing in all three tenures – a move which is unlikely to be acceptable on the Left, as was demonstrated by the reception accorded the book based on the work of the NEDO consultant who explored the idea.[6]

The Review did therefore perform a major service in demonstrating the complexity of the problem of securing financial equity. It showed, for instance, that the commitment in the 1973 Programme and February 1974 manifesto to provide the same aggregate amount of subsidy to owner occupiers and council tenants was based on much too superficial an understanding of the problem. However, the real issue, namely that the housing system *is* a major redistributive mechanism in relation to both disposable income and wealth, as well as an influence on other aspects of life chances, was ducked. In practice everyone agrees that owner occupation has proved exceedingly profitable. In a recent guide to personal investment, for instance, the *Economist* described owner occupation as 'the only secure road to riches that any employee, even one earning a very high income, will ever find in Britain'.[7] One rough examination of the comparative position of owners and tenants over the short period 1964 to 1970 suggested that the average owner would have been over £1,200 (1979 prices) better off over the period than the average tenants. Moreover, housing has become a very important element in the overall distribution of wealth, accounting for 41 per cent of gross personal wealth in 1976 compared with 20 per cent in 1960.

Owner occupation is so profitable for three reasons. First, the price
of houses has consistently risen over the longer term relative to other
goods. Second, purchase is financed with money borrowed at low and
often negative real rates of interest, and the owner's original deposit
is highly 'geared' by the large share of the cost normally financed by
borrowing. Third, generous tax concessions are available – normally
thought of as the tax relief on mortgage interest, but better viewed as
the combination of exemption from Schedule A tax on the imputed
rental income of the dwelling, together with exemption from capital
gains tax.[9] On the other hand, some other elements need to be taken
into account – such as owner occupiers' responsibility for repairs and
insurance, their high transaction costs and the excessive burden of
payments in the early years. Some marginal owner occupiers may do
much worse than most. And if council tenants' rents were low enough
and the services they received good enough, they could end up equally
well off; it must be remembered that tenants gain collectively from
being charged pooled historic cost rents in inflationary conditions.
But quite simply, no comprehensive assessment was carried out in the
Housing Finance Review. Such an assessment is indispensable if
there is to be any attempt to secure an overall balance of advantage
between the two main tenures.

The Labour movement must commit itself to securing such a
balance of advantage. It would now be generally agreed (well beyond
the Labour Party itself) that the death of the private rented sector
is to be welcomed and that long term policy need not include provision for it. Owner occupied housing is here to stay; many socialists
do not accept this with good grace, but all effectively accept it (and
to accept it with good grace would help in the process of devising
coherent socialist housing policies). The central problem is that of the
role of council housing. Traditionally, much of the Labour movement has not viewed this as a sector competing on equal terms with
owner occupation, but as a vehicle for redistributing income to a
broadly defined working class. This view is now outmoded and
dangerous. Outmoded, because the overlap in income and class
composition between the tenures is now large.[10] Dangerous, because
it reinforces the main political beliefs which are a threat to the long
term viability of the sector.

What are these beliefs? First, that council housing is more heavily
subsidised. On the contrary, the Housing Policy Review did succeed
in laying the myth that tax relief is not a subsidy. Other developments, such as the comprehensive investigation of 'tax expenditure'

in the 1979 Public Expenditure White Paper,[11] have helped further. The Review figures show that any differences in size of the subsidy are not dramatic. Moreover, extra costs imposed on local authority housing by the duty to provide for special social needs and by the concentration on high densities, difficult sites and areas with high land costs make council housing subsidies appear higher relative to owner occupation subsidies than they really are.

Second, council housing is believed to be exclusively a welfare service, aimed at underprivileged groups. This attitude not only means a withdrawal from the belief in public enterprise which has underlain the Party's efforts in housing but it also implies a concentration within the council sector of people with little bargaining power whose housing provision should be a decent minimum but no more. This has already been happening: the proportion of council tenants who are socially disadvantaged has been rising, and council tenants' incomes have been falling in relation to those of owner occupiers.[12]

Third, precisely because council housing is thought to be heavily subsidised, it is thought wrong to provide accommodation on demand for all who ask for it. Yet with the disappearance of private renting, this latter objective has become vital. Regrettably, the 1974–1979 Labour Government tolerated and even – by implication – encouraged the restriction of access to council housing of designated groups of 'undeserving' applicants including the single, the childless, the mobile and the young. It is these restrictions as much as anything else that underlay the decline of public sector building in the last months of the government.

Now it is clear that public housing must provide for the needs of the poor and disadvantaged, and that for these groups a higher rate of subsidy is required – which cannot be wholly provided through the rebate scheme. It is also clear that it would be exceptionally difficult for public housing to be competitive with owner occupation for the most prosperous groups. But if council housing (and other socially owned housing) is to take over the former role of the private rented sector, and if it is to avoid the fate of a decline into a residual welfare role, then it must be seen as broadly competitive with owner occupation, but not especially privileged, by a wide range of people with average and near average incomes. For these groups, notions of a redistributive role for council housing must be discarded.

The current situation, where owner occupiers generally do better than council tenants, cannot be condoned. Not only is this unjust in itself; it also makes it impossible for the Labour Party (especially at local government level) to take a rational view of issues such as the encouragement of owner occupation in inner city areas and the sale of council houses. But not all owner occupiers are relatively well off so it is not necessarily egalitarian simply to cut subsidies to all owner occupiers indiscriminately. The distribution of subsidy within the tenure is just as important. The Review showed that, in 1974/5, the distribution of subsidy with respect to household income in the council sector was very mildly progressive, when general subsidy and rebates are taken together. But for owner occupiers it was markedly regressive, with an average of £59 subsidy for households with an income of under £1,000 a year, rising to £369 for those with an income of £6,000 or over.[13] Not only were the most prosperous owners being heavily favoured in the distribution of subsidy, as well as in their opportunities for capital gains, but the worst off owners were getting less subsidy than council tenants on similar incomes: council tenant households with incomes less than £1,000 a year were receiving a total subsidy of £166. There has been much unproductive argument within the Labour Party as a result of this point being ignored.

Thus, the Labour Party should aim at a progressive (or neutral) distribution of subsidy within each tenure and at an overall balance of advantage between owner occupation and council renting, for a broad range of people with incomes around the average. One is not talking of mathematical equality: as explained earlier, this is an illusory goal. It is more that the choice of tenure should be widely seen as a 'toss up'. Insofar as financial aspects are concerned, the 1973 Programme commitments to a universal option mortgage scheme and to giving the same aggregate amount of subsidy to each sector were on the right lines. However, as we shall see below, the former by itself would not have gone far enough and the latter defined equality too narrowly in considering only financial arrangements (and, as we have seen, took too superficial a view of these). For what is needed is not merely a balance of financial advantage; other aspects of the two tenures are also vitally important. Policy on the level of council rents remains crucial, but the Labour Party needs to look also at such things as physical conditions, the neighbourhood environment, freedom of control and movement, and power *vis-à-vis* the managers and agents of the housing sector.

Even if the notion of a balance of advantage is accepted, there remains the difficult issue of the extent to which housing in either tenure should be subsidised. A major theme in the criticism of the Review was that subsidies ought to be cut in favour of investment, whether in housing or elsewhere in the economy.[14] Fortunately, measures aimed at making the distribution of subsidy within each tenure more equal will also tend to reduce the total subsidy bill. It is not easy, however, to see the Labour Party espousing measures to reduce housing subsidies even further. The intellectual case may be strong, but the political difficulties are no less formidable. Nevertheless, this issue needs to be taken much more seriously in the Labour movement – and not merely at parliamentary level – than it so far has been.

Table 14.1 shows how the total of subsidies moved by comparison with investment in public spending over the period of the Labour Government. The large increase in subsidies to both owner occupiers and tenants in 1974/75 was widely misunderstood at the time: it was the unavoidable result of the increase in interest rates. By 1978/ 1979 subsidies to owners had fallen back slightly, but subsidies to council and housing association tenants had continued to increase, due mainly to a fall in the real level of rents. This underlines the importance of measures to reduce subsidies to owner occupation; if the only way to bring about an overall balance of advantage is to increase subsidies to tenants, rather than by reducing subsidies to owners or taxing their capital gains, then the inevitable result is the pre-emption of considerable amounts of public expenditure and thus revenue from taxation. Nevertheless, the increase in subsidies did not take place at the expense of investment. Public investment in Great Britain was estimated at £2,834 million in 1978/9, compared with £2,414 million in 1973/4, an increase of £420 million, although improvement grants were £177 million down. This overall increase was possible because the public spending cuts in 1976 were deliberately concentrated on the local authority home loans scheme in order to minimise their impact on employment. (For the same reason, within investment, cuts were focused on acquisitions.)

Overall improvement in housing conditions depends on private as well as public investment. Here there was a substantial fall, from £3,150 million in 1973/4 to £2,590 million in 1977/8 (both at 1978 survey prices). In fact the National Dwelling and Housing Survey at the end of 1977 showed a dramatic reduction since 1971 in the number of households unsatisfactorily housed: from 3.8 million in 1971 to 2.0 million in 1977.[15] No comprehensive assessment is available of the outlook in 1979. However, the medium term forecast in

Table 14.1   *Public expenditure on housing in selected years*
(£ million at 1978 survey prices)

	1973/4	1974/5	1978/9[a]
Current expenditure			
Mortgage interest tax relief and option mortgage subsidy	1,140	1,310	1,265
General subsidies to public sector housing	928	1,391	1,609
Rent rebates and allowances	430	423	496
Administration	36	54	53
Total current expenditure	2,534	3,178	3,423
Capital expenditure			
Local authorities, new towns and Scottish Special Housing Association:			
investment in land and new dwellings	1,318	1,701	1,501
acquisitions	100	369	62
improvements	716	582	639
other	75	86	74
sales less associated net lending	− 145	− 61	− 167
repayment of principal[b]	− 265	− 261	− 255
Improvement grants by local authorities	327	279	150
Net local authority mortgage lending	205	692	− 122
Grants and net lending to housing associations	205	342	558
Other net lending	− 6	198	− 3
Total capital expenditure	2,530	3,927	2,437

[a] 1978/9 investment figures are subject to shortfall.
[b] Author's estimates. For the case for treating repayments of principal from housing revenue accounts in this way, see D. Webster, 'Overtaking into Account', *Roof*, May 1979.
Source: *The Government's Expenditure Plans 1979–80 to 1982–83*, Cmnd 7439.

the Review envisaged a reduction to 720,000 by 1986 in the number of households unsatisfactorily housed.[16]

Owner occupation

A conspicuous failure of the 1974–79 Labour Government was its refusal to implement the universal option mortgage scheme adopted in the 1973 programme. By giving every mortgagor the tax relief he would have received if he had been paying the standard rate of tax, this would have had the effect of modifying the markedly regressive pattern of subsidies to the sector although it would still give more relief to those buying more expensive homes. The excuse given was that the tax system is otherwise progressive. Even if this claim were not itself highly debatable, it is not defensible to give relief in a way that heightens inequalities in the command over land and urban space, with all their other implications.

On the other hand, three other developments have reduced the degree of inequality in assistance to owner occupiers: abolition in 1974 of tax relief on second homes; the limit of £25,000 on the amount of mortgage eligible for tax relief (which affected only a negligible number of house purchasers when it was introduced in 1974 but because of inflation now affects a substantial minority); and the increase due to inflation in the impact of stamp duty. However, the latter two penalties on those buying expensive houses are extremely vulnerable to repeal by a Tory Government; enduring reform needs to be of a more structural character. The universal option mortgage scheme would have met that test.

The government also refused to take any real action to improve access to credit for those discriminated against by the building societies. It continued the Joint Advisory Committee set up by the Tories, and acted with determination in regulating the fluctuations in the supply of credit which were so conspicuous in the early 1970s. But, succumbing to the influence of dogmatic monetarism, it shied away from setting up any form of public mortgage agency as promised in the October 1974 manifesto. Its Support Lending Scheme has done little more than make up for the effective abandonment of local authority mortgage lending with the 1976 IMF package, in which cuts were concentrated on lending in order to preserve investment and thus employment. (As Table 14.1 shows, by 1978/79 the local authority mortgage scheme was producing more in repayments from borrowers than was being paid out in new lending.) The Savings Bonus and Loan Scheme will undoubtedly help many marginal owner occupiers (along with many others), but in its present form is a minor, populist measure and does not face up to the need for structural change.

The council sector

A similar pattern to that of 1964–70 was seen in the commitment of resources to the council sector: a substantial increase at the outset, followed by reductions almost to the initial level as a result of economic difficulties (although the picture looks better when the expansion in housing association investment is taken into account). Extra cuts in the form of underspending of Housing Investment Programme allocations have been substantial, with the blame to be divided between Tory councils deciding not to spend and the cumbersomeness of the procedures devised by central government. Starts in 1978 had fallen to 107,200 for councils and housing associations combined, compared with 173,800 in 1975 and 112,800 in 1973, the previous low point. These figures do not mean much in themselves since what matters is the balance between supply and demand, with the latter depending on the rate of household formation, but they are somewhat below the level envisaged in the Review's medium term forecast. The government's worst failing was constantly to reiterate the view that there was no longer any overall shortage of housing, while allowing local authorities to refuse housing to 'undeserving' groups such as the single and childless couples.

In the allocation of resources, there was one notable early blunder, in the form of the cutback in local authority improvement spending, under the (Labour) Section 105 of the 1974 Housing Act. Like RAWP in the Health Service, this was intended to be an exercise in the egalitarian redistribution of public spending towards the less well off; in this case, improvement resources were to be shifted from the council sector with its generally good conditions to the private rented sector with its generally bad conditions. But leaving aside the question of the effectiveness of the 1974 Act measures for the private rented sector, the critical problem was the use of obsolete indicators of the degree of relative need. The indicators of housing obsolescence were based on the typical problems found in the private rented sector: lack of basic facilities and decaying physical structure. But many dwellings in the public sector were suffering from obsolescence of quite different kinds, unmeasured by any census: high density, 'non-defensible' design, bleak appearance of the dwelling and its estate, obsolete kitchen and heating installations, small rooms, poor sound regulation, windowless corridors – to mention only a few of the sadly over familiar features of many council estates, old and (unfortunately) new. In the event, the cuts of March 1975 were met by a wave of anger from Labour councils all over the country and the policy modified. But in no year was council improvement spending as high as in the last year of the Heath government, and in the worst year (1976–77) it was over one-third less. By 1979 the government had still not got round to a policy of comprehensive improvements to the living environment on council estates, in spite of a promising speech in June 1978 by Peter Shore and a Labour Party policy document, *A New Deal for Council Tenants*, published the following month. The Housing Policy Review showed that by 1977 only 40 per cent of pre-war council dwellings had received any improvement at all. From the point of view of securing an overall balance of advantage between renting and owner occupation, the importance of this issue can hardly be exaggerated. Fortunately, in respect of new construction, the government did act to raise standards by laying down in 1975 that densities should not exceed 100 habitable rooms per acre and that all family dwellings should be at ground floor level.[17]

An indication of the ground needing to be made up to provide conditions comparable with those of owner occupiers was given by the National Dwelling and Housing Survey of 1977. 90 per cent of owner occupiers were 'satisfied' or 'very satisfied' with their accommodation, and only 4 per cent 'dissatisfied' or 'very dissatisfied'. The corresponding figures for council tenants were 74 per cent and 14 per cent.[18]

The subsidy arrangements of the 1975 Act were quite generous overall and achieved their twin purposes of facilitating a (temporary) revival of council housebuilding and holding down council rents. Over the period October 1973 to October 1978 the average weekly unrebated council rent in England and Wales rose from £3.70 to £5.95.[19] Had it kept pace with the increase in average earnings of all employees, this figure would have been £8.09.[20] There was thus a fall in real terms of about one-quarter – which went some way towards improving the relative advantage of council renting compared with owner occupation; whether far enough only a very comprehensive assessment would show. However, the Act did not remove anomalies of treatment between authorities and it offered a much better deal to those making little investment than to those with real problems. There remain striking differences in the value for money received by tenants of different local authorities (as measured, for want of something better, by differences in gross rateable values). National rent pooling has been proposed as a solution to this problem[21]; it would largely achieve the objective of equity within the council sector but would entail some authorities making historic cost profits on their housing revenue accounts. Provided the level of rents were such as to achieve an overall balance of advantage with owner occupation, this would not in itself be unfair, although many tenants would undoubtedly feel it to be so. The new subsidy scheme proposed by the government in the 1979 Housing Bill would not have achieved the objective of equity within the council sector, though it would have gone some way in that direction. Since it leaves the amount of subsidy to be determined by the Secretary of State, it could be used either to worsen or to improve the relative position of council tenants. Some statutory principles on the overall level of subsidy to maintain comparability with the owner occupied sector seem essential; the only device proposed in the Review (the 'subsidy floor' whereby every authority would receive subsidy at least equal to the standard rate of income tax on its interest payments) was criticised on the grounds of equity within the sector and subsequently abandoned.

In the wake of criticism of the overall tenor of the Review, the government appeared in its last months to attach more importance to its proposals for a Tenants' Charter than it did at first. These ought to have built on pioneering work by local councils and tenants' groups (as in Basildon and Brent) and by the National Consumer Council to a greater extent than they did. As published in the Housing Bill, the Charter was a fairly weak package; the only respect in which it was substantially strengthened was the late inclusion of a statutory national mobility scheme. Separate from the Tenants' Charter, but nevertheless crucial for the quality of service received by tenants, is the issue of the level of training of housing staff. In this respect, the housing service has been left behind other local government services; for instance, the annual training budget per worker is only about one fifth that in social work.[22] The Labour Government set up an initiative on training in 1975, but very little had happened by 1979.

The private rented sector
Energy in tackling the problems of private rented housing in poor condition, using the old style methods of large scale clearance, was a distinguishing mark of the previous Labour Government. By 1974 these methods were clearly inappropriate in most cases. However, it is sad to note that the methods embodied in the 1974 Housing Act

generally proved slow and relatively ineffectual, although those local authorities who have tried it have found a combined policy of Housing Action Area declaration and aggressive acquisition quite effective. In 1974 the Labour Government came in pledged to increase municipalisation, for the first time since the demise of the policy in the 1950s, and was helped by the public mood in the aftermath of the property boom. However, municipalisation was never carried out on anything but a small scale and the budget was soon cut back under the pressure of economic events. (Only 10,317 units were purchased in 1977/8, and the peak figure was 25,600 in 1974/5.) It is hard not to concur with the very hostile view of the new policies taken by the National Community Development Programme.[23] Nevertheless, the National House Condition Survey of 1976 showed a dramatic fall in the number of dwellings in 'other tenures' (mainly privately rented) lacking basic amenities since the 1971 census, from 1,084,000 lacking at least one basic amenity in 1971 to 585,000 in 1976. The explanation for this rapid rate of progress is that purchase and improvement by owner occupiers, and demolition by councils and others, played an important role in addition to grant-aided improvement by local authorities and housing associations.

In its policies for the private rented sector, the government laid great emphasis on the role of housing associations. It was always clear that the 1974 Rent Act, felt to be justified on balance by its benefits in freeing tenants from eviction and the fear of eviction, would intensify the growing problem of access to housing. Given the Labour Party's hostility to any revival of the private rented sector – which was unlikely to be possible anyway – a policy on access had to walk on two legs. One was to reduce the restrictions on entry to the local authority sector. As we have seen, the government's record on this was poor; and in any case, there is little reason to dispute Anthony Crosland's oft-repeated view that a local authority monopoly of rented housing would pose insoluble political and administrative problems. Thus another leg was needed. This the government saw in the expansion of the housing association movement proposed both by the Tories' Housing Bill and by the 1973 Labour programme. In Labour hands, tougher safeguards against corruption were built into the Bill, and Reg Freeson later devoted much effort to encouraging the growth of housing co-operatives within and outside the housing association movement. This growth has remained extremely modest, but other housing associations have expanded dramatically, accounting for nearly one-fifth of total public sector starts in 1978. It is hard to quarrel with the overall logic of the government's actions; other entrepreneurs to run the new 'social housing' were simply not available. But we are left with the problem that tenants of housing associations usually have little control over the way their dwellings are managed and normally pay substantially higher rents than council tenants in their area. The latter problem is now becoming too visible to ignore. It is hard to see how it can be solved in the absence of a more uniform basis for the fixing of council rents.

Other aspects of inequality

The Labour Government rediscovered the inner city in 1976. This was profoundly important; the disparity in living conditions between residents of the decaying inner urban areas and those elsewhere is an important dimension of inequality. Unfortunately, the launching of the inner cities programme coincided with the introduction of tight controls over capital expenditure. Inner city programmes themselves have been negligible in size, however effective they may have been in concentrating attention on the problems and helping to define them. Capital allocations under the HIP system are known to have made some gesture towards the inner cities, but in the event they do not seem to have fared better than before – although the secrecy of the allocation process makes it difficult to say for certain. But there is no doubt that the assault on the inner city problem has been hampered by financial constraints. Perhaps more importantly, it is the inner cities which have suffered most from the lack of effective policies to deal with unsatisfactory housing in the private rented and local authority sectors.

The government was not able to make councils in peripheral areas build for the needs of the inner city.[24] This matters not only because of the unequal prospects of decent housing of tenants in the two types of area but also because of the high costs and high densities imposed on local authorities in the inner area. As we have seen, it was an important influence on the lack of success of much council housing built in the 1960s, although for the time being the problem appears to be acute only in London. The equalisation of housing opportunities could only be achieved by legislation for a statutory redistributive nominations scheme. In fact, the government went to the opposite extreme and cut back potential opportunities for outward movement by the poor by winding down the new and expanded towns schemes – in spite of something approaching official endorsement for the Lambeth inner area study's notion of a 'housing trap' for those on low incomes.

Finally, let us look at the government's policies towards some of the people who, in the words of the Review, 'face special difficulties in getting suitable housing'. A drive was launched to increase provision for the physically disabled, particularly in the local authority sector, and cost yardsticks were revised to make this easier.[25] This resulted in an increase in starts of specially designed local authority and housing association dwellings to 8,107 in 1977 compared with a total of 2,488 in the whole period August 1970 to December 1975.

Elderly people suffer disproportionately from poor conditions in the private rented sector, and the rather complicated pattern of progress here has been discussed. It is worth noting that over one-quarter of the local authority homes completed between 1974 and 1976 (and therefore planned and started before Labour came into office nationally) were specially designed for the elderly – showing that they were already receiving a substantial share of councils' housing efforts.[26] During the government's term of office, two important studies (in London and Birmingham) revealed the extent of discrimination, largely unintended but to some extent probably deliberate, against coloured people in the allocation of council housing.[27] There is little that central government can do directly about this. But ethnic minorities will have been disproportionately affected by the cutbacks in local authority mortgages, because they rely especially heavily on them.

Among the worst-off of all are the single homeless, particularly those who have become chronically reliant upon hostels. In theory, the Housing (Homeless Persons) Act should have helped many of those who are elderly or unwell; in practice, provision has continued to be mainly by the Supplementary Benefits Commission, with its reception centres, and by owners of private lodging houses. The Supplementary Benefits Commission now bluntly states that its present responsibility for providing accommodation should be taken over by local authorities.[28] But there has been very little progress and its clients continue to endure probably the worst conditions suffered by anyone in the country.

Prospects

The failure of the Housing Policy Review to tackle seriously the problem of equity in the distribution of housing subsidies has undoubtedly been a serious setback in the search for greater equality. It should be remembered, of course, that much of the disappointment over the Review is felt by those who wish to see a cutback in subsidies to housing overall. Moreover, no formula exists or can be devised for guaranteeing mathematical equality between owners and tenants. Nevertheless, it has been argued here that it remains vital to aim, first, at a progressive structure of subsidies within each tenure. The way forward clearly lies in implementing the universal option mortgage scheme – in itself likely to be a widely popular measure. Once implemented, there would be no need to keep the rate of subsidy identical with the standard rate of income tax – a lower rate and, most promisingly, a sliding scale would be perfectly possible. Indeed, the need for further measures is shown by the modest impact which the proposal in its original form would have on the total of owner occupier subsidies – a yield of only £120 million in 1976/7 according to the Review.

The £25,000 limit could also be used in an incremental way. With further study, other measures might prove viable. The 'single annuity' scheme proposed by the Housing Centre Trust is one possibility, though in its present form it would hit poorer owner occupiers as well as richer.[29] And it is worth noting that further development of the Savings Bonus and Loan Scheme would strengthen the case for cutting back indiscriminate tax relief. Unfortunately, there are so far no proposals for a viable method of taxing home owners' capital gains.

Second, an overall balance of advantage between the tenures must be established. It is vital to carry out a fundamental review of the ways in which the overall 'package' of opportunities offered to the council tenant could be improved and to carry through a determined programme of reform rather than the present half-hearted 'Tenants' Charter'. Some of the items of such a programme have already been listed, and the emerging 'consumerist' movement within the council sector – a profoundly important development – will suggest more. The most important are probably freedom of movement, a broadly based improvement programme of the kind proposed earlier, an improvement in space standards, consumer sovereignty in design, and the provision of more satisfactory means than are presently available for tenants to accumulate wealth in a manner parallel to that in the owner occupied sector. It is also vital to distinguish more clearly between subsidies which genuinely benefit council tenants on average incomes and those which result from the use of public housing to meet special social needs or to fulfil special planning requirements.

It remains to be seen how significant the proposals of the present Conservative Government for council house sales will prove to have been. If an overall balance of advantage were to be achieved in the long run then there should be no objection in principle to sales and indeed a rational socialist housing policy would involve both purchase and sale by the public sector. But indiscriminate sales worsen housing opportunities for those who need to rent; they seriously lower the overall quality and attractiveness of the council housing stock; and in some cases they may threaten the survival of existing communities. Certainly, the Labour Party ought not to contemplate large scale sales as an alternative to redressing the balance of advantage between the two tenures, as has sometimes been proposed; such a strategy would be bound to leave the remaining tenants in an even worse position.[23] And it will need to be ready to make good any adverse effects of sales on the quality of the stock by acquiring dwellings from the private sector.

On the all important question of rents, it is essential to introduce the notion of explicit comparisons with owner occupiers. Regular monitoring could be carried out by a statutory agency similar to the Comparability Commission. The fact that comparisons of pay between different groups of worker can only be made in a rough-and-ready way has not prevented comparisons being made; there is no reason why this notion should not be extended to housing.

The Labour movement also needs to put its weight behind a demand that a bonfire should be made of all the restrictions on entry to council housing and that the availability of rented housing on demand should be a normal expectation. We have pointed out the difficulty of reducing subsidies across the board. But it is sheer hypocrisy to make housing subsidies available and yet to fail to meet the additional demand thus created. The impact of such a failure falls disproportionately upon those who are poorest and least powerful. The treatment given to the homeless may now often be better than it was when the film 'Cathy Come Home' was made; but homelessness is still a deeply degrading and emotionally devastating experience for those who go through it, and the problems of many who will never be declared officially 'homeless' are often as bad. Only by facing councils with the full blast of demand from those who lose out under the present system can they be made to build and acquire on the scale needed.

15 Urban Deprivation
by Malcolm Wicks

For most of the period 1974–79, not one deprived person benefited from the Labour Government's new area policies. In fact it was not until 1977 that the government announced a new strategy for the inner cities that at least offered out some hope to the deprived, and even here the odds were heavily stacked against success. The record, by any measure, is a miserable one and it reflects badly on Labour's claim to be the party that cares for the weak and disadvantaged. It is important to study this episode for it demonstrates the difficulty of devising effective policies without strong political leadership, shows up the inadequacies of the central government system, with its heavy emphasis on departmentalism, and illustrates the danger of developing policies in secret.

The main aim of this chapter is to present a brief history of the development of area policies during the period of the last Labour Government and then to discuss the lessons that emerge. However, before this, it is important to briefly review the policies of the past decade, account for the interest in area approaches, analyse different views about the causes of urban deprivation and then consider the questions of redistribution that are involved in the light of evidence about the spatial distribution of deprivation.

Proliferating policies
The late 1970s saw a revival of interest in the problem of urban deprivation and in area policies to tackle it. The most important new initiative was outlined in the White Paper *Policy for the Inner Cities*.[1] The special 'Partnerships' now being developed in seven inner city areas are the most visible part of the new strategy. However, policies aimed at deprived urban areas (varying from those with small populations of less than 10,000 to large, local authority wide initiatives) have been an evolving feature of public policy over the last decade or more.

Since the late 1960s there has been a proliferation of area based policies designed to tackle urban deprivation. Educational Priority Areas were designated in 1968 and were based on the concept of 'positive discrimination'. The Urban Programme was initiated in the same year for areas having 'special social need', and this was closely followed by the Home Office's 12 'action research' Community Development Projects (CDPs). Special help to immigrant areas had already been provided under Section 11 of the 1966 Local Government Act. The Home Office also funded two deprived area projects under the auspices of the Greater London Council, and in 1974 the new Comprehensive Community Programmes were announced. Meanwhile, during this period, the Department of the Environment undertook a study of six towns, including the three inner area studies in Liverpool, Birmingham and Lambeth, and set up two area management schemes. To the outside observer (and even to the insider), it appeared that one policy followed another in rapid succession. How can we explain this developing interest in area based programmes to tackle urban deprivation?

In a recent paper, I argued that a wide range of social, economic and administrative ideas and interests led important committees (such as Plowden, Milner Holland and Seebohm), professional groups, policy makers and others to advocate area strategies[2]. They include a concern to combat the alienation of deprived area residents, an interest in participation and better communication, a concern for a better relationship between central and local government, a general emphasis on smallness (including small areas) as a counterweight to a society that seems to be increasingly dominated by 'bigness' (including big units of local government and health service administration), the relative concentration of ethnic minority groups (leading to anxiety about the disadvantages faced by such groups and concern about the potentiality for racial violence) and the influence of the American War on Poverty, no more successful than the War on Vietnam but having an impact on British thinking: 'ideas drifting casually across the Atlantic, soggy on arrival and of dubious utility'.[3]

Causation

While government policies, or the officials who develop them, seldom set out clearly their views about the underlying causes of deprivation, there have been several 'explanations' that influenced policy. Prior to Labour's return to office in 1974, the views of Sir Keith Joseph and his concept of a 'cycle of deprivation', were influential. His policy emphasis on family planning and 'preparation for parenthood' illustrated the focus on reforming the individual (rather than the wider society).

A second view places the emphasis on the area itself. The concept is that, in certain localities, attitudes and life styles develop which mitigate against self-improvement. For example, saving, continuing education past the school leaving age or even holding down a steady job may all be frowned on. An emphasis on the 'sub-culture' of poverty is usually associated with the name of Oscar Lewis[4] but in a less well articulated form it influenced the Home Office's CDPs.

Another view holds that it is policies and services that are largely to blame for continuing area deprivation. Thus emphasis is on the need to improve the various systems that originate, administer and deliver services of different kinds. The answer is not (necessarily) to spend more money or to develop new services. Rather there is a need for better management, greater cost-effectiveness, research and intelligence, corporate planning, more co-ordination and a comprehensive approach. This thinking has strongly influenced the development of area strategies over the last decade: Peter Walker's 'total approach' with the 'Making Towns Better' and inner area studies, the DOE's Area Management schemes and the Home Office's Comprehensive Community Programmes. It is an approach that appeals to officials, at both central and local government levels (perhaps because it *seems* to be apolitical and *certainly* because it is cheap).

The final view about causation is often termed the 'structural' approach. This emphasises the need to understand the position of the deprived individual, or deprived locality, in the context of the wider society. The structural view emphasises the need to understand, and then effectively tackle, the ways in which such factors as industrial decline and unemployment impoverish whole urban areas. Rather than seeing deprived areas as remaining 'pockets of poverty', blemishes on an otherwise smoothly running and just society, it points to the inequalities that exist throughout society and demands radical change.

Why an 'area' approach?

Early arguments in favour of an area approach to urban deprivation were often based on two inter-related assumptions. The first is that deprivations of various kinds are concentrated geographically in certain (and quite small) urban areas. A second assumption is that policies to alleviate area deprivation would be confined to the area itself, involving such measures as extra teachers and educational aids, play groups and adventure playgrounds, advice services and the employment of community workers to encourage self-help and participation.

These assumptions were hardly questioned in the early days of area strategies, but there is now evidence – much of it deriving from area programmes themselves – which has produced more scepticism and caution regarding the relative concentration of the deprived and which fundamentally questions the policy assumptions. One of the most important pieces of research was carried out by Sally Holtermann at the Department of the Environment, who explored Census information to show the extent of deprivation geographically throughout Great Britain. One of its major conclusions was that 'the national picture is dominated by Scotland, whose cities, particularly Clydeside, apparently contain areas of severe urban deprivation on a scale not matched in England and Wales'.[5] The other major conclusion was that, while there were many areas with high levels of both housing deprivation and unemployment, 'spatial coincidence of these problems is far from complete; and further, that although there is some degree of spatial concentration of deprived people into the "worst areas", there are large numbers of deprived people who live outside them'.[5] An analysis of housing indicators reached a similar conclusion: 'the spatial concentration of housing deprivation was found to be far from complete and the issue of equitable treatment between households who are covered by area policies and those who are not is therefore potentially serious'.[6] Research based on Educational Priority Areas points in the same direction. Indeed, Jack Barnes noted that: 'area policies can only meet the needs of people in poor areas; but most poor people do not live in poor areas; and most of the people in poor areas are not themselves poor'.[7]

Some critics have argued that the evidence about the spatial distribution of deprivation undermines the credibility of area strategies entirely. It certainly has undermined any simplistic acceptance of area policies, regardless of local circumstances. However it can be argued that, while the lessons from research experience need to be applied, the area approach itself remains a valid (and indeed largely untested) element of public policy. In certain urban areas there are heavy concentrations of deprivation, Glasgow being the starkest example. However, generally concentration is not so great that a majority of deprived people will be found in such areas. It follows that any area based policies cannot replace general policies aimed at the whole population or specific client groups. One of the major effects of research findings has been a move away from *small* area strategies towards a focus on larger, perhaps local authority wide initiatives, and it is now generally recognised that action to combat area deprivation will often involve action outside the area itself and on a scale much larger than that envisaged by the early advocates of area programmes. This argument can be illustrated by considering the kind of inequalities within urban areas that socialists are concerned to eradicate.

Always the key issue (and one that grew in importance over the lifetime of the Labour Government) is the command over economic resources. The problems of unemployment, insecure employment and low pay are likely to be present in most of these areas. Partly due to the poor performance of the economy generally, but more specifically as a result of shifts within the manufacturing sector which have important implications for the spatial distribution of employment opportunities, attention has increasingly focused on the problem of inner cities.

The poor quality of the physical environment is another key characteristic of deprived areas and, although not the only aspect, poor housing is the major factor here. Such areas are likely to have more than their fair share of dwellings that are unfit or lack basic amenities, and the housing opportunities (with often little chance of access to the owner occupied market) will be significantly poorer than in other localities. Such housing is matched by inferior buildings of other kinds – schools, clinics, shops and factories – and will be interspersed with large tracts of derelict and vacant land. These conditions are poor for the inhabitants and also inhibit a better future for, as the 1977 White Paper noted: 'They combine together to make these areas unattractive, both to many of the people who live there and to new investment in business, industry and housing'.[1]

Low economic resources, poor housing and an inadequate environment will all too often be matched by other disadvantages. Educational opportunities in such areas will be relatively poor. Many children will leave school with either very low or no qualifications and will be equipped only for low paid jobs or a place in the growing ranks of the young unemployed. Social services of different kinds will often fail to match the needs of these areas, recreational facilities will be sparse and many residents (particularly the elderly) will be ill-at-ease in what they feel to be a deteriorating and insecure environment.

The Labour Government 1974–79

The new Labour Government of 1974 had no clear plans for tackling urban deprivation. However, it is worth noting that Roy Jenkins, who became Home Secretary for the second time in 1974, had made a series of speeches in 1972 which focused, in part, on problems of poverty and deprivation.[8] These speeches showed a concern and an idealism that offered hope to the poorest and weakest members of an unequal society. Thus, in one speech, he argued that: 'The next Labour Government can be content with nothing less than the elimination of poverty as a social problem. It is a formidable but not insurmountable objective.' In another, he called for an expanded Urban Programme. 'An eightfold expansion of the whole programme would cost only about £120 million per year. This is not too heavy a price to pay to attack the manifold squalor in areas where poverty abounds.'

Comprehensive community programmes
How does the record compare with such notable aspirations? When Roy Jenkins returned to the Home Office in 1974, the Urban Deprivation Unit was engaged in an inter-departmental policy review. Its conclusions were reported to ministers in the summer of 1974 and the major proposal was for 'a new strategy to tackle urban deprivation'. This involved the setting-up of Comprehensive Community Programmes (CCPs), on a 'trial run' basis in six areas with populations of approximately 10,000 people. The proposal was that in these areas a special team would (a) analyse the needs in the locality (but with the emphasis on a relatively quick appraisal, rather than a lengthy research exercise); (b) study the impact of existing policies; and (c) produce a 'comprehensive' programme of action (with implications for both central and local government and other agencies). 'Its essential purpose is to bring about, through the co-ordinated efforts of central government, regional water and health authorities, voluntary bodies and residents, a reordering of priorities in favour of those living in the most acutely deprived areas'.[9]

Despite the emphasis on co-ordination, much of the thinking behind CCPs in 1974 was based as much on a structural analysis as a technocratic one, with a strong orientation towards employment and the need to redirect main spending programmes towards the needs of deprived areas. Certainly in the summer of 1974 there was some hope that CCPs might become not just another cosmetic area strategy but an effective means of combating urban deprivation. Sadly the CCP story since then is one of dismal failure. In the years that followed, CCP disintegrated into an area variation on corporate management, implemented at a pace that would embarrass any self-respecting snail.

The CCP in 1974 appeared to the casual observer to be a well thought out policy. There were certainly grounds for this view. It had been discussed and accepted by a Permanent Secretaries committee, considered in Cabinet committee and announced in parliament. And yet, almost immediately, cracks started to appear in the policy's structure which were to lead to its radical overhaul. That these problems emerged so early on in the life of a policy which had been developed by an inter-departmental review over a period of a year may cause some surprise. What were these problems?

Perhaps the most important concerned the emphasis on areas of approximately 10,000 people. In the search for suitable 'trial run' authorities, local government officers argued either that there was more than one such area within their boundaries or that virtually their whole area was deprived (and not amenable to 'small area' treatment).

Other problems concerned finance. It was originally proposed that each CCP area should be allocated £1 million per annum in addition to existing resources. However, as the economic problems facing the administration worsened, Home Office officials decided that such sums of money could not be wrested away from the Treasury. There was no fight with the Treasury about this. It was rather a basic assumption that, in a climate of public expenditure cuts, additional sums for deprived areas could not be found. Certainly the alternative argument, that at times of difficulties the weakest should be protected (a common piece of rhetoric in 'crisis' politics during this period) had no impact in practice. On this and other important questions, ministers were not involved at an early stage (and certainly showed no interest in being involved). Rather they were presented with the officials' conclusion and then, dutifully, they acquiesced.

Another problem concerned the Whitehall response to the comprehensive programmes that would be presented by CCP authorities. Certainly a major selling point in favour of CCP was the implication that Whitehall – the whole range of social and economic departments – would respond corporately to the needs of a deprived area. (A common complaint of local authority Chief Executives was that there was no one place in central government where they could talk about the overall problems facing local authorities.) Similarly, another attractive feature of CCP was the implication that mainstream programmes could be redirected, strengthened or perhaps made more flexible to better enable local councils to tackle their problems. Could CCP deliver on these matters?

Urban deprivation was perhaps the most obvious example of the need for a 'joint approach to social policy', then being advocated by the CPRS'. A determined Home Office, wishing to make sense of its co-ordinating role in this policy area, might have achieved a break-through. But on this matter, Home Office officials showed no real interest in developing the role of the Urban Deprivation Unit and getting other departments to make a genuine effort to help deprived areas. It became clearer and clearer that the Home Office did not view its urban deprivation brief as a priority. Indeed there was a lack of understanding about the issues and certainly no sense of urgency.

Meanwhile negotiations with local authorities dragged on and the CCP concept was reformulated. The focus moved away from small deprived areas towards tackling deprivation in general and the need to redirect main programmes. But no extra money was to go to CCP authorities immediately. Rather the Home Office agreed to pay the salaries and related expenses of a small team who would develop the CCP in each area. This new approach was discussed with local authorities and the talking went on ... and on. From time to time, interested backbench MPs would enquire about what was happening to CCPs. Such PQs would be skilfully dealt with by Home Office civil servants and their spokesmen in the House of Commons, the ministers (and it was *spokesmen* that they became), would report that satisfactory progress was being made or that discussions were being held with local authorities. In no way did parliament penetrate the defences of the Executive to reveal the drift, the lack of energy and commitment and the feebleness which had suffocated the 'new strategy for tackling urban deprivation'.

Three years after CCPs had been announced in the House of Commons in 1974 (earning media headlines at the time like 'Labour to give from urban rich to poor' – *The Guardian*; 'Jenkins plans new deal for the poor' – *Sun*), only one CCP had been initiated in England (Gateshead) and one in Scotland (Motherwell) and *not one* deprived person had benefited from Labour's new strategy. There are many reasons for the abysmal failure. They include the Labour Government's general lack of commitment to tackle inequality, the obsession with expenditure cuts, the feeble performance of the Home Office (whose traditionalist approach and major interests – police, prisons, immigration – made it ill equipped to tackle urban deprivation), a conservative civil service, and the heavily departmental (and therefore narrow) approach of central government. But the failure of political leadership is also clear. In this respect the CCP story provides a salutary lesson for the Labour Party. For 1974 to 1977 were the wasted years, the years when poor and deprived people must have wondered if anyone in the government cared about their plight.

In his 1972 speeches, Roy Jenkins called for a 'positive victory' for Labour at the next election: 'Only that will enable us to carry through a programme which will give us pride in our party and confidence in our processes of government'. The history of CCP, during Jenkins' Home Secretaryship, did little to restore our pride or our confidence.

Towards a policy for the inner cities

While the Home Office remained the lead department on urban deprivation until the summer of 1977, it had been losing ground in its long standing contest with the DOE. An inter-departmental committee of civil servants had been set up in 1975 to review urban problems and, significantly, this committee was under the chairmanship of a DOE official. The department was also in a key position because of its responsibilities for housing, planning and local government. Additionally, the DOE-sponsored Inner Area Studies (altogether more respectable and acceptable than the Home Office's politically controversial CDP) were nearing completion and were providing useful material and ideas for policy makers in the department.

In September 1976, the Prime Minister announced a major review of policy relating to inner urban areas. A committee of junior ministers was set up under the chairmanship of Peter Shore, then Secretary of State for the Environment, and its report led to the publication in June 1977 of the White Paper *Policy for the Inner Cities*.

The White Paper adopted a broad analysis of the problem of urban deprivation and it included both economic and social factors. Its approach was entirely a structural one and took on board many of the arguments of the critics of past area strategies. While recognising the existence of a general problem of urban deprivation, it gave priority to the needs of the inner city areas. It argued that 'the decline in the economic fortunes of the inner areas lies at the heart of the problem' and pointed to the higher rates of unemployment and a '... mismatch between the skills of the people and the kinds of jobs available'. It is noted that in 1971 unskilled and semi-skilled men accounted for 38 per cent of the labour force in inner Birmingham, 38 per cent in inner Manchester and 34 per cent in inner Glasgow, compared to a national figure of 23 per cent. There had been a loss of jobs in traditional industries, such as the docks and the railways, and many firms had either closed or moved. These losses in employment had not been made good by new investment as new enterprises had tended to locate themselves away from the inner city. Apart from economic decline, the White Paper noted the physical decay in the inner city, the preponderance of social disadvantages of different kinds and a rapid rate of population decline. Between 1966 and 1976, Glasgow had lost 205,000 people (21 per cent); Liverpool had lost 150,000 (22 per cent) and inner London had lost 500,000 (16 per cent). The government's major proposals can be usefully divided into three: main policies and programmes; strengthening the economies of inner areas; and a new area approach. The government proposed in the White Paper to 'give a new priority in the main policies and programmes of government so that they contribute to a better life in the inner areas'. It is hoped that not only DOE policies but also the policies of other government departments would be given an inner city orientation in the future.

Regarding the economic base of inner city areas the White Paper noted: 'an inner area dimension is essential in the fields of industrial and employment policies, since it is a matter of high priority to strengthen the economies of the inner areas. The aim must be to see that these areas make a viable contribution to the prosperity of their cities, and that suitable job opportunities are available for people living there'. It pointed to the importance of the location of industry and, while noting that regional policy is of continuing importance, it called for an 'intra-regional emphasis to policy designed to help inner areas'. In future inner London and inner Birmingham would take precedence, after the Assisted Areas (and before the New and Expanding Towns), in the awarding of Industrial Development Certificates.

The White Paper also stated that local authorities could do much more to improve the employment prospects of their areas. 'Briefly, local authorities should administer all their powers, including those for housing, planning and the environment, so as to facilitate the growth of employment in inner areas'. (Following the publication of the White Paper, the Inner Urban Areas Act was passed in 1978 which gave additional powers to local authorities to encourage the growth of employment opportunities in inner city areas.)

The third major element in the White Paper was the announcement of a new area approach. Its key feature was the setting up of 'Partnership' schemes. These would be set up in only a few selected areas: 'Spread too thinly, any special efforts will achieve much less'. The Partnership authorities announced were Liverpool, Birmingham, Manchester/Salford, Lambeth and Docklands. Shortly afterwards, Newcastle/Gateshead and Islington/Hackney were added to this select list. As the name implies, 'Partnerships' involve close collaboration between central and local government (and, indeed, a range of other agencies). The Partnership is intended to underline 'the government's commitment to the inner areas and to instil confidence in their future; it will help to bring national experience to bear; it will enable ways of unifying the actions of central and local government to be worked out. The initial task of the Partnerships will be to draw up an inner area programme for early implementation, based on an analysis of local conditions'.

In addition to the Partnership schemes, the DOE invited 15 authorities to devise Inner Area Programmes. These are: North Tyneside, South Tyneside, Sunderland, Middlesbrough, Bolton, Oldham, Wirral, Bradford, Hull, Leeds, Sheffield, Wolverhampton, Leicester, Nottingham, and Hammersmith. These 'Programme' authorities will have the powers to make loans and to declare Industrial Improvement Areas and will receive favourable treatment under the Urban programme. However, they have a very much lower status than the Partnership authorities.

Another feature of the new area approach is a reform of the Urban Programme. This is transferred from the Home Office to the DOE, extended to cover industrial, environmental and recreational provisions (as well as social service projects) and its spending was to be increased from under £30 million per annum to £125 million in 1979/80.

Facing the challenge
How should the policies for the inner cities be judged? Some critics

were quick to portray it as just another dose of an all-to-familiar mixture. However, a more sympathetic response is justified. The move of responsibility to the DOE is a step forward and, under the political leadership of the then Secretary of State, Peter Shore, more energy and commitment was given to the attack on urban problems. The analysis of the White Paper is wide ranging and recognises the structural causes of urban deprivation. There has undoubtedly been a shift in thinking since the 1970–74 Conservative Government.

However, there must be major doubts about the feasibility of successfully implementing the area policy. There are two key questions, both of which are recognised in the White Paper. The first concerns the economic rejuvenation of inner areas. The difficulties here are immense and relate directly to some of the most important questions facing the British economy, such as the balance between manufacturing industry and the service sectors, and the impact of technological change on jobs.

The other important challenge recognised in the White Paper concerns 'mainstream' policies and programmes. A great weakness of past area approaches was their isolation from the major policies and services in such fields as education, housing and health. This led to the absurd spectacle of area policies, with grand names like the 'Urban Programme' and equally grand objectives, being allocated pitifully low resources. The proposal to 'give a new priority in the main policies and programmes of government so that they contribute to a better life in the inner areas'[1] was therefore very significant – indeed potentially much more so than the increased funding of the Urban Programme. However, it is an immensely difficult policy to implement. The DOE has succeeded in redirecting its own policies to the needs of the inner city (indeed the New Towns policy has already been cut back and housing investment programmes can be related to inner city needs without much difficulty) but other major spending departments will take some persuading – to put it mildly.

In brief, how can the inner city policies become a *government* strategy, rather than merely a *DOE* one? Certainly inner city needs cannot be met by the heavily departmentalised, and consequently disjointed, approach to public policy that abounds in Whitehall. There is no better example than urban deprivation to prove the need for the 'joint approach' advocated by the Central Policy Review Staff and their call for: 'better analysis of, and policy prescriptions for, complex problems – especially when they are the concern of more than one department'[10].

Since the adoption of the new policy there is little evidence to suggest that the challenge to redirect main spending programmes has been taken up. Indeed there is a danger that the allocation of extra money to the Urban Programme (in itself a welcome move) will stand in the way of this happening. The first full year of the new Partnerships seems to have been largely devoted to spending this money inevitably on small scale projects which, however useful, are directed at the symptoms and not the causes of urban deprivation.

Another key problem for the new strategy relates to the nature of the 'Partnership' between the two tiers of government. Area policies involve an interesting, and somewhat two edged, relationship between central departments and local authorities. On the one hand, defining an area as deprived suggests a recognition by central government that it requires *more* resources. However, while the local authority will put emphasis on the need for redistribution *to* its own area (often at the expense of other local authorities), Whitehall in its turn will stress the need for a local authority to redistribute its own resources within its own boundaries – from the better off suburbs to the inner area. Central departments also look for a greater sensitivity to the needs of the deprived in local policy making and administration, in housing allocation for example, and also for more and better communication between Town Hall and the local people. Thus, area programmes involve a problematic partnership between the two main tiers of government. Whitehall will want to prevent councils from taking the money and running, while local councillors and officials will often be wary of strings and argue that more local discretion (rather than less) is the answer.

These are inevitably political questions, but they become overt in some authorities when deprived area programmes are effectively controlled by councillors representing the interests of the outer areas. One of the major tests for the new inner city policy is whether the extraordinarily complex committee systems that have been devised in the new Partnership areas can become arenas in which genuine co-operation between tiers of government takes place.

Another question concerns the participation of local people in the new programmes. The need for community involvement in deprived area projects has been a common feature of policies over the last decade, but has rarely been realised. The White Paper argued that 'involving local people is both a necessary means to the regeneration of the inner areas and an end in its own right. Public authorities need to draw on the ideas of local residents, to discover their priorities and enable them to play a practical part in reviving their areas'. However, as experience shows, this is easier said than done. One report found that there had been scarcely any local participation in drafting the new area programmes in the first year of the policy in the 'Partnership' and 'Programme' authorities.[11] Some authorities have clearly gone to great lengths to stimulate community involvement but the actual impact on policy development has been disappointing.

Behind closed doors

There are then major barriers standing in the way of a successful implementation of area deprivation policies and they involve some important and complex questions. But the main issues are essentially political. Although urban deprivation policies are often discussed in an apparently neutral language (with much talk of 'co-ordination', 'consultation' and better management), there is no way in which these more technical questions can be successfully addressed without a commitment to greater equality and social justice. For most of the period of the last Labour Government, this commitment was missing and, in its absence, it was civil servants who did most of the thinking about urban deprivation, developed the ideas and fashioned new programmes. Even in the best of circumstances this may be inevitable; however, the closed and secretive nature of such policy making is not inevitable but merely traditional and convenient for the small élites who determine policy in Britain. Such secrecy is the enemy of democratic decision making, it makes a mockery of parliamentary government and often produces ill thought out and ineffective policies. Only occasionally is the public given an inkling of what is happening within Whitehall. Thus during the period of 1974–79 there were *three* major reviews of urban deprivation policy, *none* were published and only *one* was publicly announced. Major problems were discussed behind closed doors and yet there were many outside Whitehall who could have usefully contributed to such discussions. Even backbench MPs stood no chance of successfully questioning the Executive about developments. Parliamentary questions were taken seriously, but often answered misleadingly, being drafted with more regard to the needs of the department than the rights of the House of Commons.

Conclusions

There are two tragic features about the recent history of area deprivation policies. The first is that for three years, 1974–77, time was wasted and the development of the Home Office's CCP suffered from a lack of urgency, imagination and commitment, at both ministerial and civil service levels. Despite a promising start, CCP fizzled out into a mere variation on corporate management (and is now being developed in only three areas). It is only since 1977 that the Labour Government began to develop a policy that potentially matched up to the major structural causes of urban deprivation, although, as noted, the barriers standing in the way of successful implementation were considerable.

The second tragic feature of contemporary policy is the advent of the Conservative Government in 1979. For, while Labour would have had to struggle hard to implement the inner city policy, the will to do so existed in some quarters. This cannot be said now. The private market philosophy, which pervades the current administration, does not augur well for an initiative that critically depends on public intervention. Its electoral support derives primarily from outer areas (and from the South) and this is likely to prevent action – such as the redirection of major spending programmes – in favour of the inner areas (which are mainly in the North). And its determination to cut back public expenditure will prevent it meeting the needs of deprived areas that require greater public spending.

16 The Personal Social Services

by Adrian Webb

An absence of concern for equality?

The post-war debate on equality and redistribution has virtually by-passed the personal social services. Unlike such services as education, housing or even health, relatively few attempts have been made systematically to gather data which would answer such questions as: who benefits; or, do these services reinforce or modify wider patterns of inequality? This neglect reflects the generally low status accorded to these services; even now their 'take' of public expenditure, compared with that of the more established social services, is insufficient to exert much impact on national inequality.

There is a widespread assumption that the 'benefits' of the personal social services do find their way to the poor and the working classes. Any intention there may have been at the time of the Seebohm report of producing a universal service to set alongside the NHS has been destroyed by the twin forces of rising demand and public expenditure restraint which characterised the second half of the 1970s. Despite a few faltering steps towards a universal service, the personal social services have not fully escaped from the residual model of their Poor Law origins. The constant concern is to identify the most needy as a basis for allocating scarce resources, rather than to offset the 'overly successful' use of services by the middle classes. There are middle class clients, there are real issues of inequality and there is real interest in the pursuit of equality, but the very failure to establish a comprehensive service in the universal mould means that one of the major preoccupations in other services – the distribution of services between classes or income groups – is less fiercely debated.

What are the personal social services?

For the purposes of this chapter, the personal social services are taken to comprise the work of local authority social services departments and of voluntary and informal care and provision for similar client groups. This approach excludes the probation and after-care service, but it includes a great mass of imprecisely defined non-statutory work. One must also recognise the importance of privately purchased or produced services, ranging from elderly and disabled people who buy domestic help on the 'open market' to socially dependent people who live in hotels, private boarding houses or 'homes', rather than in a private household.

The personal social services can only be understood and analysed if they are conceived as part of a 'mixed economy of welfare'. The balances and shifts between the various components of this 'mixed economy' must be counted as a central issue in any discussion of equality. In 'real' manpower terms, at least, the 'professional' statutory services are overshadowed by the volunteer sector.[1] The informal care provided by kin, neighbours and friends is extensive and diverse, although not easily quantified.[2] Changes in the statutory sector must therefore be expected to ripple throughout a much wider 'system' – and *vice versa*.

Equality as a dimension of analysis
The concept of equality has been used in several principal ways in post-war debate on social policy. They are not of equal significance for the personal social services and they are by no means always distinguished in debate. It is therefore important to identify them as a basis for analysis.

The first and strongest notion of equality involves the political objective of transforming the tendency of society towards material inequality. This approach locates equality at the core of a theory of fundamental social change; it concerns the range of inequality in earned incomes, the distribution of income generating opportunities (access to the labour market) and the distribution of wealth generating opportunities. It is most pertinent to those social services which do, or are believed to, affect access to the labour market. It has limited significance for the personal social services in the sense that the quality of care provided to the elderly, handicapped, mentally ill or the delinquent child is unlikely to affect the distribution of initial incomes.

However, a second and related approach emphasises the peculiar disadvantages which affect minorities in the labour market: deprived and delinquent children; the physically and mentally handicapped and mentally ill; ethnic groups subject to discrimination and women. The call is for positive discrimination of a kind which will improve access to jobs. Within any given labour market, certain groups and individuals may need special support if they are to overcome disadvantages placed in their way by 'the hand of God' or by social forces. They include many of the clients of the personal social services. One of the major problems is that the personal social services, and social work as a profession, have not been strongly oriented to problems of employment and labour market access. It is an area of potential in which skills have been developing far too slowly in relation to the size of the task. It is also a field of activity which is highly vulnerable to high unemployment.

A third approach to equality is to move more deeply and to emphasise inequalities of power as themselves productive of and reinforced by material inequality. One way in which this emerges in the personal social services is as a concern with decision making. Participation in decision making, the mobilisation of community and consumer interests, attempts to counteract 'professional dominance' and the search for alternatives to professional bureaucratic services all give expression to a dissatisfaction with inequalities of power.

A fourth notion of equality emphasises the redistribution of material resources as a means of modifying the distribution of income set by the market. It is this notion of equality which is most fully reflected in the measures of service distribution noted earlier. The focus is on benefiting two groups: those who are excluded from, or who are no longer participants in, the labour market; and those who are penalised in the labour market – the low wage earners. The first category should be highly relevant to the personal social services. The second should be much less pertinent. The personal social services are not primarily intended as agencies which subsidise low wage families. In practice, however, the position is greatly complicated by the fact that it is nonetheless possible to subsidise low incomes, especially through the provisions of the Children and Young Persons Act, 1963. Some argue strongly that social security policies and practices have greatly enlarged this role of the personal social services as a substitute social assistance service.[3] Local authorities differ considerably in the way they use their power to provide material aid[4] but doubts about future changes in social assistance policies and their implications for the personal social services have contributed to a sense of uncertainty.

A fifth notion of equality moves beyond material inequality to consider social isolation and exclusion. Townsend has identified inequalities of social integration as the heart of this perspective.[5]

By this he referred not merely to the unavoidable isolation of the bereaved, which may be offset somewhat by support, but also the avoidable isolation and exclusion of the chronically sick and disabled, the mentally ill or handicapped person discharged from hospital and the young person stigmatised by delinquency, family breakdown or inadequate parenting. The personal social services have a large potential role in removing these social inequalities or in compensating for them where the basic problem is irremediable – by providing friendly visitors for the bereaved, or subsidised communications (telephone and television) for the house bound, and other isolated people.

At least five senses of equality of social integration can be identified as relevant to current policies: the avoidance of the unnecessary and inappropriate use of residential institutions; the avoidance of institutionalisation, social isolation and an impoverished social life among people who have necessarily to live in some form of institutional care; the prevention and reduction of social isolation among people living 'in the community'; the compensation of people suffering unavoidable isolation; and the removal of stigma attached to the use of services. Each of these has a somewhat different implication for service development and they are not necessarily compatible – especially in the face of resource shortages. The action equivalents of each might be briefly characterised as: expansion of community care services; the improvement of the *quality* of residential care of all kinds; the improvement of the *quality* of community care services and the expansion of their preventive functions; the use of community based services to substitute for more 'normal' social networks and patterns of integration; and the 'de-labelling' of stigmatising conditions, types of intervention and services (not least by moving towards the provision of universal services which acquire status from their middle class clients).

Pursuing these rather different strategies simultaneously and within a limited budget is not the only problem. There are also profound areas of ignorance and uncertainty surrounding method: how best can one prevent delinquency by removing causes, while also rehabilitating the presently delinquent; how best can one prevent social isolation in old age, or among the mentally ill and handicapped; how best can one remit the worst effects of bereavement and loss? How great is the danger of providing token help of a kind which conceals the fact of systematic exclusion of people: of the retired by a rigid exclusion from the world of work; of the elderly by subjecting them to a universal 'label' and stereotype; of the handicapped by denying them the means to independence? Perhaps the most pertinent feature of the personal social services, in any consideration of equality, is the impossibility of confining discussion to material parameters. Once one moves into the field of equality of social integration, the concepts, strategies and criteria of evaluation become even more problematic than at the level of material inequality.

Any discussion of equality and the personal social services must therefore identify different approaches to equality and address several fundamental issues: which concepts of equality, if any, inform professional philosophies, theories of problem causation and the selection of solutions – or methods of intervention; to which problems of equality are the personal social services most pertinent and how relevant and effective are the methods of intervention currently available; how adequate are resources in relation to the scale of the task?

Trends and policies, 1964–70
Although the personal social services as we now know them did not come into being until 1970/71, there were important changes during the mid- and late 1960s. Despite the pressure for community based care of the elderly, mentally ill and mentally handicapped which had been building up since the late fifties, less was spent in the early 1960s in this field (0.7 per cent of all public expenditure in 1963) than on school meals, milk and welfare foods.[6]

The 1960s were years of growth, but the personal social services did not command more than 1 per cent of public expenditure until the beginning of the 1970s. Their share of local authority expenditure rose by 52 per cent in the seven years after 1965: in 1965 £1 was spent for every £13 spent by local education authorities; by 1970 the ratio was one to eight; by 1973 it was one to seven. But the ludicrously small expenditure base has to be kept in mind to put such a change into perspective. It should also be remembered that in the 1960s an enormous backlog of unmet need was known to exist and that extra resources were the very essence of moving the burden of long term social care from the health services.

Changes in approach beginning in the 1960s were perhaps more important than the increase in resources. Juvenile crime was being radically reinterpreted as socially caused – a product of poverty deprivation and of 'labelling'. The chosen solutions were less obviously radical than the new model of causation implied: child care policy was not directly addressed to the removal of deprivation, that was assumed to be effected elsewhere. The emphasis within the personal social services was on the reduction of institutional care and on community based support for their families. If the approach was in the first instance one of no longer blaming the victim, the search for community alternatives to institutional punishment did express a more fundamentally egalitarian aim. Children of deprived families were to be compensated; they were to be the beneficiaries of positive discrimination. All that was apparently needed to give effect to this philosophy of the Children and Young Persons Act, 1969, was resources and energy.

The change of philosophy within child care spilled over into a more general change in the casework model. Material deprivation and powerlessness were seen as the core problems of the socially battered families and communities with which social work had long been engaged. The favoured solutions were: to improve access to other social services for the multiply deprived via information, advice and advocacy; to focus on whole areas and not merely on individuals and families, through community work but also more generally throughout the work of the new local authority departments; and to exert influence on other agencies more able to attack the social causes of need – a strategy which paralleled the movement towards corporate planning.

Although, as Townsend argued,[5] the Seebohm Report failed in not advocating a new philosophy centred on the pursuit of equality, changes in perspectives and legislation provided a greater opportunity for such an approach to flourish than had previously existed. In addition to the positive discrimination embodied in child care policy, a move towards a universal model of service was enshrined in the Chronically Sick and Disabled Persons Act, 1970, and in the commitment to extending domiciliary and other community based services.

In short, by the end of the 1960s the opportunities for promoting equality through the personal social services were surprisingly good. Expenditure was rising and this could in itself be expected to have egalitarian effects. The expansion of community care services would reduce inequalities of material and social integration. Insofar as growth resulted in a more socially diverse clientele, the direct egalitarian effect would diminish at the margin but the indirect effect predicted from a more universal service would be expected to come into play. However, growth could also be expected to improve the quality of residential care and compensate for the disadvantages suffered by residents.

Nevertheless, the challenge was real. The reform of the personal social services entailed two assumptions, each containing an egalitarian component: that these services could take their place alongside the four main social service systems as a comparatively universal and therefore non-stigmatised means of intervention; and that they could positively discriminate in favour of the hardest pressed.

Trends and policies, 1970–74

The first three years of the 1970s were the brief hey-day of the reorganised personal social services. Expenditure growth per annum in real terms ranged from approximately 8 per cent and 11 per cent on fostering children and field social work respectively, to 17 per cent, 18.5 per cent and 19 per cent on residential care for the mentally handicapped, day care and meals on wheels respectively.[7] Overall, a comparatively impressive growth rate of approximately 12 per cent per annum was being achieved on what was by now a more substantial expenditure base (the much higher growth rates were primarily in the least well developed sectors of the services). Capital expenditure rose by more than 30 per cent per annum at constant prices in 1972/3 and 1973/4.[8] During this period all client groups were attracting growth. The largest and most rapidly expanding group – the elderly – was especially benefiting from an expansion in domiciliary care, but even residential care for the elderly – the largest single area of expenditure – was growing at a rate of 9 per cent per annum. Nevertheless, the overall rate of growth left room for matching performances in services for the mentally ill, handicapped and families and children. The problem of priorities was muted.

However, there are a number of reasons for taking a more critical view of this period. First, it was a very brief boom which had repercussions in subsequent years – especially arising from capital expenditure. Second, it was essentially a period of uncontrolled growth; a longer period of steady growth with adequate time for planning would have been preferable. Third, it only began to reduce a little of the backlog of need while creating the impression that the personal social services were no longer the 'poor relation' of the welfare state. Growth had been seen to have happened and there was little opportunity once the expenditure squeeze arrived to reflect on the extent to which this growth corresponded with indicators of need. Indeed, the burst of enthusiasm for studies of 'need' came to rather an abrupt halt by the mid 1970s. Fourth, the Conservative Government had adopted policies which blunted the reformative impact of expansion. Crucial sections of the Children and Young Persons Act, 1969, were not implemented and progress in services for the chronically sick and disabled was patchy and often slow. Fifth, despite the merits of steady but prolonged growth, there are developments which cannot be taken slowly if they are to succeed and the Children and Young Persons Act was just such a measure. The pressure of many competing initiatives on finite resources was undoubtedly one of the factors underlying the disappointing impact of this Act.

Nevertheless, these years were certainly characterised by progress and the epitome of this period of optimism, the introduction in 1972 of a ten-year planning cycle by DHSS, was also an attempt to guide and shape expansion. The actual plans which were developed were, however, made redundant almost immediately. By 1973 the honeymoon was over and the first real evidence of severe public expenditure constraint was manifest, although actual effects were patchy depending on local authorities' willingness to finance spending from the rates.

Bearing in mind the extent of the local variations, the early 1970s can be summarised in the following terms. A brief period of nationally unco-ordinated growth was followed by an optimistic programme of planned growth, beginning in 1972. This rapidly collapsed into a rather chaotic retreat from growth, from 1973 onwards, in which the first tactic was to load cuts onto capital expenditure. On the current expenditure side, a series of circulars included inconsistent and *ad hoc* suggestions about how local authorities might effect reductions: by directly cutting growth in social work staff, home helps, day centres, meals and holidays; by restricting improvements in standards of residential accommodation and adult training centres; and by cutting such support services as research and planning staffs.

Trends and policies, 1974–79
The two major issues which emerged in 1973 dominated the period of Labour Government: the extent to which the personal social services should bear cuts; and the search for national guidance to local authorities on how they might adjust to this new economic

climate. Although local variations in the impact of expenditure restraint and in the response to national statements of priority continued to undermine generalisations, a fairly coherent national strategy emerged. This strategy consisted of two major components – the phasing of cuts in planned expenditure and the development of clear service priorities within DHSS. Looking first at the expenditure component, the pattern of spending for main services is set out in Table 16.1.

Table 16.1   Current expenditure on social services, England (£ million, 1978 prices)

	1975/6	1977/8
Services mainly for the elderly and physically handicapped		
Residential care	180.6	183.4
Home help	112.1	115.8
Meals	16.2	16.4
Aids/adaptations/phones	13.6	12.7
Services for the disabled	50.7	44.1
Services for the mentally handicapped		
Residential care	20.3	26.5
Day care	30.8	34.3
Services for the mentally ill		
Residential care	4.6	5.8
Day care	3.6	4.3
Services for children		
Residential care	148.7	153.9
Boarding out	17.7	23.4
Day nurseries	33.4	36.7
Intermediate treatment	1.0	2.0
Social work service	111.6	119.1

Source: DHSS

In order to preserve a limited rate of growth to set against the backlog of unmet need and the pressure of increasing need (especially among the elderly, mentally handicapped and mentally ill), the health and personal social services were partially protected from the full

force of retrenchment compared with some areas of public expenditure. This first element of an expenditure strategy was
supported by the decision to severely cut capital to help preserve
current expenditure. This approach was underpinned by both the
Public Expenditure White Papers of 1975[9] and 1976.[10]

The 1975 White Paper included short and medium term cuts in
planned expenditure compared with the previous year and the 1976
White Paper further cut these reduced totals. The capital programme
cuts of 1973 were continued with a further cut of at least 20 per
cent in 1974/5. The 1975 White Paper envisaged a slower decline
in the capital programme thereafter, but by 1976 the further need
to retrench resulted in projected cuts of considerable magnitude in
the late 1970s. Current expenditure was planned to fall over a period
of several years to a real growth of just over 2 per cent per annum.
This rate of decline was dramatic and the period of adjustment was
crucial. But the target rate of growth for the late 1970s was also
critical because the official estimate of the growth needed just to
keep pace with demographic and other pressures was also 2 per cent
per annum. The cushioning of the personal social services was strictly
a short term concession, therefore, with virtually no provision in
the longer term for a faster growth in services than in officially
recognised need. This short term respite was itself totally overshadowed by the revenue consequences of the earlier capital boom.

The 1977 White Paper intensified the medium term pressure on
the capital programme but retained the phased reduction in current
expenditure, which was not expected to fall to 2 per cent before
1977/78.[11] In the event, actual current expenditure fell significantly
below planned levels in 1976/7 to a rate of growth of 2.4 per cent
per annum. The introduction of cash limits had affected 'excessive'
savings and the experience was to be repeated subsequently.

During 1977 the first effects of a change in policy on the capital
side became apparent. Support for the construction industry included modest additions to personal social services capital expenditure throughout the 1970s. To this was added further planned
increases in the early 1980s designed to promote residential and
day care provision. But the immediate experience was the same on
the capital as on the current side – local authorities were underspending.

This divergence of planned and actual trends became clear in the
1978 White Paper.[12] Current as well as capital expenditure was now
being boosted somewhat in recognition of the extreme pressure which
the services were labouring under and – from 1981/2 onwards – to

ensure that growth exceeded officially estimated increases in need by nearly 1 per cent. In terms of planned expenditure, the worst period of retrenchment and adjustment from growth had been negotiated. In terms of actual expenditure, the squeeze was still biting quite firmly with a continued shortfall in capital and current spending – and great variation in the experience of individual social services departments.

Expenditure plans can only be judged in terms of their actual effects on services and against longer term trends: some attempt was made to cushion these services, but was it sufficient? The adjustment from rapid growth was difficult enough, but the long history of neglect meant that 'unmet need' was far from being a rhetorical cry. Similarly, the underlying growth in need was not fully reflected in the official estimates. The care of the elderly is a case in point. The fact of demographic change is now so widely recognised as to be easily underestimated. The crucial feature of the increasing number of the very old is that it is an unrelenting pressure: it will probably continue into the third decade of the next century. Increasing age is a far greater challenge than simply the increase in the numbers of the elderly which is already a spent force in planning terms. The very old are far more likely to be highly socially dependent and therefore to need either intensive domiciliary support or residential care of a particularly expensive kind. To maintain the 1973 *proportion* of the elderly population in residential care would involve an expansion in residential places of 32 per cent by 2001. To meet the demands of more elderly residents implies better staff ratios and training, and each of these contributions to the quality of care has to be achieved in the light of rising expectations of good conditions of work among staff.

The problem of the care of the elderly therefore illustrates three factors against which the planned levels of expenditure have to be assessed: the necessity of capital expenditure to any programme of community care for the socially dependent; the real expenditure implications of the growth in need; and the tendency for unit costs to rise faster than is allowed for in public expenditure surveys. The first of these is apparent and a belated recognition of its importance was at least built into Labour's plans for the 1980s. The same was not so obviously true of increasing need. The official estimate of this factor does not, for example, include the full consequences of deepening unemployment and poverty for the needs of families and the handicapped – even if it allows fully for demographic change. The third issue – that of unit costs – has been officially acknowledged[11] but it strikes at the very heart of the strategy of providing some protection for these services. Either unit costs have to be held back by reducing the quality of service, or the volume of service produced by a given level of expenditure must fall.

Despite a slightly more optimistic note in the plans for the early 1980s, the Labour record on expenditure was poor when viewed from the wider perspective of actual service production and trends in both needs and provision. The experience of retrenchment caused local and national assumptions about how best to improve the well being of clients to be reviewed and there can be little doubt that some forms of existing expenditure have been less than cost effective. There is a real need for far more systematic evaluation of provision against specific objectives. Nevertheless, the scale of outstanding problems and the implications of substantially developing the social care of the elderly, mentally ill, mentally handicapped, chronically sick and disabled – not to mention families under stress – underline the continuing need for prolonged and steady growth in real expenditure. In the late 1960s, Labour policy advisers recognised the greater 'productivity' at the margin of expenditure on these services compared with income maintenance services; the protection afforded to the latter during the 1970s has entailed a real cost in the former.

One further feature of the expenditure strategy must be noted. In 1976, allowance was made for a small pool of monies to be spent on projects of benefit to the health services but in collaboration with local authorities. These joint financing monies (starting at £4 million and rising to £29 million in 1978/9) were a long overdue attempt to ease the transfer of responsibility for clients needing social support from hospital to community services. The scale of the exercise, though growing, is minuscule in relation to the size of the task, but it has provided an additional element of 'growth' in the personal social services. Despite widespread initial anxieties, it is now generally accepted as a worthwhile innovation and it has helped to sustain services for the elderly, in particular, to some degree. Whether it has fostered joint planning in a broader sense is a moot point. What is clear, however, is that joint financing cannot be a panacea, even if expanded considerably. The 'distortion effect' on personal social services budgets limits its potential. In a period of severe constraint, even a modest programme of joint financing projects can dominate the margin for growth in social service departments and virtually ensure that all new developments will be geared to the needs of just the interface with health.

In view of the severe limitations of the expenditure plans, how successful was the search for priorities? The publication in 1976 of a Consultative Document was undoubtedly a significant step forward. The priorities and objectives were eminently 'rational': the declared intention was to safeguard standards of service for the elderly and families in the face of rising need and to improve services for two of the neglected groups – the mentally handicapped and mentally ill. Given that provision was bound to fall below what was desirable, the first question was whether the balance of priority between client groups seemed appropriate. People became concerned about a relative decline in capital expenditure on residential care for the elderly in favour of the mentally ill and handicapped and the neglect of community services for the younger physically handicapped. As we have seen, subsequent capital expenditure proposals might have modified the first trend if Labour had remained in power. However, in the case of aids, adaptations and community services for the disabled, substantial cuts in expenditure were effected in 1976/7 and were maintained in 1977/8. The number of telephones installed was halved between 1975/6 and 1976/7. Although a decline in this service was to be expected as the backlog was met, it was one of the easiest areas to cut. Likewise, home adaptations for the disabled were expanded, but not rapidly. Holidays for the elderly and disabled were substantially reduced over the same period. These are prime examples of services designed to mitigate inequalities of social integration.

Local authorities' performances in specific areas of provision reflected the national priorities to a considerable extent. In terms of both expenditure and places provided, residential and day care for the mentally handicapped and ill made some progress in the mid seventies although from a very low base. Any growth has to be set in context of the overwhelming inadequacy of the services in 1977/8. Even with this protection we were only spending £10.1 million on community care of the mentally ill. Day care also improved for the elderly and physically handicapped. The picture was quite different in community services for the elderly, however, where expenditure on home helps and meals increased by only 1 per cent in 1976/7. The number of home help cases increased in 1975/6 and 1976/7, but home help hours fell by 1.79 million between 1974/5 and 1976/7. The number of meals served per 1,000 of the elderly population rose by 5 per cent between 1974/5 and 1975/6, but this performance was not repeated subsequently and projected expenditure implies a decline.

The fastest rate of growth in services for families and children has been in the boarding out of children – in terms both of expenditure and provision. Expenditure on residential care has grown more slowly, but from a larger base. The number of fieldwork staff per 1,000 of the population had increased by 24 per cent between 1974/5 and 1976/7, but changes in the accounting categories for these figures mask the changes in trainee and para-professional numbers. By 1976, the rate of increase in expenditure on fieldwork staff was low and was projected to remain so. Secondment of staff for training was cut markedly. The numbers and quality of field staff are clearly crucial to services for children and families and the improvements needed simply to match changing demand are difficult to assess, as the issue of non-accidental injury to children has emphasised.

In summary, performance in the mid-1970s reflected (in small measure) the priority given to the mentally ill and handicapped, but a price was paid, especially in services for the elderly. These priorities may seem appropriate in relation to the recent past, but compared with the objectives outlined in the Consultative Document and apparently re-confirmed in *The Way Forward*,[13] the actual level of provision is too low. For example, far from being a period of increasing social integration for children 'at risk', the seventies have been marked by an increasing level of inappropriate incarceration, with the hopes vested in intermediate treatment being almost totally undermined. Despite continued enthusiasm among some members of the social work service, and within some local authorities, expenditure on intermediate treatment has remained pitifully low and was not projected to rise substantially under Labour's plans. The hopes raised by the 1975 Children's Act have not been realised in practice.

The opportunities to substantially reduce material and social inequality were lost following the cuts made from 1973 onwards. The subsequent introduction of cash limits, together with rising unit costs, has undermined the 'defensive' strategy adopted of simultaneously safeguarding standards of service for the elderly and for families while off-setting unmet need among other groups. Another indirect casualty has been policy analysis. The preoccupation with resource utilisation – which is appropriate and potentially beneficial to clients – has left little room for traditional measures of need. The fear must be that if severe constraints continue, planning will be increasingly preoccupied with inputs, not outputs, and with resource allocation, not objectives.

Equality: the outstanding dilemmas

A concern for equality has characterised the personal social services throughout the past decade or so, despite the lack of quantitative studies of redistribution. The impact has been on the ideologies and nascent theories which underpin practice rather than on specific or general objectives. An increase in resources could remove some of the disappointments. Both residential and community care services could be extended, improved in quality, and made more flexible. The status of 'simple' care could be enhanced by focusing more attention on the role of domiciliary, day and informal care. An enhanced share of training opportunities for care staff would be a key to such improvements. Similarly, greater imagination and collaboration, backed by extra resources, could bring more advisory, supportive and socially and culturally enriching care to the handicapped, the mentally ill and to the elderly. Resources are a necessary means of moving away from the 'emergency service' syndrome which afflicts this most neglected of the social services.

Nevertheless, there is a sense of failure and disillusionment among many personal social services staff – admittedly counter-balanced by optimism and sheer determination – which is too fundamental to be explained wholly by the shortage of resources. It is intimately connected with the concern for equality.

Even at the level of general philosophy, some problems were already apparent from the beginning of the seventies. A structural view of causal processes and policy solutions is highly likely to lead to frustration: structural change depends essentially on the effectiveness of social and economic policies outside the control of the personal social services. The paradox of commitment and impotence surfaced in the Community Development Projects, and more indirectly in corporate planning and the growth of community work within social services departments. Impotence in the face of frustrated hopes has been a large part of the experience of personal social services staffs throughout the seventies.

This experience has raised a fundamental question of legitimacy. The structural view of causality was sufficiently widely accepted for the wider failure to fund egalitarian policies to undermine the legitimacy of much social service work from within. The experience of failure to achieve the more ambitious hopes of more optimistic days has been generalised. The attempt merely to ameliorate inequalities – material and social – tends to be derided or undervalued. But amelioration, in context, is a legitimate and necessary function of the personal social services.

Similarly, by reference merely to the raised expectations of visible outcomes instead of the underlying causes and increased social stress, public and political reactions have signalled a lack of confidence in these services from without. The problem which these reactions high-light is partly one of morale, but also one of theory and philo-sophy and of a lack of widely shared understandings. The personal social services are beginning to reverberate to the question: what are we achieving with the use of even those scarce resources we possess? Part of the response must be the evolution of a more sophisticated analysis of the different types of egalitarian objectives which can appropriately be pursued through the personal social services. The quality of the analysis which is needed can be revealed by noting just four issues of equity.

The first concerns power. For example, the implication of the Children's Act, 1975, was that the rights of children would be strengthened at the expense of those of their parents or other adults responsible for their care. The well being of the child was placed less ambiguously at the heart of child care policy – especially in relation to fostering and adoption. This approach can be attacked for ignoring the importance of inequality as a prime source of family stress and breakdown, but this does not negate the Act. There was, and remains, a need to reassess and change the balance of power en-shrined in traditional concepts of the family and of parental rights. The expression of traditional mores in police practices, which has been a recurring feature of the family violence debate, is but one further reflection of this. But whatever the merits of the Act in strengthening the rights of children, its implementation has been undermined by the pressure on fieldwork resources.

A second issue, that of charges and means tests, raises a problem which has not been made explicit – that of equity between consumers and potential consumers. If charges are a source of stigma and non-uptake of service, they offend against one of our concepts of equality; if they enable service to be extended, they may promote equality. The personal social services include a variety of different contexts in which charges are, or can be, applied. Charges for residential care for the elderly primarily represent a substantial transfer of resources from the social security system to local authorities and are compara-tively non-controversial. Those imposed on the parents of children in local authority residential care are potentially far more controversial and may represent a source of additional stigma for families who are reluctant users of child care services. Charges on domiciliary services occupy a middle ground: they are controversial but they do not contain 'punitive' overtones. Charging policies differ enormously and there is unfortunately little factual evidence, as opposed to assumptions and assertion, on which to base policy. Even the economic viability of charging for some services (such as home helps) is unclear. At present, the question of charges poses an apparent and unresolved choice between the equality to be achieved through a possibly more extensive, but means tested, service and that achieved through a universal, free, but admittedly under-financed, service.

A third problem – that of territorial inequalities – is by no means simple or receding. The national concern for inner city areas reflected in the rate support grant formula may be an appropriate re-distributive strategy, but not all shire counties have the resource base from which to provide good services in rural areas and by no means all of those which have, do so. Rural deprivation has been greatly neglected and it bears heavily on the personal social services in many county districts. The physical isolation induced by declining rural transport services exacerbates the problems of the elderly and disabled in particular and adds to the cost of maintaining services. Since local government reorganisation in 1974, most shire counties have been faced with inequalities of service between the old county and the old county borough areas and territorial justice has been a key policy issue for some of the new social services departments.

A fourth example of complexity centres on the growing enthusiasm for informal and voluntary care. At worst it is unreflective jingoism, but this worst manifestation was a predictable reaction to 'resource shock'. The potential, and the limits, of alternatives to state services are beginning to attract more serious attention. Whether the right questions are yet being asked in a coherent way – from the equality, or other, perspectives – is another matter. The danger presently remains that these alternatives could be developed and used with too high an expectation of saving money in the state sector. To para-phrase Richard Titmuss's famous dictum on selectivity, we most urgently need to establish that infrastructure of universal, publicly financed provision which will enable the non-statutory alternatives to grow in appropriate ways. This is profoundly a matter of philo-sophy and objectives and not merely of giving a bit more public money to voluntary agencies or beseeching families and neighbours to do more for the socially dependent.

One final problem for the future arises from the tendency of an inadequately financed policy of community care to transfer the burden of care to the families, neighbours and friends of the people in need of care – or to volunteers. Surprisingly, there has been little attempt to document the extent and consequences of this pheno-menon.

Notes and References

Chapter 1

1. Peter Townsend and Nicholas Bosanquet, *Labour and Inequality*, Fabian Society, 1972.
2. *Labour's Programme: Campaign Document*, 1974.
3. See, for example, A. B. Atkinson, *The Economics of Inequality*, Clarendon Press, 1975.
4. *Public Expenditure on Income Maintenance Programmes*, OECD, 1976.
5. *Ibid.* For 1975, the UK was ranked eighth of the nine EEC countries in expenditure on social benefits as a per cent of net national disposable income; *Report on the Development of the Social Situation in the Communities in 1976*, EEC, 1977.
6. H. L. Lydall, *The Structure of Earnings*, OUP, 1968.
7. M. Ellman, *Socialist Planning*, Cambridge University Press, 1979. See also, M. Mathews 'Top incomes in the USSR: towards a definition of the Soviet elite', *Survey*, Vol 21, No 3, 1975.
8. A. McCauley, 'The distribution of incomes and earnings in the Soviet Union', *Soviet Studies*, April 1977.
9. M. Ellman, *op cit.*
10. For a short account, see *The Contract Observed? A Critical Review of Government Policies and the Social Contract*, Society of Civil and Public Servants, May 1977.
11. *Control of Public Expenditure*, Cmnd 1432, HMSO, 1961.
12. See H. Glennerster, *Social Service Budgets and Social Policy*, Allen and Unwin, 1975. See also, Lord Diamond, *Public Expenditure in Practice*, Allen & Unwin, 1978; and Sir R. Clarke, *Public Expenditure, Management & Control: the Development of PESC*, Macmillan, 1979.
13. DHSS, *Priorities for Health and Personal Social Services in England*, HMSO, 1976.
14. Report of the Resource Allocation Working Party, *Sharing Resources for Health in England*, HMSO, 1976.
15. See also other consultative documents, such as *The Way Forward*, 1977 and *A Happier Old Age*, HMSO, 1978.
16. F. Wright, *Public Expenditure Cuts Affecting Services for Disabled People*, Disability Alliance, 1977.
17. *Hansard*, 12 November 1974.
18. *Economic Trends*, January 1977, February 1978 and January 1979; FES Reports for 1974 and 1977.
19. See, for example, D. Piachaud and J. Muellbauer, 'Written Evi-

dence to the Royal Commission on the Distribution of Income and Wealth', *Selected Evidence Submitted to the Royal Commission for Report No 6: Lower Incomes*.

20. *Wealth Tax*, HMSO, August 1974.

21. C. Sandford, 'The wealth tax debate', in F. Field (ed), *The Wealth Report*, Routledge and Kegan Paul, 1978.

22. Royal Commission on the Distribution of Income and Wealth, *Report No 3*, Cmnd 6383, HMSO, 1974. See also Peter Townsend, 'How the Rich stay Rich', *New Statesman*, 1 October 1976.

23. See, for example, R. M. Macleod, *Treasury Control and Social Administration*, Bell, 1968.

24. The hurt and astonishment expressed by many socialists is illustrated in H. Glennerster (ed), *Labour's Social Priorities*, Fabian Society, 1976.

25. M. Meacher, 'The men who block the corridors of power', *The Guardian*, 14 June 1979.

Chapter 2

1. H. George, *Progress and Poverty*, Kegan Paul, 1884.

2. R. Dinwiddy and Derek Rees, *The Effects of Certain Social and Demographic Changes on Income Distribution*, Royal Commission on the Distribution of Income and Wealth, Background Paper No. 3, HMSO, 1977.

3. Royal Commission on the Distribution of Income and Wealth (the Diamond Commission), Report No. 6, *Lower Incomes*, Cmnd 7175, HMSO, 1978.

4. R. Bacon and W. Eltis, *Britain's Economic Problem: Too Few Producers*, Macmillan, 1976.

5. D. Smith, 'Public consumption and economic performance', *National Westminster Bank Quarterly Review*, November, 1975.

6. D. Healey, *Letter to IMF*, 15 December 1976.

7. See J. Westergaard, 'Social policy and class inequality: some notes on welfare state limits', in R. Miliband and J. Saville (eds), *The Socialist Register 1978*, Merlin Press, 1978.

8. H.M. Treasury, *The Government's Expenditure Plans, 1979/80–1982/3*, Cmnd 7439, HMSO, 1979.

Chapter 3

1. C. A. R. Crosland, *The Future of Socialism*, Jonathan Cape, 1956.

2. *Young People and Work*, HMSO, 1978.

3. For a more detailed discussion of the potential impact of alternative policies chosen within the framework of orthodox demand management techniques, see M. J. C. Surrey and P. A. Ormerod, 'Demand management in the UK, 1964–81', in M. V. Posner (ed), *Demand Management*, Heinemann, 1978.

4. The Attack on Inflation, Cmnd 6151, London, HMSO, 11 July 1975.

5. The Government's Expenditure Plans (to 1979–80), Cmnd

6393, London, HMSO, February 1976.

6. 'The Right Debate' in Howard Glennerster (ed), *Labour's Social Priorities*, Fabian Society, 1976.

7. The Government's Expenditure Plans 1979/80–1983/84, Cmnd 7439, London, HMSO, 1979.

8. See, for example, a letter in the *Financial Times* of 5 February 1979.

9. J. S. E. Laury, G. R. Lewis and P. A. Ormerod, 'Properties of macroeconomic models of the UK economy – a comparative study', *National Institute Economic Review*, February 1978; Jeremy Bray, 'Cracking open the secrets of the Treasury's Black Box', *New Statesman*, 14 July 1978.

10. For a recent comprehensive survey, see D. Savage, 'The channels of monetary influence', *National Institute Economic Review*, February 1978.

11. *Trade and Industry*, 5 January 1979.

12. C. A. Enoch, 'Measures of competitiveness in international trade', *Bank of England Quarterly Bulletin*, vol 18, no 2, June 1978.

13. See, for example, the Chancellor's April 1975 budget speech.

14. A detailed discussion of wage bargaining behaviour in the UK is given in S. G. B. Henry, M. C. Sawyer, P. Smith, 'Models of inflation in the UK', *National Institute Economic Review*, August 1976, and of the effects of incomes policies in S. G. B. Henry and P. A. Ormerod, 'Incomes policy and wage inflation: empirical evidence for the UK, 1961–1977', *National Institute Economic Review*, August 1978.

15. R. Skidelsky, *Politicians and the Slump*, Macmillan, 1967.

Chapter 4

1. D. Seers and P. Streeten, 'Overseas development policies under the Labour Government', in W. Beckerman (ed), *The Labour Government's Economic Record 1964–72*.

2. D. Morawetz, *Twenty Five Years of Economic Development 1950–75*, World Bank, p. 30.

3. *World Bank Development Report*, 1978.

4. For an analysis of the origins of British aid, see Peter Atkinson, 'Aid to developing countries as an issue in British politics', Ph.D thesis, University of Oxford, 1978, Ch. 1.

5. *Trade and Aid*, First Report from the Select Committee on Overseas Development, December 1977.

6. R. D. Mckinley and R. Little, 'Foreign policy models for the distribution of bilateral aid', *European Journal of Political Research*, 1978.

7. Richard Luce and Nigel Forman, 'A Conservative approach to development policy', *ODI Review*, 2, 1978.

8. P. Atkinson, *op. cit.*

9. T. S. Bowles, *Survey of Attitudes Towards Overseas Development*, HMSO, 1978.

10. For a more philosophical dis-

cussion, see Deepak Lal, *Poverty, Power and Prejudice*, Fabian Society, 1978.

11. H. Wilson, *The War on World Poverty*, 1953.

12. For a good overall evaluation, see Adrian Hewitt, 'British aid: policy and practice', *ODI Review*, 2, 1978.

13. 'oda' is an internationally recognised measure of concessional official development assistance.

14. D. Morawetz, *op cit.*

15. *More Help for the Poorest*, HMSO, Cmnd 6270.

16. M. Gregory, P. Pearson and R. Sinha, Working Papers, University of Glasgow, 1979.

17. For some clarification, see ODI Briefing Paper, *Basic Needs*, 1979.

18. For a more positive viewpoint, see C. Stephens, *Food Aid and the Developing World*, ODI, 1979.

19. Douglas Williams, 'Economic development and human rights', *ODI Review*, 2, 1978.

20. Select Committee on Overseas Development, *The Renegotiation of the Lomé Convention*, HMSO, 1978.

21. *Ibid*; see evidence by Overseas Development Institute.

22. J. Hills, *The EDF: Proposals for the Renegotiation*, CIIR Conference Papers, 1978.

23. The complex issues are summarised in 'Britain, the new protectionism and trade with the NICs', by the present author in *International Affairs*, January 1979.

24. Labour Party/TUC, *Into the Eighties*, July 1978.

Chapter 5

1. John Edmonds and Giles Radice, *Low Pay*, Fabian Society, 1972.

2. J. Mitchell, *The National Board for Prices and Incomes*, Secker & Warburg, 1972.

3. National Board for Prices and Incomes, *General Problems of Low Pay*, Report 169, HMSO, 1971.

4. Royal Commission on the Distribution of Income and Wealth, *Lower Incomes*, Report 6, Cmnd 7175, HMSO, 1978.

5. *Op cit.* Three members of the Commission – G. Doughty, D. Lea and D. Wedderburn – took a less complacent view.

6. R. Layard, D. Piachaud and M. Stewart, *The Causes of Poverty*, Royal Commission on the Distribution of Income and Wealth, Background Paper 5, HMSO, 1978.

7. A. B. Atkinson, 'Low pay and the cycle of inequality', in Frank Field (ed), *Low Pay*, Arrow Books, 1973.

8. Alan Fisher and Bernard Dix, *Low Pay and How to End It*, Pitman, 1974.

9. Department of Employment, *New Earnings Survey 1978*, HMSO, 1978, Part A.

10. Low Pay Unit, Written Evidence to the Royal Commission on the Distribution of Income and Wealth, in *Selected Evidence for Report No. 6*, HMSO, 1978.

11. J. Hurstfield, *The Part Time Trap*, Low Pay Unit, 1978.

12. C. Pond and S. Winyard, 'A profile of the low paid', in F.

Field (ed), *Are Low Wages Inevitable?*, Spokesman Books, 1977.

13. *Department of Employment Gazette*, October 1978 plus unpublished information supplied by the Department of Employment.

14. F. J. Bayliss, *British Wages Councils*, Blackwell, 1962.

15. Department of Employment Evidence to the Royal Commission on the Distribution of Income and Wealth.

16. D. Jordan, *The Wages of Uncertainty*, Low Pay Unit, 1977.

17. Society of Civil and Public Servants, Written Evidence to the Royal Commission on the Distribution of Income and Wealth.

18. S. Winyard, *Policing Low Wages*, Low Pay Unit, 1976.

19. Department of Employment, Written Evidence to the Royal Commission on the Distribution of Income and Wealth.

20. C. Thomas, *The Charge of the Wages Brigade*, Low Pay Unit, 1978.

21. C. Pond and C. Thomas, 'Low Pay: a battle still to be won', *The Times*, 23 October 1978.

22. B. Wooton, *Incomes Policy: An Inquest and a Proposal*, Davis-Poynter, 1974.

23. F. Field and C. Pond, 'Low pay awards', *Bulletin*, 4, Low Pay Unit, July 1975.

24. C. Trinder, 'The social contract and the low paid', in P. Willmott (ed), *Sharing Inflation?*, Temple Smith, 1976.

25. Chris Pond, '*For whom the pips squeak*', Low Pay Unit, 1977.

26. C. Thomas, 'Poverty in percentages', *Bulletin*, 21, Low Pay Unit, June 1978.

27. C. Pond, 'The high paid and the crisis of living standards', in F. Field (ed), *The Wealth Report*, Routledge and Kegan Paul, 1979.

28. D. Jordan, *Short Measures for the Poor*, Low Pay Unit, 1977.

29. Chris Pond, 'No £50 target', *New Society*, 15 September 1977.

30. Chris Pond, 'Poor by authority', *Bulletin*, 24, Low Pay Unit, December 1978.

31. F. Wilkinson and H. A. Turner, 'The wage-tax spiral and labour militancy', in Turner *et al*, *Do Trade Unions Cause Inflation?*, Cambridge University Press, 1975.

32. *Hansard*, 23 March 1976, vol 908, col 135/6, updated by author.

33. F. Field, M. Meacher and C. Pond, *To Him Who Hath*, Penguin, 1977.

34. *Hansard*, 26 March 1974, vol 871, col 322.

35. *Libra*, vol 2, no 5, March 1976.

36. *Hansard*, 6 April 1976, vol 909, col 276.

37. Board of Inland Revenue, *Inland Revenue Statistics 1978*, HMSO, 1978.

38. C. Pond, 'Soaking the poor', *Bulletin*, 19, Low Pay Unit, February 1978.

39. A. R. Thatcher, 'The New Earnings Survey and the Distribution of earnings', in A. B. Atkinson (ed), *The Personal Distribution of Incomes*, Allen & Unwin 1976.

40. E. Cannan, *Wealth*, Staples Press, 3rd ed, 1948, quoted in A. B. Atkinson, *The Economics of Inequality*, Oxford University Press, 1975.
41. Quoted in Atkinson, *ibid*. For a full discussion of the causes of low pay, see Chapters 5 and 6; also E. H. Phelps Brown, *The Inequality of Pay*, Oxford University Press, 1977.

Chapter 6

1. W. W. Daniel and Elizabeth Stilgoe, *The Impact of Employment Protection Laws*, Policy Studies Institute, 1978.
2. Linda Dickens, 'Unfair dismissals applications and the industrial tribunal system', *Industrial Relations Journal*, Winter 1978/79, vol IX, no 4.
3. Bullock, *Committee on Industrial Democracy*, HMSO, 1977.
4. *New Earnings Survey*, Department of Employment, April 1978.
5. *Industrial Review to 1977, Motors*, NEDO, 1973.
6. *Incentive Payments Systems*, Office of Manpower Economics, 1973.
7. *Social Trends*, HMSO, 1977.
8. Helen Murlis, *Employee Benefits*, BIM, 1976.
9. Royal Commission on the Distribution of Income and Wealth, Report No 6, *Lower Incomes*, Cmnd 7175, HMSO, 1978.
10. Frank Herron, *Shipbuilding in Crisis*, Allen and Unwin, 1975, and W. W. Daniel, *Whatever Happened to the Workers in Woolwich?*, PEP, 1972.
11. *Britain's Medium Term Employ-ment Prospects*, Warwick Manpower Research Group, 1978.
12. *The Changing Structure of the Labour Market*, Unit for Manpower Studies, 1977.
13. *Engineering Craftsmen, Shortages and Related Problems*, NEDO, 1977.
14. *Employee's View of the Machine Tool Industry*, NEDO, 1977.
15. *General Household Survey*, HMSO, 1977.
16. *Executive Salaries and Fringe Benefits in the UK*, Inbucon-AIC Salary Research Unit, 1977 and 1978.
17. Helen Murlis, *Towards Single Status*, BIM, 1977.
18. Dorothy Wedderburn (ed), *Poverty, Inequality and Class Structure*, Cambridge University Press, 1974.
19. W. G. Runciman, *Relative Deprivation and Social Justice*, Allen and Unwin, 1966: and W. W. Daniel, *Wage Determination in Industry*, PEP, 1976.
20. Peter Reilly, *Employee Financial Participation*, BIM, 1978.

Chapter 7

1. *Royal Commission on the Distribution of Income and Wealth*, Cmnd 6999, HMSO, November 1977.
2. *Royal Commission on the Distribution of Income and Wealth*, Report 5.
3. G. Polanyi and J. B. Wood, *How Much Inequality?*, IEA, 1974.
4. A. B. Atkinson, 'The Wealthy and the Wealth Tax', *New Society*, 9 February 1978.

5. Michael Meacher in P. Townsend and N. Bosanquet (eds), *Labour and Inequality*, Fabian Society, 1972.
6. A. B. Atkinson and A. J. Harrison, *The Distribution of Personal Wealth in Britain*, Cambridge University Press, 1978.
7. Inland Revenue Statistics, 1978.
8. *Wealth Tax*, Cmnd 5704, August 1974.
9. HC 696, session 1974–5.
10. C. Sandford, 'The wealth tax debate', F. Field (ed), *The Wealth Report*, Routledge and Kegan Paul, 1979.
11. *The Times*, 20 December 1977.
12. *Hansard*, 15 March 1977, col 102.
13. *Hansard*, 16 November 1978, col 329–30.

Chapter 8

1. W. W. Daniel, *Racial Discrimination in England*, Penguin, 1968.
2. David J. Smith, *Racial Disadvantage in Employment*, PEP Broadsheet 544, June 1974.
3. Neil McIntosh and David J. Smith, *The Extent of Racial Discrimination*, PEP Broadsheet 547, September 1974.
4. David J. Smith and Anne Whalley, *Racial Minorities and Public Housing*, PEP Broadsheet 556, September 1975.
5. David J. Smith, *The Facts of Racial Disadvantage*, PEP Broadsheet 560, February 1976.
6. A fuller summary of this evidence may be found in the report, *Urban Deprivation, Racial Inequality and Social Policy*, Community Relations Commission, HMSO, 1977.
7. Sally Holtermann, *Census Indicators of Urban Deprivation*, Working Note No 6, Department of the Environment, February 1975.
8. *Race and Council Housing in London*, Runnymede Trust, February 1975.
9. *Colour and the Allocation of GLC Housing*, Research Report 21, GLC, November 1976.
10. *The Role of Immigrants in the Labour Market*, Department of Employment, 1977.
11. *Department of Employment Gazette*, November 1973 and September 1976.
12. *Unemployment and Homelessness*, Community Relations Commission, HMSO, 1974.
13. *Young People's Employment Study*, OPCS Social Survey Division, Preliminary Report No 3, January 1976.
14. *Looking for Work*, Commission for Racial Equality, October 1978.
15. Roger Ballard and Bronwen Holden, 'Racial discrimination: no room at the top', *New Society*, 17 April 1975.
16. *Application of Race Relations Policy in the Civil Service*, Civil Service Department, HMSO, 1978.
17. *Educational Needs of Children from Minority Groups*, Community Relations Commission, March 1974.
18. Alan Little, 'Performance of children from ethnic minority backgrounds in primary

schools', *Oxford Review of Education*, Vol 1, No 2, 1975.

19. *Racial Discrimination*, Cmnd 6234, HMSO, September 1975.

20. Kuttan Menon, 'Individual complaints and the industrial tribunals', and Ian McDonald, 'Individual enforcement of the Race Relations Act', in *A Review of the Race Relations Act 1976*, Runnymede Trust, forthcoming.

21. 'Race Relations Act: a review of cases in 1978 concerning employment', in *IDS Brief No 150*, Incomes Data Services Ltd, February 1979.

22. *Policy for the Inner Cities*, Cmnd 6845, HMSO, June 1977.

23. *Funding Multi-Racial Education*, a discussion paper prepared by a Working Party of Directors of Education, Community Relations Commission, May 1976.

24. *Multi-Racial Britain: the Social Services Response*, Association of Directors of Social Services and Commission for Racial Equality, July 1978.

25. *Proposals for Replacing Section 11 of the Local Government Act 1966*, Home Office, November 1978.

26. *Race Relations and Housing*, Cmnd 6232, HMSO, September 1975.

27. *British Nationality Law: Discussion of Possible Changes*, Cmnd 6795, HMSO, April 1977.

28. *A Register of Dependants*, Cmnd 6698, HMSO, February 1977.

29. *First Report from the Select Committee on Race Relations and Immigration, Session 1977–78, Immigration*, Vol 1, Report HC 303–1, HMSO, March 1978.

30. *Immigration: Observations on the Report of the Select Committee on Race Relations and Immigration*, Cmnd 7287, HMSO, July 1978.

31. 'Race and the dangers of "benign neglect"', *Runnymede Trust Report for 1975*.

Chapter 9

1. L. Hamill, 'Wives as sole and joint breadwinners', unpublished paper quoted in J. Hurstfield, *The Part Time Trap*, Low Pay Unit, 1978.

2. *Department of Employment Gazette*, June 1977.

3. *Department of Employment Gazette*, March 1979.

4. *General Household Survey*, 1977.

5. A. Hunt, *A Survey of Women's Employment*, Vol 1, HMSO, 1968.

6. M. Bone, *Pre-school Children and the Need for Day-care*, HMSO, 1977.

7. Equal Opportunities Commission, *Second Annual Report*, HMSO, 1978.

Chapter 10

1. *Better Pensions: Fully Protected Against Inflation*, Cmnd 5713, HMSO, 1974.

2. DHSS, *Social Assistance: a Review of the Supplementary Benefits Scheme in Great Britain*, HMSO, 1978.

3. *Response of Supplementary Benefits Commission to Social Assistance*, Supplementary

Benefits Administration Paper No 9, HMSO, 1979.

4. Ruth Lister, *The No-Cost No-Benefit Review*, Poverty Pamphlet 39, Child Poverty Action Group, 1979.

Chapter 11

1. Margaret Wynn, *Family Policy*, Penguin, 1972.
2. D. Bell, quoted in Margaret Wynn, *op cit*.
3. Frank Field, 'A lobby for all children', *New Society*, 29 September 1977.
4. R. Leete, 'One parent families: numbers and characteristics', *Population Trends*, 13.
5. *Hansard*, 16 May 1978.
6. Speech to Conservative Party Conference, 1977.
7. *Department of Employment Gazette*, June 1977.
8. Richard Layard *et al, Causes of Poverty*, HMSO, 1978.
9. *Hansard*, 29 March 1977.
10. Press Release, DHSS, 15 July 1977.
11. *Hansard*, 1 August 1978.
12. *Finer Report*, Cmnd 5629, HMSO, 1974.
13. *Hansard*, 3 August 1978.
14. Frank Field, *Worse off Under Labour?*, CPAG, 1978.
15. Press Release, DHSS, undated.
16. Mimi Parker, *Who Pays for the Children*, Outer Circle Policy Unit, 1978.
17. *Labour's Programme 1976*.
18. DHSS/SBC, *Low Incomes*, HMSO, 1977.
19. *Hansard*, 16 May 1978.
20. Eleanor Rathbone Lecture, 1978.

Chapter 12

1. DHSS, *Sharing Resources for Health in England*, HMSO, 1976.
2. DHSS, *Priorities for Health and Personal Social Services in England*, HMSO, 1976.
3. M. J. Buxton and R. E. Klein, *Allocating Health Resources: A commentary on RAWP*, Royal Commission on the NHS Research Paper No 3, HMSO, 1978.
4. H. Eckstein, *The English Health Service, its origins, structures, and achievements*, Harvard University Press, 1964.
5. *A Review of the Medical Services in Great Britain* (Chairman, Sir A. Porritt), 1962.
6. *Health Service Financing*, BMA, 1970.
7. DHSS, *National Health Service*, HMSO, 1970.
8. *Democracy in the National Health Service*, DHSS, 1974.
9. HM Treasury, *The Government's Expenditure Plans 1979/80–1983/84*, Cmnd 7439, HMSO, 1979.
10. *Management of Financial Resources in the NHS*, Royal Commission on the NHS, Research Paper No 2.
11. West Midlands RHA, *Towards a Strategy for Health, 1978/9–1987/8*.
12. *The Right to Health*, the Labour Party, 1977.
13. 'Direct benefit to patient care', *Nursing Times*, 15 March 1979.
14. A. H. Snaith, 'Sub-regional resource allocations in the NHS', *Journal of Epidemiology*

and Community Health, 1978, no 32.

15. For London, see J. S. Yudkin, 'Changing patterns of resource allocation in a London Teaching District', *British Medical Journal*, 28 October 1978.

16. DHSS, *The Way Forward*, HMSO, 1977.

17. Royal Commission on the NHS, Research Paper No 3.

18. DHSS, *Planning Guidelines for 1971–80*, HC (79) 9.

19. DHSS, *Better Services for the Mentally Ill*, Cmnd 6233, 1975.

20. DHSS, *Better Services for the Mentally Handicapped*, Cmnd 4683, HMSO, 1971.

21. DHSS, *Prevention and Health*, Cmnd 7047, HMSO, 1977.

22. R. E. Kendall, 'Alcoholism: a medical or a political problem?', *British Medical Journal*, 10 February 1979.

23. Department of the Environment, *Drinking and Driving*, HMSO, 1976.

24. 'Twice wrong', *The Economist*, 2 June 1979.

25. DHSS, *Prevention and Health*, HMSO, 1976.

26. Dr David Owen, *In Sickness and In Health*, Quartet, 1976.

27. A. Maynard and A. Walker, *Doctor Manpower, 1975–2000: Alternative Forecasts and their resource implications*, Royal Commission on the NHS, Research Paper No 4.

Chapter 13

1. James Coleman, *Equality and Educational Opportunity*, US Government Printing Office, Washington DC, 1966; and C. Jencks, *Inequality*, Allen Lane, 1973.

2. M. Rutter *et al*, *Fifteen Thousand Hours*, Open Books, 1979.

3. Rudolf Klein *et al*, *Social Policy and Public Enterprise*, Centre for Studies in Social Policy, 1974.

4. Howard Glennerster, 'Education and Inequality', in Peter Townsend and Nicholas Bosanquet (eds), *Labour and Inequality*, Fabian Society, 1972.

5. CPRS, *Services for Young Children with Working Mothers*, HMSO, 1978.

6. *Hansard*, 25 May 1978.

7. Unpublished work by Fulton, Gordon and Williams at Lancaster University.

Chapter 14

1. For comprehensive documentation of many of these changes, see Chapter One of the *Housing Policy Technical Volume*, Cmnd 6851, HMSO, 1977.

2. House of Commons, Expenditure Committee, Tenth Report, 1972–73, *House Improvement Grants*, HMSO, 1973.

3. The White Paper, *Policy for the Inner Cities*, Cmnd 6845 was published in June 1977. It was preceded by a major speech by Peter Shore on 17 September 1976.

4. Terms of reference, *Housing Policy Consultative Document*, Cmnd 6851.

5. See Chapter 5 of the *Housing Policy Technical Volume* (*op cit.*)

6. A. Grey, N. Hepworth and J.

Odling-Smee, *Housing Rents, Costs and Subsidies*, Chartered Institute of Public Finance and Accountancy, 1978.

7. 'Survey of personal finance', *The Economist*, 24 March 1979.

8. Stewart Lansley and Guy Fiegehen, *One Nation? Housing and Conservative Policy*, Fabian Society, 1974.

9. For a discussion of the problem of defining the subsidy to owner occupiers, see Grey, Hepworth and Odling-Smee, *op cit*. If the subsidy to owner occupiers is defined in this way, consistency demands that the subsidy to council tenants should be defined as the difference between the rent paid and the current value of the housing services received.

10. Cf. A. E. Holmans, 'Housing tenure in England and Wales: the present situation and recent trends', *Social Trends*, No 9, HMSO, 1978.

11. *The Government's Expenditure Plans, 1979/80 to 1982/83*, Cmnd 7439, HMSO, 1979.

12. Cf. *Housing Policy Technical Volume*, Chapter 8, and Stewart Lansley, *Housing and Public Policy*, Croom Helm, 1979.

13. *Housing Policy Technical Volume, op cit.*

14. Bernard Kilroy, *Housing Finance – Organic Reform?*, Labour Economic Finance and Taxation Association, 1978.

15. As reference 11.

16. As reference 13.

17. Press Notice, Department of the Environment, 16 July 1975.

18. Department of the Environ-

ment, *National Dwelling and Housing Survey*, HMSO, 1979.

19. *Housing and Construction Statistics*, No 28, 4th quartet 1978, Supplementary Table XIX.

20. *Department of Employment Gazette*, vol 87, no 2, February 1979.

21. For a fuller discussion, see *Housing Finance Review: Evidence to the Secretary of State for the Environment*, The Housing Centre Trust, 1975; and David Webster, 'Local authority rent pooling: some hard evidence', *Centre for Environmental Studies Review 5*, January 1979.

22. Housing Services Advisory Group, *Training for Housing Work: A Consultative Document*, Department of the Environment, 1978.

23. National Community Development Project, *The Poverty of the Improvement Programme*, 1975.

24. The long battle by Labour administrations on the GLC to achieve the objective of 'opening up the suburbs' is well chronicled in Ken Young and John Kramer, *Strategy and Conflict in Metropolitan Housing*, Heinemann, 1978.

25. *Hansard*, 4 February 1975.

26. *Housing Policy Consultative Document, op cit.*

27. J. Parker and K. Dugmore, *Colour and the Allocation of GLC Housing*, GLC Research Report No 21, 1976; Hazel Flett, *Black Council Tenants in Birmingham*, Research Unit in Ethnic Relations, 1979.

28. Supplementary Benefits Commission, *Annual Report 1976*,

Cmnd 6910, HMSO, 1977.
29. Housing Centre Trust (reference 21); *Housing Policy Consultative Document, op cit.* and *Housing Policy Technical Volume, op cit.*
30. This case for council house sales was put from within the Labour movement by Frank Field in *Do We Need Council Houses?*, Catholic Housing Advisory Service, Occasional Paper 2, 1975.

Chapter 15

1. *Policy for Inner Cities*, Cmnd 6845, HMSO, June 1977.
2. Malcolm Wicks, 'Social policy for the inner cities', in Muriel Brown and Sally Baldwin (eds), *The Year Book of Social Policy in Britain 1977*, Routledge & Kegan Paul, 1978.
3. A. H. Halsey, *Times Educational Supplement*, 9 February 1973.
4. See, for example, Oscar Lewis, *The Children of Sanchez*, Penguin, 1964,
5. 'Census indicators of urban deprivation', Working Note Number 6, Great Britain. EcUR Division, Department of the Environment, 1975.
6. 'Census indicators of urban deprivation', Working Note Number 13, Areas of Housing Deprivation. EcUR Division, Department of the Environment, 1976.
7. Jack Barnes in H. Glennerster and S. Hatch (eds), *Positive Discrimination and Inequality*, Fabian Society, 1974.
8. *What Matters Now*, Collins Fontana, 1972.

9. 'New Government Plans to Tackle Acute Deprivation', Press Notice, Home Office, 18 July 1974.
10. *A Joint Framework for Social Policies*, HMSO, 1975.
11. *The Inner City Programme: Community Involvement*, National Council for Social Services, 1979.

Chapter 16

1. A. L. Webb *et al*, *Voluntary Social Service Manpower Resources*, Personal Social Services Council, 1976.
2. Report of the Wolfenden Committee, *The Future of Voluntary Organisations*, Croom Helm, 1978.
3. B. Jordan, *Paupers*, Routledge & Kegan Paul, 1973; and B. Jordan, *Poor Parents*, Routledge & Kegan Paul, 1974.
4. J. Heywood and B. Allen, *Financial Help in Social Work*, Manchester University Press, 1971.
5. Peter Townsend, *The Fifth Social Service*, Fabian Society, 1971.
6. R. Klein *et al*, *Social Policy and Public Expenditure*, Centre for Studies in Social Policy, 1974.
7. DHSS, *Priorities for Health and Personal Social Services in England*, 1976.
8. *Public Expenditure to 1978/79*, Cmnd 5879, HMSO.
9. *Ibid.*
10. Cmnd 6393.
11. Cmnd 6721.
12. Cmnd 7049.
13. *The Way Forward*, DHSS, 1977.

Index